THE SELF-PORTRAIT

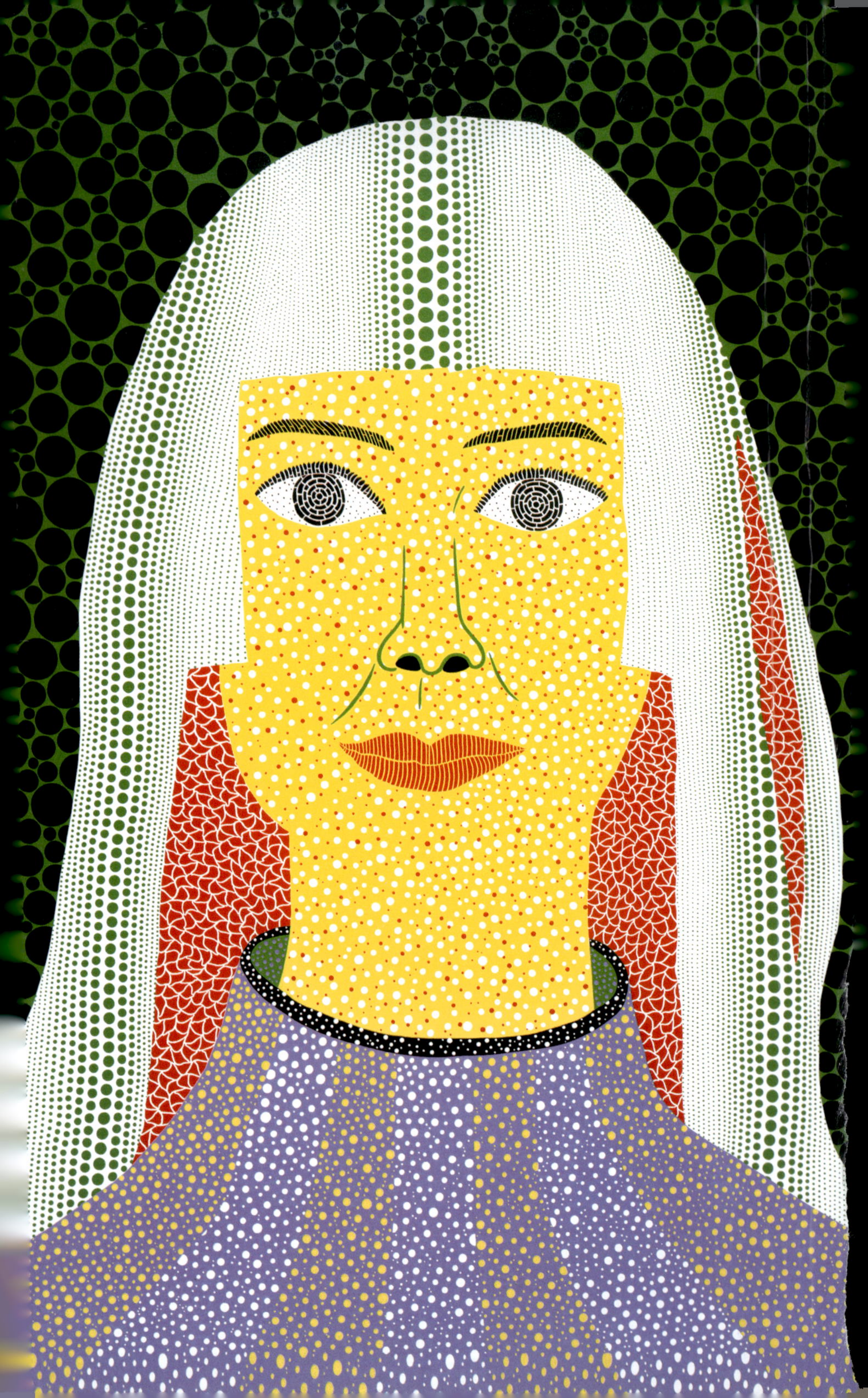

ART ESSENTIALS

THE SELF-PORTRAIT

—

NATALIE RUDD

—

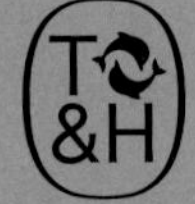

CONTENTS

INTRODUCTION

On any street, in any town, on buses and trains, at landmarks and beauty spots, you will see people taking pictures of themselves using smartphones, sharing their imagery globally, often seeking recognition. Some of the images appear unmediated. Others are modified using filters, blurring reality and fiction. Welcome to the world of the selfie: a democratized form of self-portraiture, disseminated in an instant.

At a time of widespread interest in self-representation across our culture, this book provides an opportunity to review the fascinating genre of self-portraiture. For centuries, artists have found ways to include themselves in their work. Evidence of their presence can be found in paintings, drawings, prints, architectural features and sculptures and, more recently, in films, photographs, performances and installations. Artists have produced self-portraits for a wide variety of reasons, from the practical to the philosophical.

A self-portrait can draw in lucrative commissions, as it offers proof of an ability to capture a likeness. Some artists have used self-portraiture to convey inner states, deep crises or searing revelations. Others have explored the chameleonic potential of this genre, finding boundless opportunities to play, to hide, to mask, to transform.

Spanning Renaissance art to the present day, this book provides a fresh view of self-portraiture. Each section explores the work of a different artist, enabling specific insight into sixty individual practices and approaches. The early chapters follow a loose chronology, tracking developments across time and place. Towards the end of the book, the structure opens out to embrace thematic concerns, reflecting concurrent developments in modern and contemporary practice.

A spirit of enquiry and open-mindedness informs these pages. Consideration is given to work that at first glance might disrupt preconceptions of what a self-portrait should look like. New voices and perspectives are introduced; fresh thinking is welcomed. This inquisitive approach tests the limits of self-portraiture, ensuring its ongoing relevance. A supple and responsive genre emerges, one able to accommodate expanding definitions of identity and shifting notions of selfhood in an ever-changing globalized world.

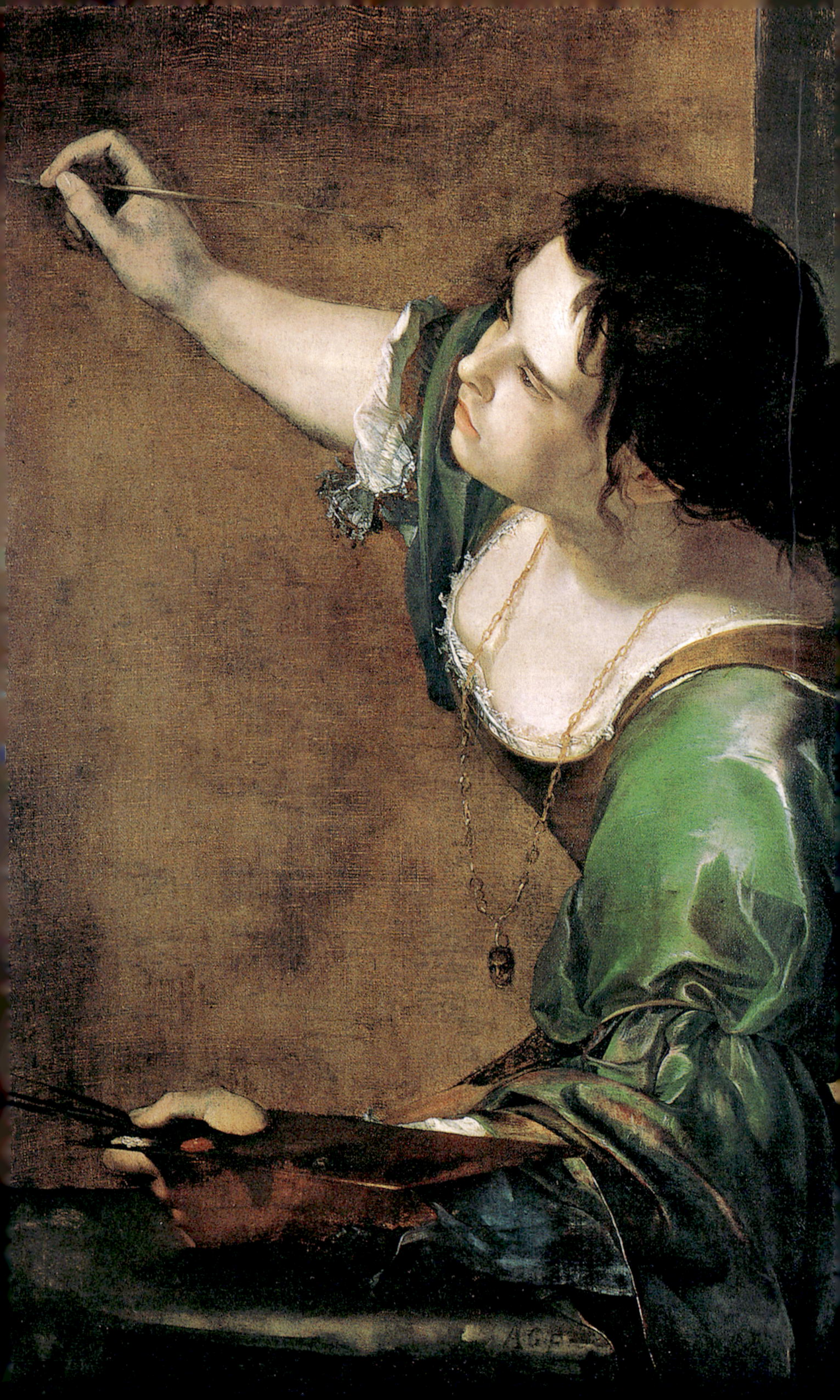

FROM CAMEO TO CENTRE STAGE

-

**The mirror, above all —
the mirror is our teacher.**

-

Leonardo da Vinci

JAN VAN EYCK
active 1422–died 1441

Jan van Eyck was a Flemish painter renowned for his technical mastery of oil paint and for his significant contribution to Early Netherlandish art. A leading figure of the Northern Renaissance, he combined symbolic imagery with meticulous realism to create intense visions of heaven and earth. Based in Bruges, Van Eyck enjoyed the support and companionship of Philip the Good, Duke of Burgundy, who gave him a generous income for his work as court painter and allowed him space to develop his ideas. In addition to producing major religious scenes and altarpieces, Van Eyck also worked as a portraitist, receiving numerous commissions from the growing merchant classes.

The *Arnolfini Portrait* (1434) is one of the earliest surviving portraits of non-royal subjects and the first to depict a domestic setting. It represents Giovanni Arnolfini, a wealthy merchant of textiles and luxury goods, holding hands with his betrothed, Giovanna Cenami. They stand side by side in a bedroom in an undisclosed location and appear to be in the process of getting married. Giovanna hitches up her elegant garments to create an upfront bump, suggesting fertility rather than pregnancy. Other symbolic objects are positioned strategically around the room: a small dog occupies a central position to represent fidelity, while the apples on the windowsill warn against sinful temptations. Every detail, every surface is illuminated with Van Eyck's mystical representation of light. This couple bask in the radiance of God. In the fifteenth century, the presence of a priest was not necessary for marriage; the joining of hands was sufficient if recorded by a witness. Just above the couple's joined hands lies the self-portrait. 'Jan van Eyck was here, 1434' is written on the wall, in ornate calligraphy, below the chandelier. Beneath, a circular convex mirror hangs in the centre of our field of vision. Here, in miniature, we find the reflected image of the artist standing alongside another witness. This double portrait therefore operates as a group portrait, a self-portrait and a signed certificate of marriage.

Flat, foil-backed mirrors were not widely available outside of Venice until at least the 1500s. Curved convex mirrors were much easier to obtain and it is likely that Van Eyck owned one. To create a

Unlike the *Arnolfini Portrait* with its complex structure and symbolic iconography, this portrait appears understated. The dark jacket fuses with the featureless background to focus all attention on the head and face. There is an honesty to this portrait, a 'warts-and-all' directness.

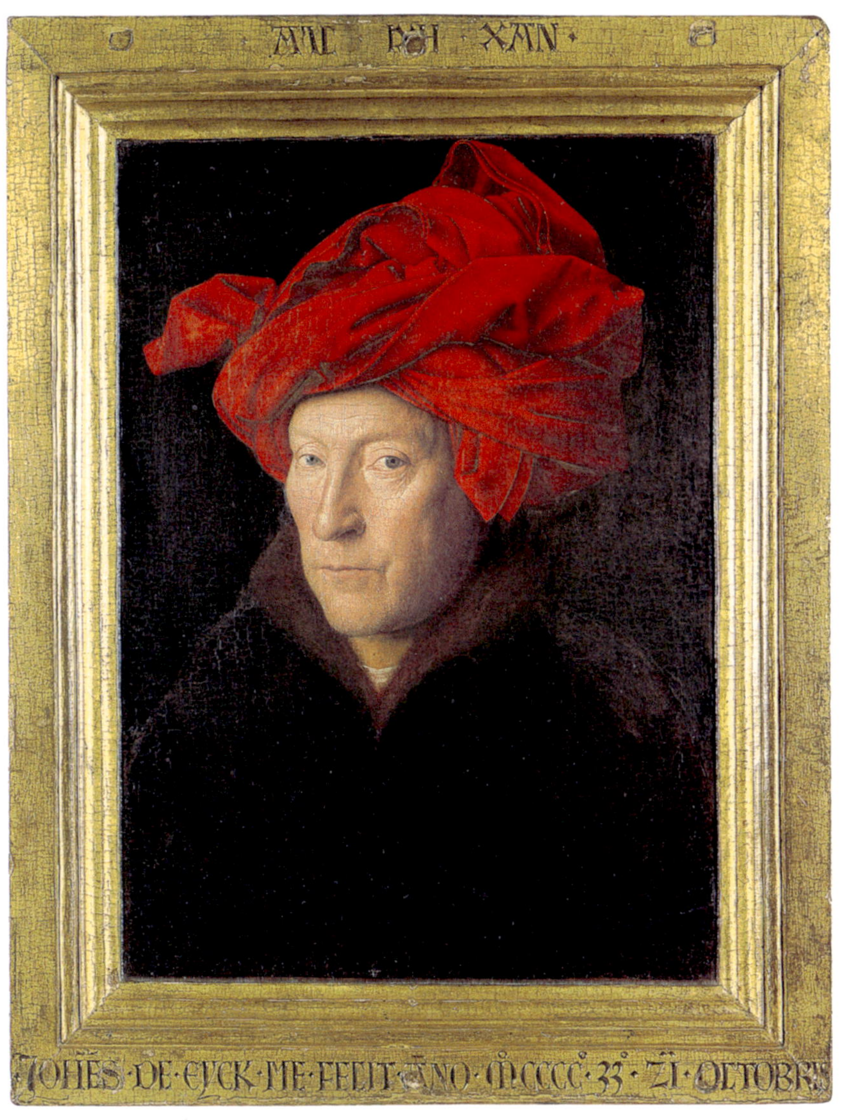

self-portrait using a primitive mirror of this kind would have involved considerable skill. The artist would need to look beyond the cloudy surface to search for his likeness, and to make substantial adjustments to correct distortions similar to those found when staring into a festive bauble. *Portrait of a Man* (1433) is thought to have emerged from precisely this process. Although this man remains unidentified, many experts consider him to be Van Eyck, making this the earliest autonomous self-portrait (one with the

11

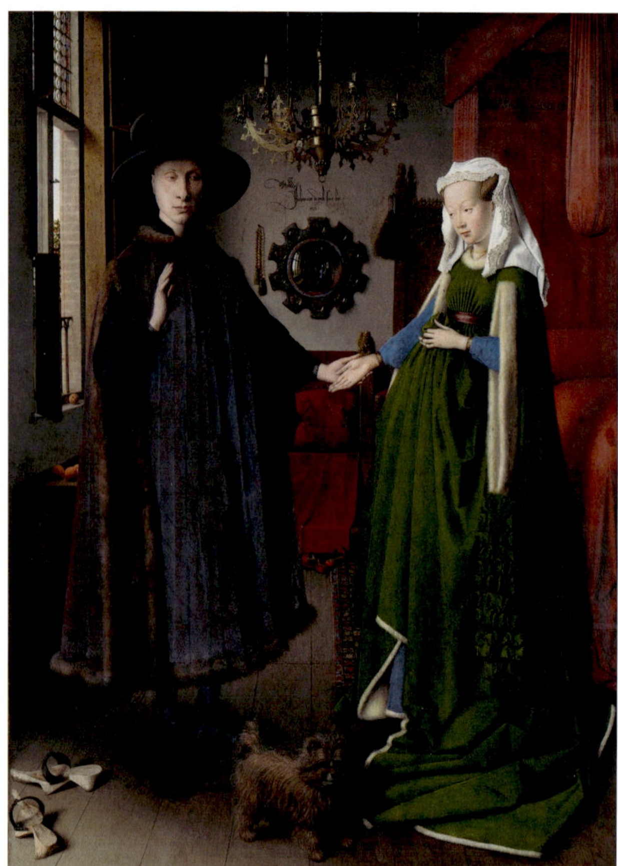

Jan van Eyck
Portrait of Giovanni(?) Arnolfini and his Wife, 1434 (detail opposite)
Oil on oak,
82.2 x 60 cm
(32⅜ x 23⅝ in.)
National Gallery, London

Van Eyck was fascinated by reflective surfaces. In *Portrait of Giovanni(?) Arnolfini and his Wife*, the mirror takes on a religious significance, surrounded by ten tiny scenes from Christ's Passion. Two years later, Van Eyck concealed a tiny image of himself in the altarpiece *Virgin and Child with Canon van der Paele*, reflecting his image in the shine of St George's shield.

artist as the central focus) in existence. Nobody is quite sure why the artist chose to make this image, nor what status it held within his wider practice. There is no subplot, no role-play within a wider religious scene, no contractual obligation. There are no signs of his tools, no boastful expressions of wealth. Van Eyck simply sits and observes. His three-quarter profile pose turns as if to consult the mirror. The piercing stare and the pursed mouth conspire to convey a serious intensity, for the viewer is also under scrutiny. Van Eyck's trademark attention to detail is evident in his growing stubble, the meandering veins in his eyes and the rich folds of his turban. The image is again bathed in Van Eyck's magical light, radiating from the top left of the image. The gilded frame adds a further shimmer. On the top plane of the frame, in the place normally reserved for the sitter's name, the artist has painted the words 'ALS ICH KAN', rendered as if carved. This trompe-l'oeil inscription translates as

'AS I CAN'. The playful correspondence between the words Ich ('I') and Eyk provides further proof of Van Eyck's interest in self-identification, if any were needed.

OTHER KEY WORKS

Virgin and Child with Canon van der Paele, c.1434–6, Groeningemuseum, Bruges, Belgium

---

KEY FEATURES

Miniature self-portraits hidden within larger scenes: the artist plays a cameo role

Autonomous self-portraiture: the artist takes centre stage

Use of convex mirrors

Acute observation and attention to detail

Direct gaze and a focus on the eyes

Strong use of chiaroscuro

Use of portraiture to convey both religious and secular ideas

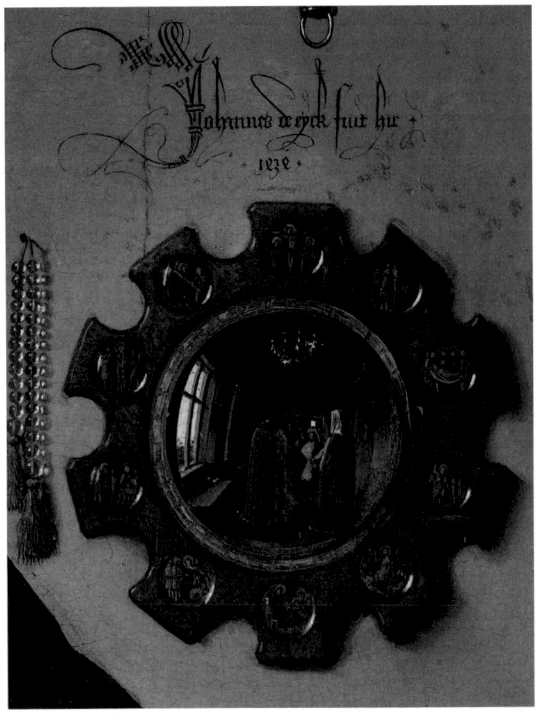

FILIPPO LIPPI
c.1406–69

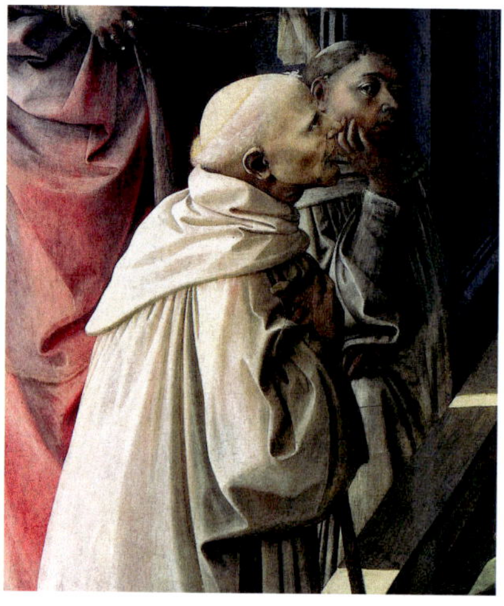

Until the nineteenth century, visitors to the Benedictine Chapel of Sant'Ambrogio in Florence were met with a heavenly vision. Now in the Uffizi Gallery, Fra Filippo Lippi's sumptuous altarpiece depicts Christ crowning his mother, Mary, the Queen of Heaven. A jubilant crowd bears witness to this ceremony. Everyone is engaged with the action, all except for one curious witness kneeling in the bottom left-hand corner of the composition. With his head resting casually on his hand, this self-assured character turns to look at the viewer. His intriguing expression is part cocksure, part dreamy. Many believe this figure is a portrait of the artist. If the figure could speak he might say, 'Look! I can summon the kingdom of Heaven in my mind, sharing my vision through paint.' Lippi plays the role of an anonymous bystander. His place within the action highlights the relevance of religious narratives for contemporary audiences: I am here, this is now.

Assistenza self-portraits are often found in Early Renaissance art. These discreet insertions into a larger commissioned scheme act as calling cards or signatures. Their concealed nature reflects the obligations of working for a patron. *Assistenza* self-portraits also reveal a growing desire among artists to be recognized not as tradespeople, but as inspirational individuals with special talents. The Carmelite friar Filippo Lippi worked in and around Florence and was regarded as an exceptionally gifted artist. This status gave him

Filippo Lippi
Coronation of the Virgin, 1439–47 (detail above)
Tempera on wood, 200 x 287 cm (87¾ x 113 in.)
Uffizi Gallery, Florence

Early Renaissance art reveals a growing understanding of various methods of representation, from proportion and perspective to the depiction of human gestures and emotions. A public commission was an excellent opportunity to showcase a range of skills. Lippi's depiction of a crowd enables him to represent various poses and expressions. The inclusion of an architectural setting indicates his developing understanding of perspective.

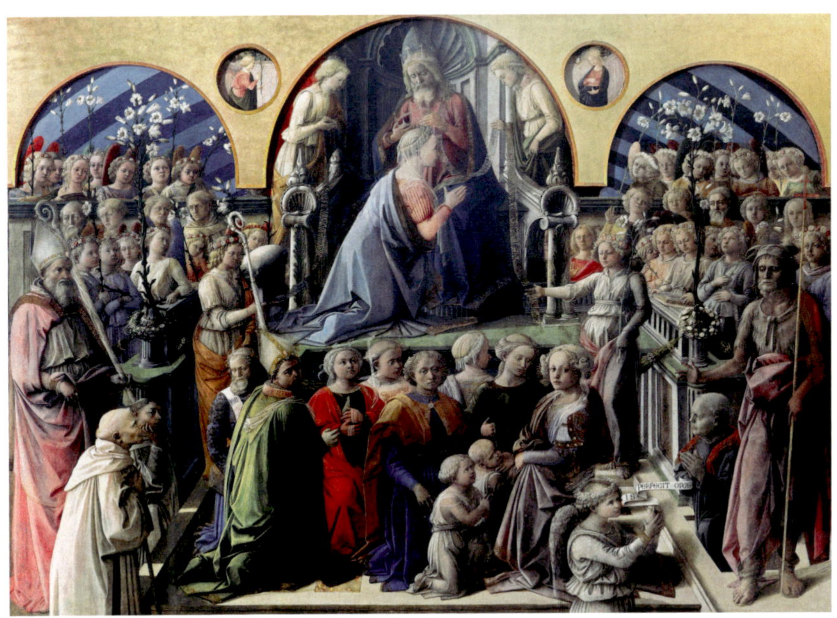

license to pursue a liberal lifestyle despite his religious orders. In the bestselling book *Lives of the Artists* (1550), Giorgio Vasari portrays Lippi as a colourful character driven by two passions: his art and his personal relationships. In a further mirroring of art and life, many of Lippi's later representations of the Madonna and Child feature novice nun Lucrezia Buti as the Virgin. Buti was the mother of Lippi's two children.

OTHER KEY WORKS

Scenes from the Life of the Virgin Mary, 1469, Duomo,
   Spoleto, Italy

KEY FEATURES

Assistenza self-portraiture: the discreet and anonymous
   insertion of the self into a larger scheme
Self-portraiture as a signature within a commissioned work
Increasing awareness of the role and status of the artist
   within society
Early Renaissance interest in capturing individual identities,
   emotions and expressions and a growing understanding of
   how figures occupy deep space

ADAM KRAFT
c.1460–1509

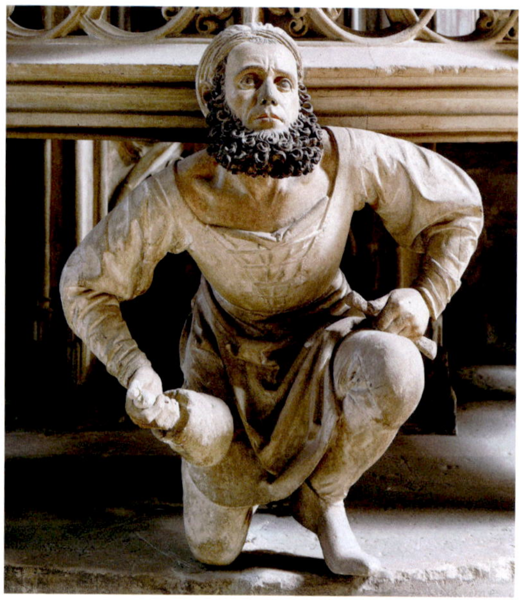

Adam Kraft was a stone sculptor and builder, renowned for ambitious architectural schemes made in a Late Gothic style. A contemporary of Albrecht Dürer (see pages 18–21), Kraft lived and worked in the German city of Nuremberg, a prosperous trade centre. Kraft enjoyed lucrative commissions that enabled him to showcase his skills on an impressive scale. In 1493 he was approached by Hans Imhoff, one of Nuremberg's wealthiest noblemen. Imhoff invited Kraft to design and build a tabernacle for the medieval church of St Lorenz. Imhoff stipulated that the tabernacle must be 'beautifully made'. Kraft responded with an astonishing sandstone structure standing over 18 metres (59 feet) tall. It rises up from the ground like an ornate finger pointing to heaven. Intriguing life-size representations of the artist and two assistants occupy the base. These figures appear to bear the colossal weight of the tabernacle on their shoulders. Kraft makes light work of this heroic task: he glances upwards with a serene expression, perhaps in gratitude for his God-given talent. His body is athletic. Gripping the hammer and chisel with purpose, he looks ready to break into a sprint. In German, the word 'Kraft' denotes vigour and strength: Kraft by name, kraft by nature.

Adam Kraft
*Self-Portrait at the Foot
of the Tabernacle*, c.1496
Sandstone,
life-size
Lorenzkirche, Nuremberg

**The tabernacle would
originally have been
painted to spectacular
effect. Much of this
colourful finish has been
lost over time. Due to
the overall height of the
tabernacle, Kraft's heroic
self-portrait is thought to
be the largest in western
art history.**

Discreet self-portraiture was often employed by craftspeople as a signature device – a way of leaving one's mark without upstaging a patron. Kraft, however, was the first to carve such a prominent position for himself. He appears gigantic when compared with the smaller religious figures found further up the tabernacle and even dwarfs the Imhoff coat of arms. This unusual self-portrait indicates the growing status and aspirations of the artist within society. Although Kraft's tools and workwear highlight his position within a trade, his self-conscious posturing indicates a strong desire to be identified as a unique artist capable of intellectual thought.

KEY FEATURES

Heroic self-portraiture on an epic scale

Sculptural ingenuity and innovation

Ease of action: an increasing sense of movement and flow
    within sculpture

An acknowledgement of the increasing status of the artist
    within society

Self-portraiture as a signature within a larger commissioned work

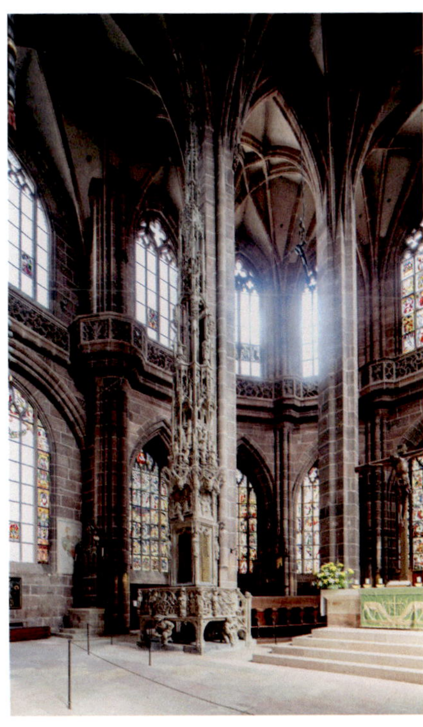

ALBRECHT DÜRER
1471–1528

It is hard to overstate Albrecht Dürer's contribution to the development of self-portraiture. This leading painter and printmaker from Nuremberg in Germany was the first artist to capitalize on the significant creative potential of the genre. He created sixteen self-portraits during his lifetime, experimenting with different materials and compositional devices. Dürer was also aware of the power of his brand. He used his outstanding skills as a printmaker to disseminate his work internationally and he incorporated his initials into an instantly recognizable logo signature: 'AD'. Few Northern Renaissance artists were able to break into the Italian scene, but Dürer did just that, embarking on a perilous journey across the Alps to make a name for himself in Venice. He also shared his self-portraits with fellow artists, including Raphael, in a quest to be remembered.

Dürer produced self-portraits using a variety of approaches. He sometimes presented himself as a bystander in a larger religious scene, but more often he chose a central role, playing himself. A number of his autonomous self-portraits were intended as standalone works of art. Others served a more practical function, with the artist striking a pose so that he could master a technical or anatomical aspect. His body was simply the most readily available point of reference. Dürer even used self-portraiture for diagnostic purposes: an intriguing pen and ink wash drawing of 1512–13 (Kunsthalle, Bremen) shows the artist pointing to the source of pain in his abdomen, presumably to assist his physician. Allusions to the experience of intellectual thought abound in Dürer's intriguing 1514 etching *Melencolia I*. In this work, a brooding winged figure is surrounded by an assortment of ambiguous symbols and craft tools. Although Dürer is physically absent, *Melencolia I* could be read as a proxy self-portrait. The work also anticipates romantic notions of the artist as an isolated, misunderstood figure. Collectively, Dürer's self-portraits operate as a revelatory visual diary, providing clues at key moments in his life.

Dürer's precocious talents were evident from a very early age. His *Self-Portrait at the Age of 13* (1484) highlights his astonishing skills, handling the unforgiving medium of silverpoint with incredible confidence. His journey to maturity is captured in three painted self-portraits of 1493, 1498 and 1500. The *Portrait of the Artist*

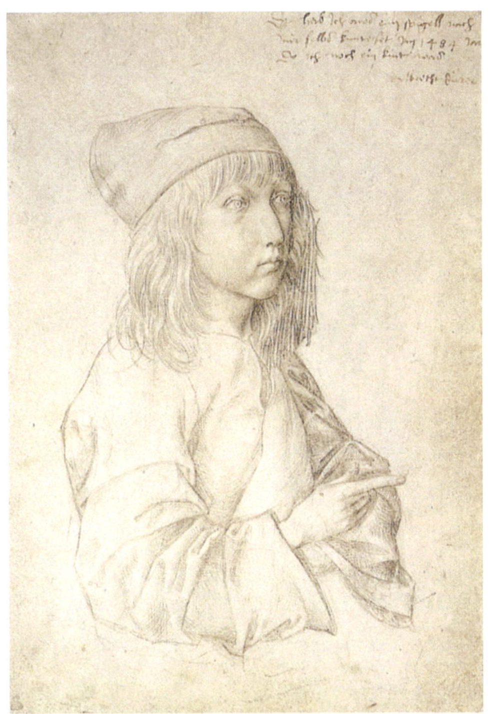

Albrecht Dürer
*Self-Portrait at the
Age of 13*, 1484
Silverpoint,
27.5 x 19.6 cm
(10⅞ x 7¾ in.)
Albertina, Vienna

**The young artist used a
looking glass to make this
work and chose a tricky,
three-quarter pose. His
sidelong glance follows
his determinedly pointed
finger. What is the source
of his interest and where
is he headed? This very
early drawing highlights
Dürer's precocious talents
and his considerable self-
belief, even at the age of
thirteen.**

Holding a Thistle (1493) shows a beseeching young man wearing
sensuous, billowing garments. Dürer painted the work during family
negotiations in the year leading up to his marriage to his fiancée,
Agnes. The *Self-Portrait* of 1498 represents the twenty-six-year-old
artist in a confident three-quarter profile pose. A majestic Alpine
view is visible through the window behind him. There is nothing here
to suggest Dürer's role as an artist. Rather, he appears as a wealthy
young nobleman in fine clothing, his doeskin-gloved hands clasped
together with powerful confidence. Dürer had just returned to
Nuremberg following his trip to Venice, a place where artists were
celebrated and valued. The *Self-Portrait* of 1498 acts as a conscious
attempt to raise the status of the artist in his home city; it also
reveals Dürer's growing personal success and wealth.

Two years later, the twenty-eight-year-old Dürer returned to
self-portraiture once again, this time assuming a daring, full-frontal
pose and a sombre, direct stare. His hair is painstakingly rendered,
perhaps alluding to references in the Bible connecting long hair
with spiritual thinking. His right hand is raised as if to clasp his
luxurious jacket or, perhaps, to point to his heart. Dürer appears
from the darkness as if from nowhere. The pose is almost divine.

The reference to representations of Christ seems undeniable. Is this a blasphemous image? Even Dürer didn't seem entirely sure, for he kept the portrait hidden in his studio during his lifetime. This is an expression of heightened status like no other: no longer just a gentleman, Dürer has become a beautiful vision, made in God's image. The *Self-Portrait* of 1500 was Dürer's last painted autonomous self-portrait. One senses that the twenty-eight-year-old artist had said all that he had to say.

OTHER KEY WORKS

Portrait of the Artist Holding a Thistle, 1493, Musée du Louvre, Paris, France

Self-Portrait of the Sick Dürer, 1512–13, Kunsthalle Bremen, Bremen, Germany

Melencolia I, 1514, Metropolitan Museum of Art, New York, USA

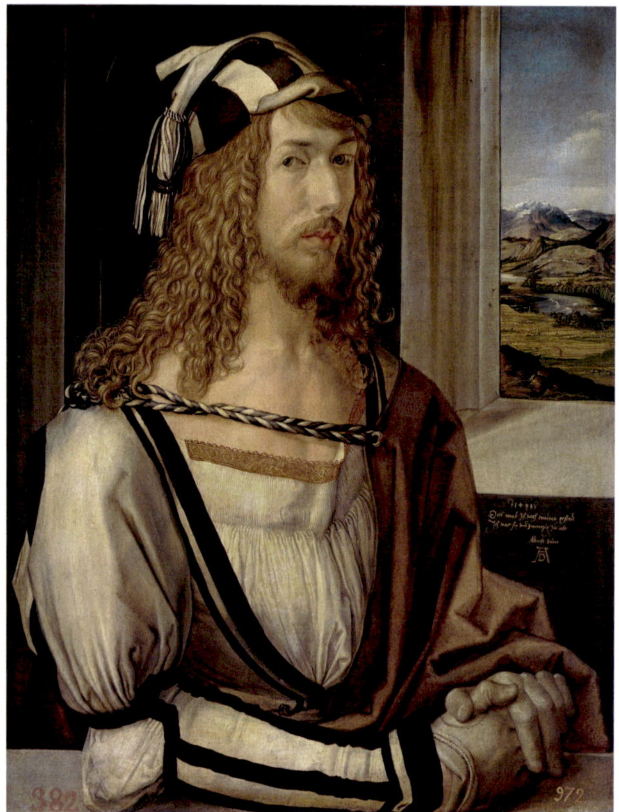

Albrecht Dürer
Self-Portrait, 1498
Mixed media on limewood,
52 x 41 cm
(20½ x 16⅛ in.)
Museo Nacional del Prado, Madrid

Dürer cuts an extraordinary figure in this self-portrait. Robed in black and white striped finery, his garments sit dazzlingly low to reveal his upper chest. Every attention is given to the sensuous rendering of his flowing hair. The Alpine landscape reinforces Dürer's identification as a cosmopolitan man with a far-reaching perspective.

Albrecht Dürer
Self-Portrait, 1500
Oil on wood,
67 x 49 cm
(26⅜ x 19¼ in.)
Sammlung Alte
Pinakothek, Munich

The underlying composition of this painting provides a further Christian reference. A strong vertical line connects Dürer's hand, chin, nose and fringe. Horizontally, the written inscriptions occupy the artist's eye line. The structure of the painting is therefore underpinned by a cruciform.

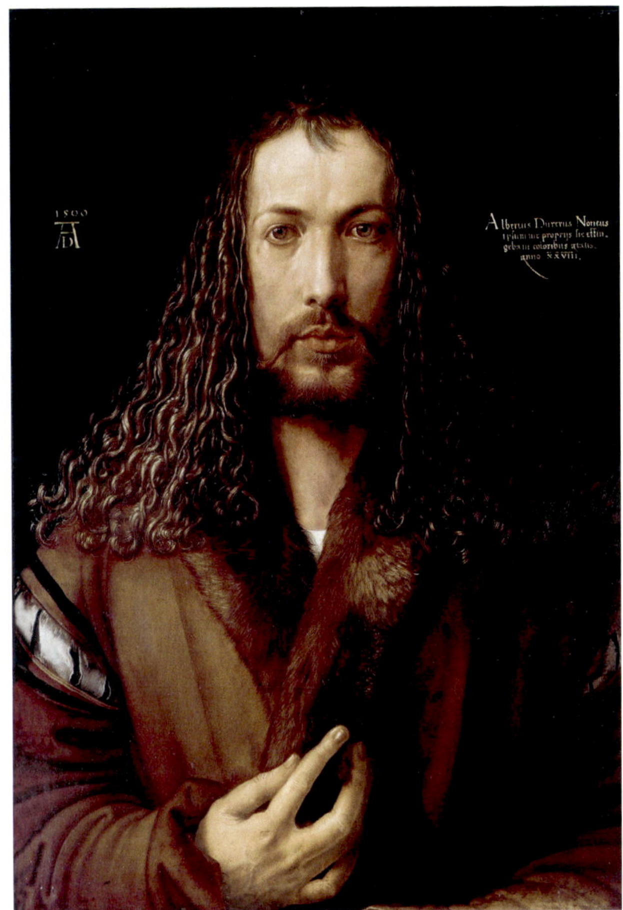

KEY FEATURES

Sustained and inventive approach to self-portraiture

Deployment of a wide variety of media, including paint,
  silverpoint and pen and wash

Varied use of the genre including *assistenza* and autonomous
  self-portraiture, anatomical practice and to aid diagnosis

Status elevation: representation of the artist as a nobleman and
  an icon

Self-conscious development of a logo to create a recognizable
  artistic brand

MICHELANGELO
1475–1564

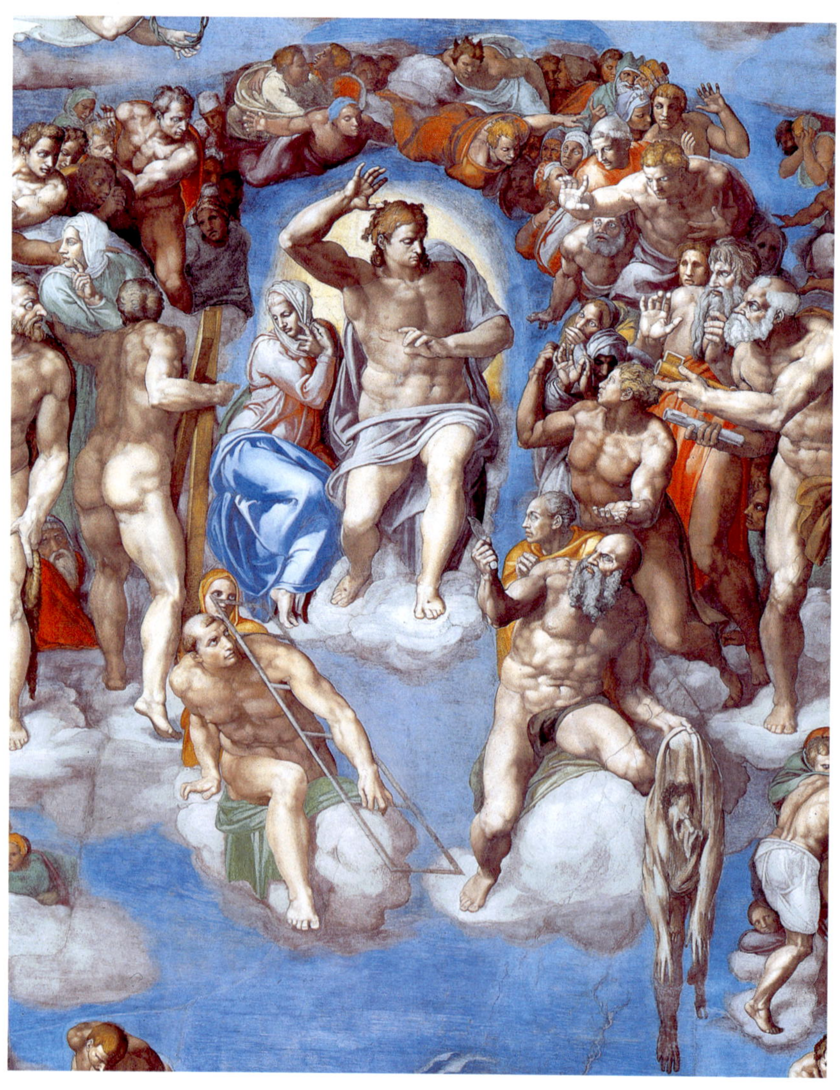

Michelangelo
The Last Judgement
(detail), 1536–41
Fresco
Sistine Chapel, Vatican

Michelangelo had little time for portraiture, viewing it as a lowly genre fixated on individual quirks. His contribution to self-portraiture is therefore limited to anonymous cameo roles. Despite his first-hand knowledge of human dissection, Michelangelo's representation of flayed skin in this work is surprisingly sketchy, verging on caricature. Deliberately grotesque and guilt-ridden, this self-portrait is the equivalent of hanging out your dirty laundry.

Michelangelo is one of the most celebrated figures in western art history. Venerated during his lifetime, he was the archetypal 'Renaissance Man', excelling across sculpture, painting, poetry and architecture. His works mark a pinnacle in High Renaissance art. They feature masterful and idealized representations of the body, informed by classical art and first-hand knowledge of the world. Michelangelo's understanding of human anatomy, for example, stemmed from classical sculpture and from his involvement with human dissection.

Michelangelo is renowned for his spectacular fresco paintings in the Sistine Chapel. Having completed the ceiling in 1512, the artist returned to the chapel twenty-five years later to depict *The Last Judgement* on the wall behind the high altar. Towards the centre of this complex composition, St Bartholomew is shown with a knife in one hand and his own flayed skin in the other – a reference to the saint's martyrdom. Although this gruesome sheath is only lightly sketched, the severed face looks familiar. The trademark broken nose and rugged appearance bear an uncanny resemblance to Michelangelo himself.

Why would an artist famed for figurative perfection paint himself as repulsive, limp skin dangling precariously above hell? Michelangelo completed this fresco at the age of sixty-seven. Now entering old age, he was besieged by mortal thoughts. His poetry of this time references the process of skin shedding as a metaphor for cleansing and rebirth. This self-portrait might be Michelangelo's attempt to present his true identity to God in the hope of forgiveness. Or it could represent his total commitment: the martyr-like dedication of his whole body to art. The vulnerability of this self-portrait also highlights the artist's sensitive, thin-skinned nature. Some experts consider the features of the seated St Bartholomew to resemble the writer Pietro Aretino (1492–1556), Michelangelo's arch-rival and critic. He handles Michelangelo's skin with a seeming lack of care and respect.

KEY FEATURES

Assistenza self-portraiture: the discreet insertion of the self into
   a larger scene
High Renaissance interest in large narrative compositions and
   complex human interactions
Deliberate uglification of the self
Interest in grotesque caricature
Use of role-playing to reference personal subplots and narratives

PARMIGIANINO
c.1503–40

In 1524, a handsome young artist from Parma arrived in Rome with big ambitions. Francesco Mazzola, commonly known as Parmigianino – Italian for 'little one from Parma' – carried with him a small circular painting depicting himself gazing into a convex mirror. This mesmeric showpiece is roughly the size of the glass he would have used, and painted on a slightly convex piece of wood to intensify the illusion. We expect to see our reflection in the glass but instead discover the childlike face of the artist staring back with an expression of intense focus, deeply engaged in the process of painting. Intriguingly, Parmigianino's features are immune from distortion, as is his neat, fashionable haircut. A blemish-free hand emerges from stylish clothing, lingering to rest in the foreground, elegantly elongated. The pose may reflect the cultish fascination with beautiful boyhood which predominated during these years, as the artist offers his hand with knowing courtly refinement. The focus on the hand could also be read as an expression of originality, suggesting that only the artist's hand can achieve such fine work. The hand also operates as a physical barrier, adding to the curious combination of intimacy and distance at the heart of this mysterious self-portrait.

Parmigianino was a young man on a mission. He used his self-portrait to advertise the advent of a new style of painting called Mannerism. Influenced by Michelangelo (see pages 22–3) and Raphael, Parmigianino advocated for an art with heightened grace, flowing, languorous poses and elongated limbs: extreme youth, extreme beauty. Soon after arriving in Rome, he gave his self-portrait to the recently elected Medici Pope Clement VII. It was a clever strategy. *Self-Portrait in a Convex Mirror* provided an instant source of fascination. Various commissions for larger religious schemes soon followed. This intriguing work remains one of the most celebrated and referenced self-portraits of the sixteenth century.

Giorgio Vasari gave this self-portrait special mention in the second edition of his book *Lives of the Artists* (1568): 'And since Francesco had an air of great beauty, with a face and aspect full of grace, in the likeness rather of an angel than of a man, his image on that ball had the appearance of a thing divine … and in it were seen the lustre of the glass, the reflection of every detail, and the lights and shadows, all so true and natural.'

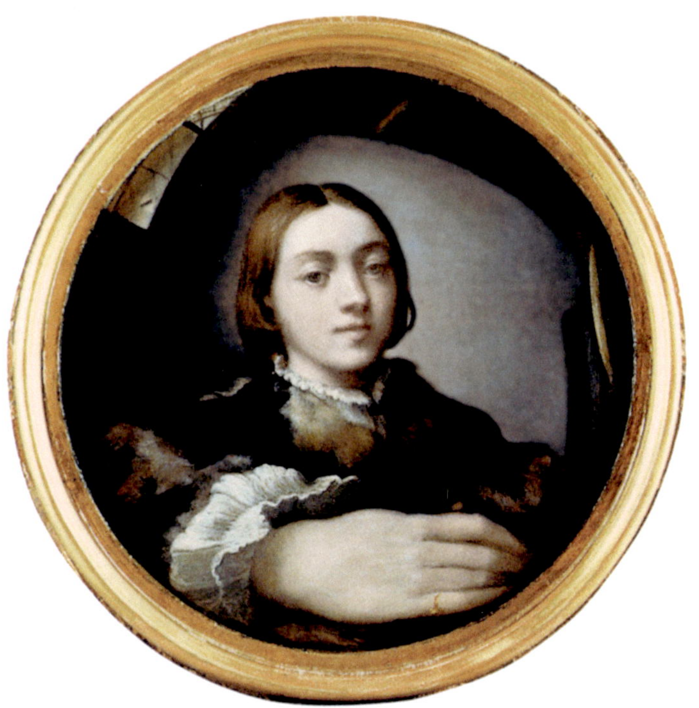

KEY FEATURES

An autonomous self-portrait, placing the artist front and centre
An early representation of an artist at work in a studio
Self-conscious fashioning and an interest in courtly styling
  and conduct
The portrait as manifesto, conveying an artist's style
  and intentions
A Mannerist approach to painting, representing exaggerated
  proportions in bodies and gestures, and extreme youth
Interest in illusion and materiality, evidenced in the distortive
  reflections and the use of a convex support

SOFONISBA ANGUISSOLA
c.1532–1625

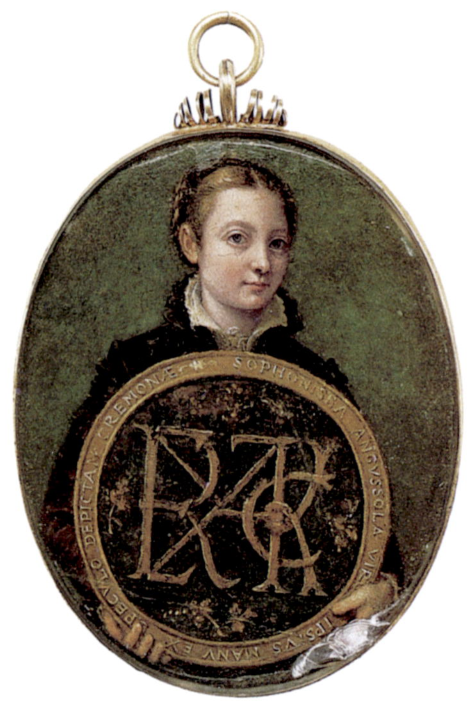

The Greek philosopher Aristotle held the view that women were fundamentally inert and passive: the pliant egg awaiting the dynamic seed. This classical philosophy informed much Renaissance thinking. The blank canvas and the pot of paint were considered feminine, whereas the actions of the artist were essentially masculine. The idea of a woman working as an artist was a contradiction in terms. Given this patriarchal context, Sofonisba Anguissola's success as a painter during her lifetime is all the more extraordinary.

Anguissola was born in Cremona, northern Italy, the daughter of Amilcare Anguissola, a nobleman of modest wealth. Anguissola had five sisters and one brother, and Amilcare ensured that each of his children received an excellent education. Anguissola's artistic talents soon emerged, prompting her father's radical decision to allow her to train with local master painters for three years. Anguissola was aware of the disadvantages she faced as a woman.

Sofonisba Anguissola
Self-Portrait, c.1556
Varnished watercolour
on parchment,
8.3 x 6.4 cm (3¼ x 2½ in.)
Museum of Fine Arts,
Boston

This miniature self-portrait is dominated by the huge medallion, which Anguissola holds tenderly in her hands: a prize possession. The central logo overlays the letters A M I L C A R E, highlighting the artist's devotion to her father. The circular border features the words 'painted from a mirror with her own hand by the Cremonese virgin Sofonisba Anguissola'.

Many of her male contemporaries had received many more years of training than she had, and her status as a woman prevented her from competing for public commissions for historical or religious paintings. She knew the risks of overstepping the mark and took the decision to specialize in the lowly genre of portraiture, attracting private commissions. Through self-portraiture, Anguissola found the freedom to explore issues of identity and gender, using her intelligence to make subtle transgressions.

Anguissola's father was an enthusiastic supporter of her work. He assumed the role of publicist, writing persuasive letters to potential patrons and making strategic gifts. He even shared her work with Michelangelo (see pages 22–3), receiving encouragement and praise in return. Amilcare would have understood the power of Anguissola's self-portraiture. Self-portraits by women were rare and therefore attractive to collectors. Amilcare's promotion of these novel images paid off. In 1559, Anguissola was appointed portraitist in the court of Philip II of Spain. She received a generous income and secured an international reputation.

Sofonisba Anguissola was the most prolific self-portraitist in western art in the years between Dürer (see pages 18–21) and Rembrandt (pages 44–5). The majority of her self-portraits were made during her early years working as an artist, when her father's promotional activity was at its height. Anguissola introduced various new motifs to the genre, including depictions of herself at the clavichord, or holding her signature aloft on a piece of paper. These cautiously groundbreaking works offered a huge source of inspiration to younger artists, including the Bolognese painter Lavinia Fontana (1552–1614). Virtue and modesty radiate from these works. Anguissola is usually depicted in dark, modest clothing, a white blouse emerging at her collar and wrists. Her hair is scraped back to form a neat, plaited bun. The facial expression is serious and demure. Strikingly, Anguissola's virginity is often explicitly stated. In her tiny *Self-Portrait* made during the mid 1550s, the artist holds aloft a medallion proclaiming, among other things, her chastity. Later in the decade, in *Self-Portrait at the Easel Painting a Devotional Panel*, Anguissola expands on this theme by representing herself at work on a depiction of the Virgin and Child, thus aligning herself with expressions of purity and virtue, whilst highlighting her ability to depict religious subjects.

Most Renaissance men avoided reference to hard toil in their self-portraits, preferring to present themselves as intellectual noblemen. Anguissola, however, was one of the first artists to capture herself at work. The decision to paint remained a radical choice for a woman, and Anguissola takes pride in her actions: I *am* a painter, this *is* what I do. Several years later, Anguissola returned to the idea of the artist at work, this time switching gender roles by representing herself as if being painted by her teacher, Bernardino Campi. This highly inventive composition serves as a fond mark of respect for her former teacher, but it also illustrates Anguissola's growing reputation. She assumes a higher, central position in the painting, and appears to steal the limelight. Is it possible to discern a playful glint in her eye? Campi supported Anguissola in her quest to become an artist, but now she is going places.

OTHER KEY WORKS

Self-Portrait with Clavichord, 1561, Spencer Collection, Althorp, UK

Self-Portrait, c.1610, Gottfried Keller Collection, Bern, Switzerland

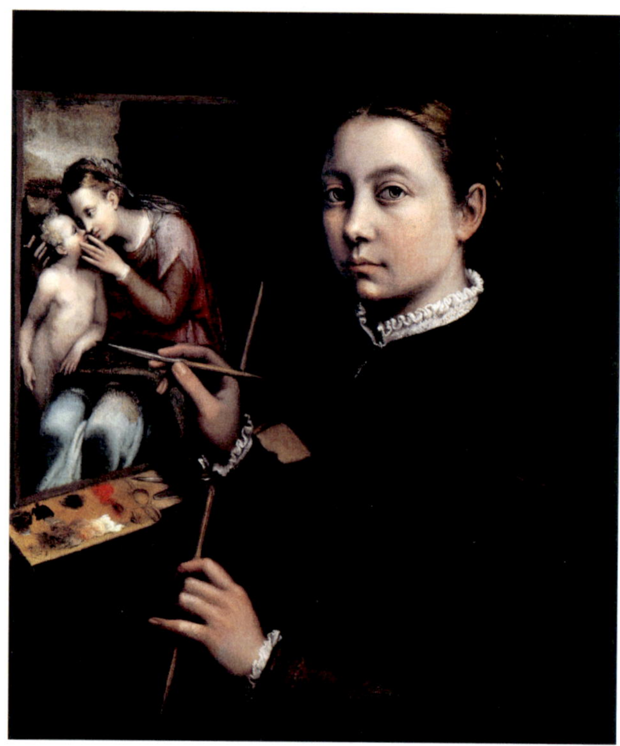

Sofonisba Anguissola
Self-Portrait at the Easel Painting a Devotional Panel, late 1550s
Oil on canvas,
66 x 57 cm (26 x 22½ in.)
Museum-Zamek, Lancut

According to legend, St Luke the Evangelist was the first person to portray the Virgin Mary. Representations of this theme were popular during Renaissance times and St Luke was considered the patron saint of artists. By assuming the role of St Luke, Anguissola seeks to legitimize her position as an artist and to showcase her skills in religious painting.

Sofonisba Anguissola
*Self Portrait as a Portrait being Created by Bernardino Campi, c.*1559
Oil on canvas,
111 x 109.5cm
(43¾ x 43⅛ in.)
Pinacoteca Nazionale, Siena

The Cremona-based artist Bernardino Campi (1522–91) was one of Anguissola's teachers. Despite his talents, Campi failed to gain representation in Giorgio Vasari's book *Lives of the Artists* **(1550). Vasari did, however, write favourably about the work of Anguissola. He made a special trip to Cremona to view her paintings ahead of publication of the 1568 edition of his bestselling book.**

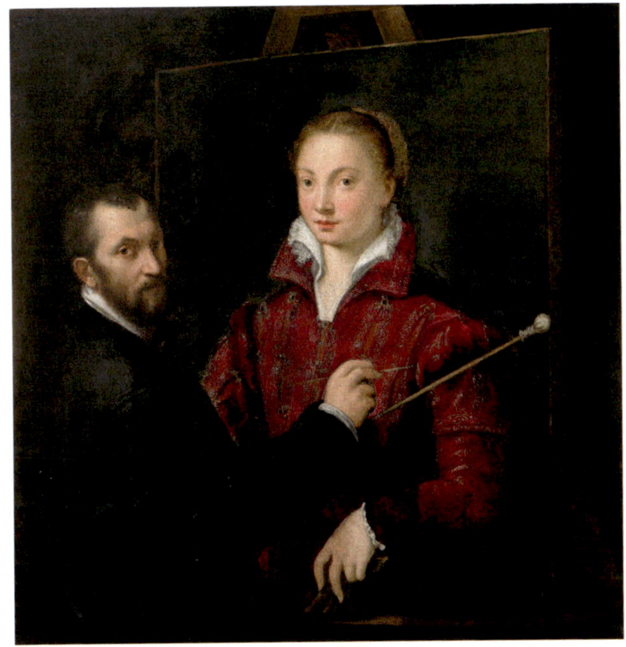

KEY FEATURES

Sustained and inventive use of self-portraiture
Innovative introduction of new motifs
Playful subversion of gender roles and norms
Sustained development of the 'artist at work' trope
Use of self-portraiture for career advancement and promotional
  purposes
Exploration of the self in old age

MICHELANGELO MERISI
DA CARAVAGGIO

1571–1610

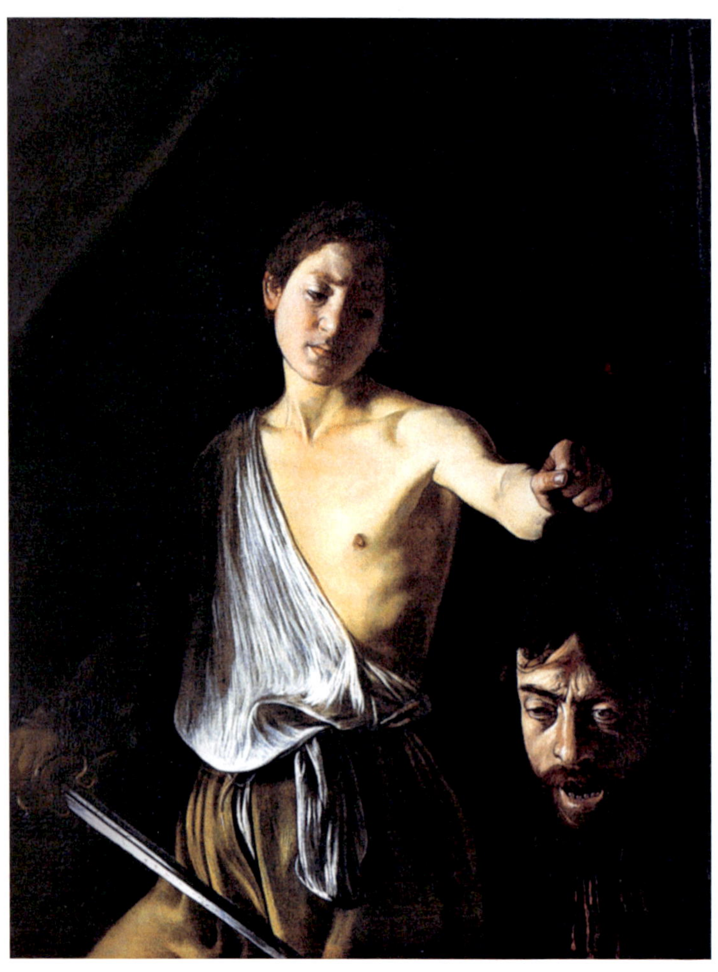

**Michelangelo Merisi
da Caravaggio**
*David with the Head
of Goliath*, 1609–10
Oil on canvas,
125 x 101 cm (49 x 40 in.)
Galleria Borghese, Rome

**Caravaggio was one of
the first artists to assume
different identities in
his paintings. In an early
painting he transformed
himself into Bacchus,
the god of wine, laden
with grapes and sick from
excess. In a later work,
he served his head on
a plate, reenacting the
execution of John the
Baptist. In all of these
images, Caravaggio
identifies as the victim.**

Caravaggio courted controversy like an old friend. He was recognized during his short life as an exceptional painter of shockingly realistic, warts-and-all scenes. Having trained in Milan, he moved to Rome in 1592 to establish himself as the originator of a daring new style. He worked fast, with impassioned intensity, and many of his paintings capture dramatic moments of violence and anguish. Shafts of light illuminate the looming darkness in his paintings, creating strong tonal contrasts known as chiaroscuro. Caravaggio was also known for his exceptionally volatile personality and for his frequent involvement in violent street brawls. One such altercation ended in the death of a young man, Ranuccio Tomassoni. With a death sentence hanging over his head, Caravaggio fled to Naples in 1606, a dead man walking.

David with the Head of Goliath (1609–10) is one of the last paintings Caravaggio ever made. It features a lithe, young David holding aloft the decapitated head of Goliath. A shaft of warm light illuminates this otherwise dark and grisly scene. Caravaggio plays the role of the slain giant. His first-hand experience of physical violence and its impact on the human body is evident in his authentic depiction of gore. His face is contorted in anguish and his ashen pallor contrasts with the deep red of his bloody, gaping mouth. This must be one of the most unflattering self-portraits in all of art history. In reducing himself to a pitiful cadaver, the penitent artist hoped for forgiveness. In 1610, the soundings from Rome were positive. Caravaggio set out for the capital to seek a papal pardon. He died en route from an unexplained illness, aged just thirty-eight. The circumstances surrounding his death remain shrouded in mystery.

OTHER KEY WORKS

Self-Portrait as Sick Bacchus, 1593–4, Galleria Borghese, Rome,
  Italy
Salome with the Head of John the Baptist, c.1609, National Gallery,
  London, UK

KEY FEATURES

Representation of the self as victim
Interest in moments of drama and violence
Use of self-portraiture to seek forgiveness
Interest in role-playing
Realistic representation of the human form
Strong use of chiaroscuro
Loose and spontaneous handling of paint

ARTEMISIA GENTILESCHI
1593–c.1652

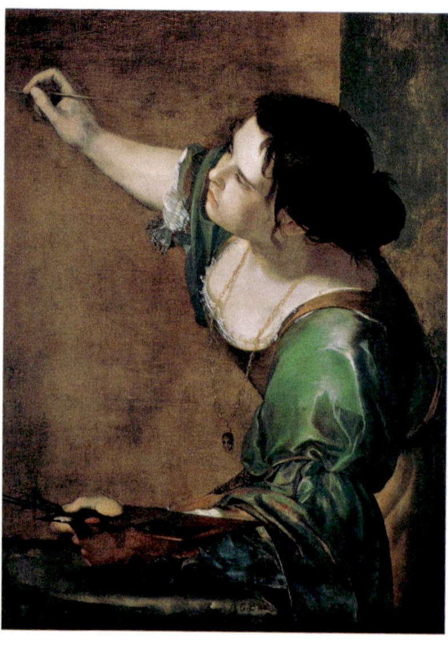

Most women who succeeded as artists during Renaissance times were the daughters of male artists. Artemisia Gentileschi trained in the painting workshop of her father, Orazio, in Rome, before pursuing her own career. Gentileschi was the first woman to gain recognition for historical and religious scenes. She pursued a Baroque style, conveying heightened emotions and actions using dramatic lighting and tonal variations. Like many artists at this time, she drew inspiration from Caravaggio (see pages 30–31), an old friend of her father's. Many of Gentileschi's paintings feature strong women engaged in acts of revenge. It is tempting to draw autobiographical connections. At the age of nineteen Gentileschi was sexually assaulted by one of her tutors, Agostino Tassi. During the humiliating trial, she was subjected to physical torture to test the veracity of her story. Although she eventually won her case, her honour had been tarnished.

Endurance and determination underpin Gentileschi's extraordinary *Self-Portrait as the Allegory of Painting* (c.1638–9). Unlike Sofonisba Anguissola's tightly controlled representations of herself at work (see pages 26–9), Gentileschi appears dishevelled and engrossed. Caring little about her hair or rolled-up sleeves, she dedicates her body and her mind to the physical process of painting. This self-portrait is without precedent. It provides an apparently

Artemisia Gentileschi
Self-Portrait as the Allegory of Painting,
c.1638–9
Oil on canvas,
98.6 x 75.2 cm
(38⅞ x 29⅝ in.)
Royal Collection, London

Gentileschi incorporates many of Cesare Ripa's symbolic references in her work, including the mask pendant and unruly hair. The daring curve of the composition directs our focus towards the paintbrush in the artist's hand. Gentileschi's mastery of chiaroscuro and drapery is evident in the dress which shimmers in the gentle light, reflecting different colours.

natural and unselfconscious representation of a woman at work. It also assumes an allegorical function, for Gentileschi presents herself as the personification of painting itself.

In 1603, Cesare Ripa published an illustrated edition of his *Iconologia*, a popular emblem book illustrating a range of personifications of concepts such as Dignity, Theory and Vice. Because all abstract concepts were considered female, Ripa's book featured many women. The powerful figure representing Painting has flowing hair to represent imagination, the pendant around her neck features a mask, symbolizing imitation, and her robes were said to change colour in a frenzy of creative energy. Ripa's illustration provided Gentileschi with the perfect opportunity to assume the leading female role, eliminating all male competition.

OTHER KEY WORKS

Judith Beheading Holofernes, c.1610, Museo Capodimonte, Naples, Italy

KEY FEATURES

Allegorical self-portraiture: use of the self to convey
    symbolic concepts
An interest in role-playing and transformation
Expressive brushwork
Dynamic compositions featuring strong lighting and
    dramatic chiaroscuro
Baroque focus on heightened drama and theatricality
Strong female identities and roles

Cesare Ripa
Detail of *Pittura* (Painting) from title page of *Iconologia of uytbeeldingen des verstands*, translated from the Italian by Dirck Pietersz. Pers, Amsterdam, 1603
Engraving
Rijksmuseum, Amsterdam

Cesare Ripa's *Iconologia* (second, illustrated edition 1603) was an important reference book for artists wishing to inject symbolic content into their work. Presented alphabetically, it illustrated hundreds of classical concepts. Painting is personified as a flamboyant and theatrical figure with wild hair and a fan of paintbrushes at her fingertips.

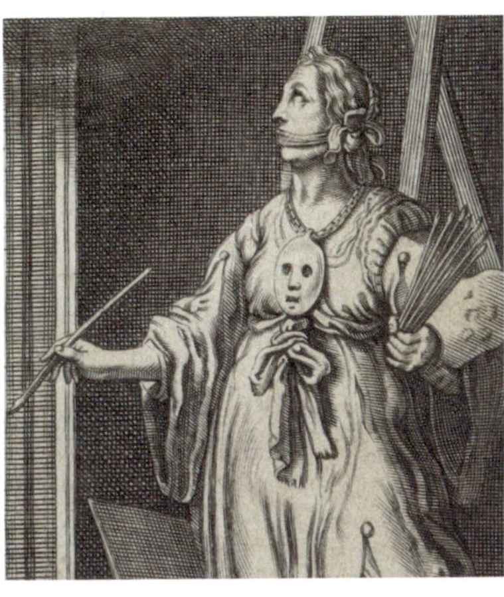

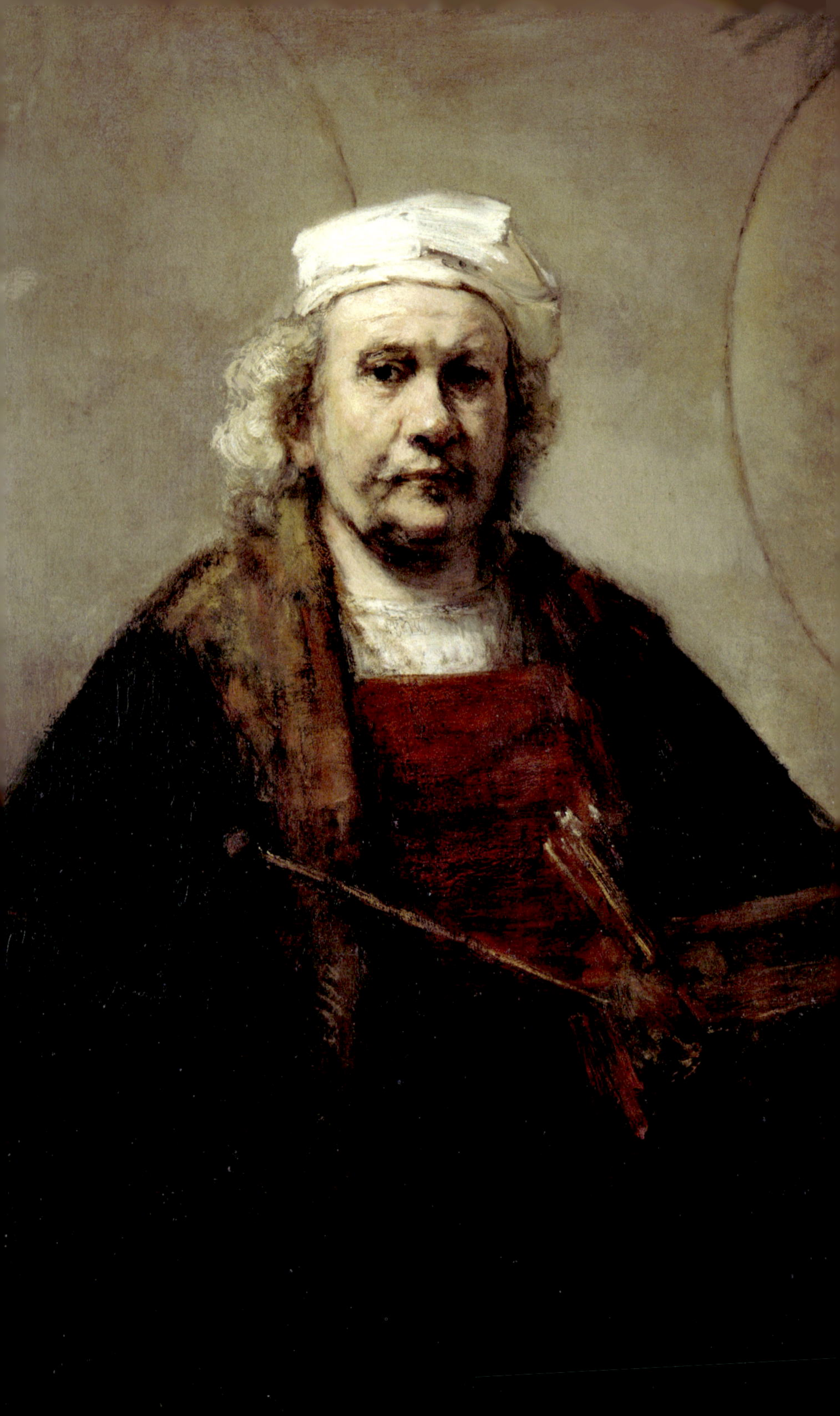

WORK-LIFE BALANCE

-

... set aside a room, just for ourselves, at the back of the shop, keeping it entirely free and establishing there our true liberty.

-

Michel de Montaigne

CLARA PEETERS
active 1607–21

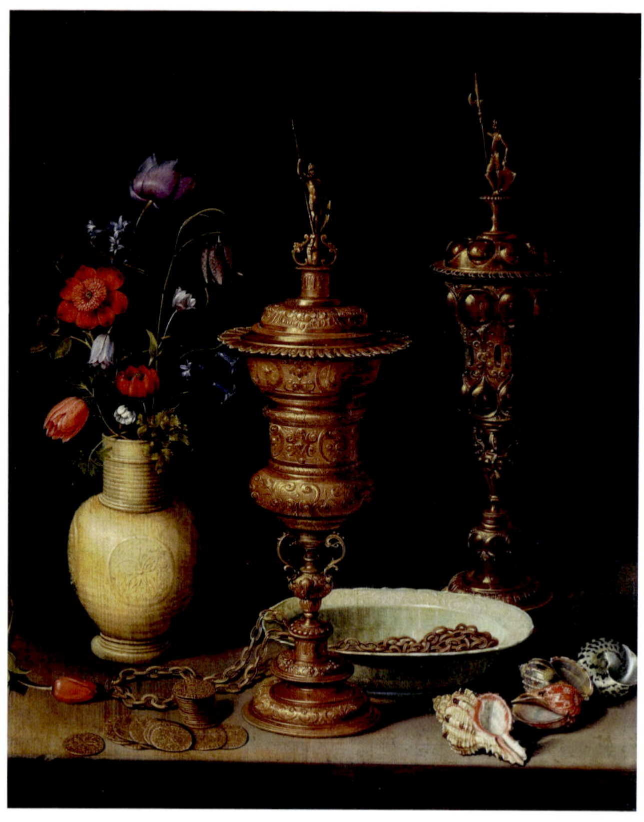

Many artists have concealed their self-portraits within larger scenes:
Filippo Lippi (see pages 14–15) slipped his face into a crowd, and
Jan van Eyck (pages 10–13) painted himself as a tiny reflection
in a small mirror. Clara Peeters took the cameo appearance to
new levels of miniaturization. Working on a tiny scale, she placed
portraits of herself within the polished surfaces of the pewter jugs
and gilt goblets featured in her still-life paintings. She often appears
multiple times across a single painting, as if inviting the viewer to
participate in a game of 'spot the artist'.

    Very little is known about Peeters. Even the basic details of her
life are lost. We do not know if she was self-taught or if she received
formal training. There is no evidence of her affiliation to an artists'

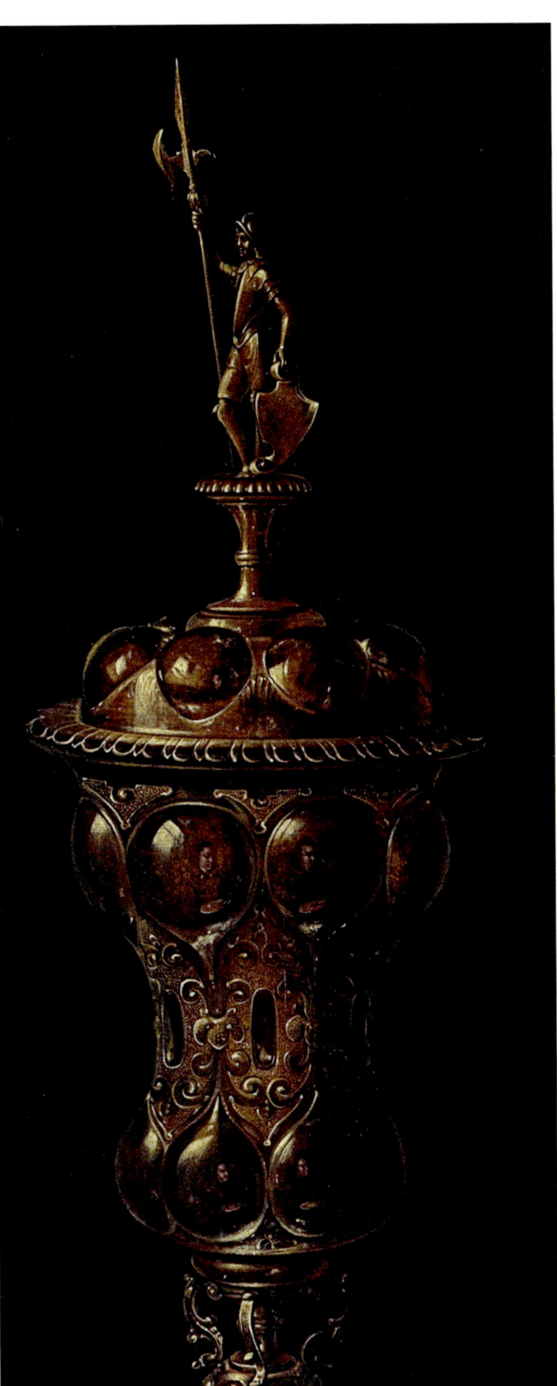

Clara Peeters
*Still Life with Flowers
and Gilt Cups*, 1612
(detail right)
Oil on panel,
59 x 49 cm (23¼ x 19¼ in.)
Staatliche Kunsthalle,
Karlsruhe

Although Peeters was
not the first artist to
feature her self-portrait
in reflective surfaces, she
was the first to include
more than one self-
portrait in any one scene.
Her exceptional attention
to detail is revealed in
these minuscule images
of herself at work in front
of a window, her features
gently distorted in the
convex surfaces. The
repeat image of the artist
adds to the decorative
qualities of the goblet.

guild. It is believed that she was born in Antwerp in the late sixteenth century and that many of her works were painted when she was a young woman. Given the limited opportunities for women within the seventeenth-century art world, it stands to reason that Peeters would draw inspiration from her immediate domestic environment. Still-life subject matter was easy to access. Approximately forty paintings by Peeters have survived. These works reveal her skilful rendering of a multitude of surfaces, from fruit, flowers, biscuits and cheese, to pewter, ceramic and glass. Her selected items are usually placed in the foreground, carefully arranged on a table for our delectation. This is mouth-watering realism.

Still-life painting was a popular genre within Dutch and Flemish art. It satisfied a growing middle-class market for easel paintings of modest proportions that could be displayed in the home. These buyers did not wish to be considered lavish and so there was a strong demand for work that combined beauty and skill with moral narratives concerning human vanity and transience. Seventeenth-century still-life paintings are laden with this *vanitas* symbolism. Fresh-cut flowers in a vase, for example, may look beautiful in the present moment, but before long they will shrivel and die.

Still Life with Flowers and Gilt Cups (1612) is an excellent example of Peeters' interest in *vanitas* themes. If the flowers and shells represent the fragility of life, then the decorative goblets, gold chain and coins reflect the futility of worldly success. This painting also indicates the artist's ability to work across artistic genres. Peeters chose a rare portrait format to capture the drama of these towering ceremonial cups, each topped with a triumphant male figurehead. The rear goblet is decorated with an ornate sequence of shiny globes. Five of these convex surfaces feature a gently distorted portrait of Peeters at work, holding her palette and brush. Each portrait offers a slightly different view of the artist, depending on its place on the goblet.

In *Vanitas Self-Portrait* (c.1610–20), Peeters no longer plays an incidental role. She occupies a prominent place at the table, as if part of the still life itself. She uses her body and her actions to play out *vanitas* narratives. The cut of her dress reveals flawless skin and her face glows with radiance, highlighting the transience of youth and beauty. The artist surrounds herself with various markers of earthly pursuits: luxury trinkets, fine fashions, jewelry, coins and dice. A translucent bubble hovers above the table, occupying a central position within the composition. This classic symbol of human frailty appears ready to burst at any moment. This work captures the spirit of the Latin phrase *memento mori*: 'remember you must die'.

Clara Peeters
Vanitas Self-Portrait,
c.1610–20
Oil on panel,
37.5 x 50.2 cm
(14¾ x 19¾ in.)
Private collection

Spheres and circles recur across this sumptuous image, from the convex decorations on the gilt cup to the prominent curve of the artist's breasts. This pictorial device not only creates a sense of harmony but also draws our attention to the bubble in the centre of the image, an ominous reminder of the brevity and fragility of life.

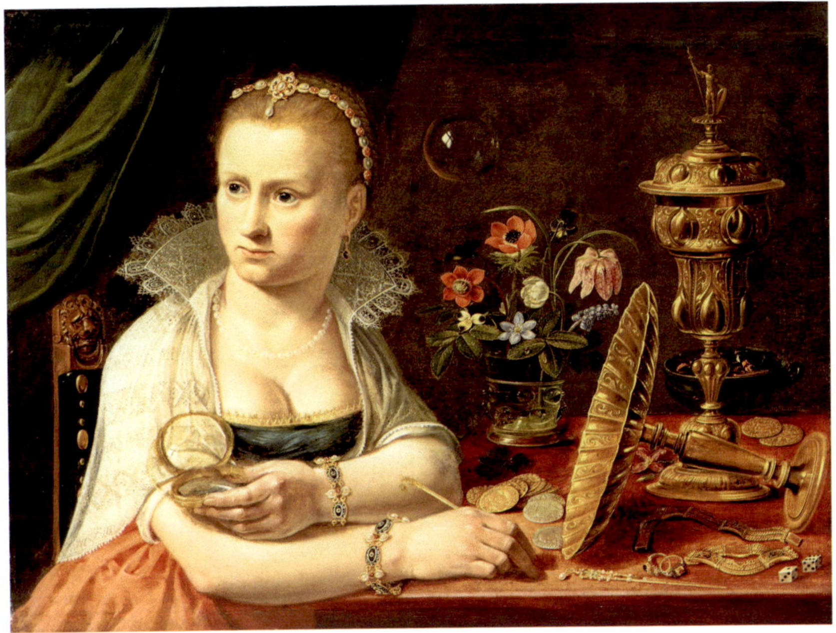

OTHER KEY WORKS

*Still Life with Flowers, a Silver-gilt Goblet, Dried Fruits,
    Sweetmeats, Bread Sticks, Wine and a Pewter Pitcher*, 1611,
    Museo Nacional del Prado, Madrid, Spain

KEY FEATURES

Miniature and concealed self-portraits
Fusion of self-portraiture with still life
Rare inclusion of multiple self-portraits in a single image
Realism: exceptional attention to details and textures
Interest in *vanitas* symbolism
Incorporation of reflective and convex surfaces

ANTHONY VAN DYCK
1599–1641

The Antwerp-born portraitist Anthony van Dyck was a flamboyant character. 'He behaved more like a noble than an ordinary person; and he shone in rich garments,' wrote Gian Pietro Bellori in his authoritative book *Lives of the Modern Painters, Sculptors and Architects* (1672). 'He therefore wore – as well as silks – a hat with feathers and brooches, gold chains across his chest, and was accompanied by servants.' Van Dyck occupied the upper echelons of society and he certainly knew how to network. The son of a silk merchant, he mastered the arts of painting and flattery at a very young age. After a stint as chief assistant to Peter Paul Rubens, he travelled to Italy to learn from the masters Titian and Veronese. Van Dyck developed an influential and enduring style of portraiture that sought to enhance the supposed elegance and authority of the upper classes. His full-length portraits idealized his sitters, adding height, haughtiness and highly expressive hands.

King Charles I, an ardent lover and collector of art, instantly fell in love with the relaxed elegance of Van Dyck's approach. The King lured him to London in April 1632, providing lavish accommodation and a handsome pension. Van Dyck was knighted just three months later, receiving a golden chain for his services as court portraitist. In *Self-Portrait with a Sunflower* (c.1633) the artist basks in the King's patronage, grasping the gold chain with elegant, elongated fingers. The sunflower symbolizes a courtier's loyalty to the monarch, however this regal bloom turns to face the princely painter as if to engage in mutual appreciation. Van Dyck breaks off to turn to the viewer. His head tips casually, enabling a haughty glance over the shoulder. There is informality, and there is an air of total superiority.

Anthony Van Dyck
Self-Portrait with a Sunflower, c.1633
Oil on canvas,
73 x 60 cm
(28¾ x 23⅝ in.)
Private collection,
Eaton Hall, Cheshire

Van Dyck produced a number of autonomous self-portraits during his lifetime, the majority of which sought to bolster his position and status. The fresh handling of paint and the rich use of colour in this work indicates Van Dyck's deep respect for Titian. His love of fashion is revealed in his sumptuous coat and the precise grooming of his influential 'Van Dyck' beard.

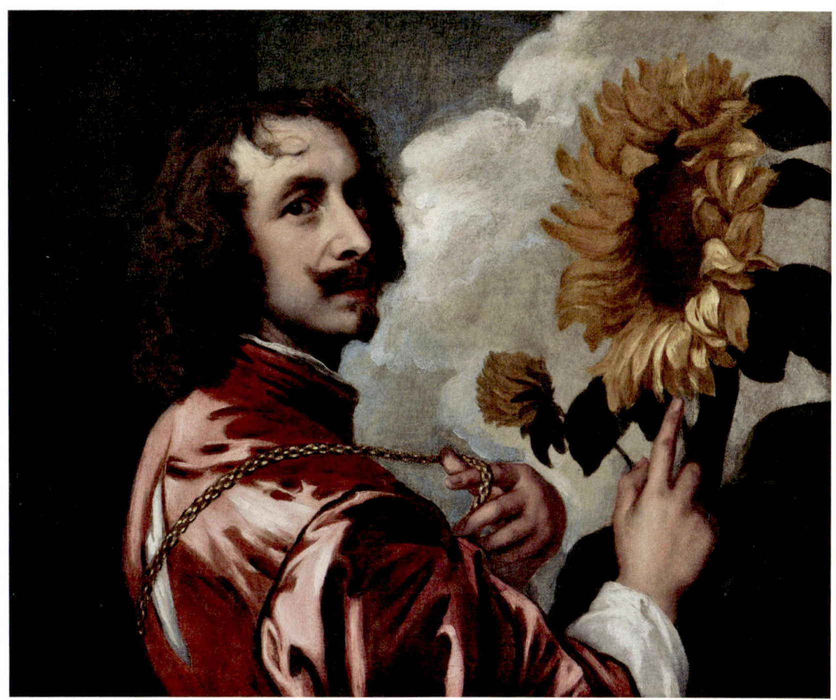

OTHER KEY WORKS

Self-Portrait, c.1620–21, Metropolitan Museum of Art,
  New York, USA
Sir Endymion Porter and Van Dyck, c.1635, Museo Nacional
  del Prado, Madrid, Spain
Self-Portrait, c.1640, National Portrait Gallery, London, UK

KEY FEATURES

Frequent production of autonomous self-portraits
Ostentatious status elevation: the painter as prince
Exaggerated elegance: elongated fingers and limbs
Acute awareness of fashion and styling
Use of symbolism to reinforce the position of the artist
Bravura technique: an expressive, loose handling of paint
Evident interest in Titian's handling of gesture and colour

JUDITH LEYSTER
1609–60

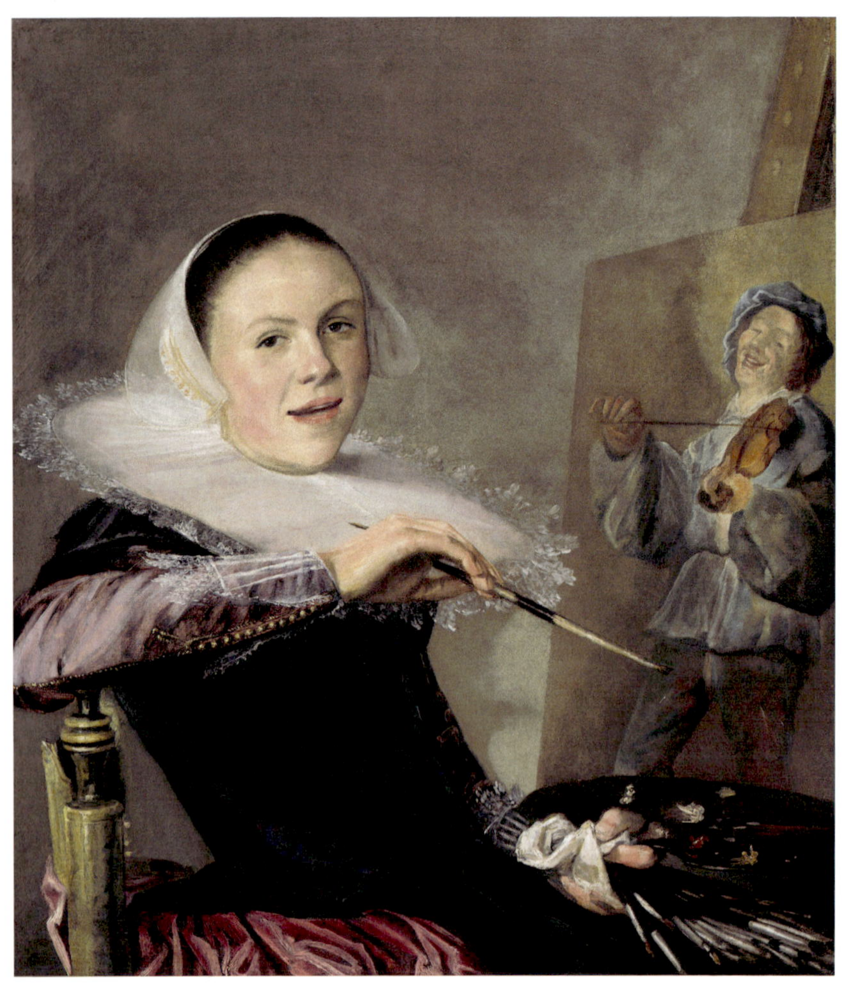

Who is this charismatic figure turning from her canvas to face the viewer? She appears ready to speak or to chuckle, perhaps both. She wears the latest fashions. Her white lace collar and cuffs are extravagant and pristine – hardly suitable for the act of painting. Clutching a fistful of brushes, this young woman looks casual and relaxed, totally at ease in her work. She smiles so broadly you can see her teeth, thus breaking all previous rules of female modesty and decorum. The logo signature shows a 'J' and an 'L' followed by a star: 'JL*'. This is Judith Leyster, a notable painter of the Dutch Golden Age.

Leyster gained recognition during her lifetime for portraits and genre scenes of people making merry. A number of her works foreground female characters and situations. After her death, Leyster's work fell into obscurity for over 200 years, with many of her paintings falsely attributed to the leading Dutch painter Frans Hals. Leyster's logo signature was eventually decoded during the late nineteenth century, finally enabling her to take her place within art history.

Leyster was one of the first female artists to join the Haarlem Painters' Guild in 1633 and it is thought that she presented this self-portrait on her admission. This work exudes freshness and vitality. The brushstrokes dance across the picture surface with assured lightness and bravura handling. X-rays reveal that Leyster had initially intended to present herself working on a portrait of a woman, perhaps herself. She later pursued a different approach, presenting instead an image of a man dressed in a *commedia dell'arte* costume, perhaps to illustrate her knowledge of theatre and poetry. In a final cheeky twist, Leyster points the tip of her paintbrush directly towards the actor's groin. Intentional? The artist's amused expression would suggest so.

Judith Leyster
Self-Portrait, c.1630
Oil on canvas,
74.3 x 65 cm
(29¼ x 25½ in.)
National Gallery of Art,
Washington, DC

Dutch Golden Age portraiture is renowned for its informality and directness, with sitters appearing cheerful and at ease. In Judith Leyster's self-portrait, the artist leans back, turning as if to speak to the viewer. This striking pose creates a strong diagonal axis – a popular compositional device evident in much Dutch Golden Age painting.

OTHER KEY WORKS

The Proposition, 1631, Mauritshuis, The Hague, Netherlands

KEY FEATURES

Confident and relaxed image of a woman working at an easel
Baroque interest in theatrical lighting and pose
Expressive, visible brush marks
Deliberate self-fashioning
Use of self-portraiture for promotional purposes
Self-conscious use of a logo signature, perhaps intentionally
   gender-neutral to avoid discrimination

REMBRANDT VAN RIJN
1606–69

Few artists have explored self-portraiture with such sustained rigour as Rembrandt van Rijn. This major figure in Dutch art produced more than forty painted self-portraits, over thirty-one etchings and six drawings across forty years of practice. His prolific contribution to the genre is shrouded in mystery; nobody is quite certain why he made so many self-portraits, or for whom they were intended. It is also unclear if the self-portraits were created in ponderous solitude, or if Rembrandt produced them in a businesslike fashion, building up stock in his bustling workshop for a growing market. Certainly, there was widespread interest in self-portraiture in Europe during these years, as evidenced by the number of Rembrandt's self-portraits entering important collections during his lifetime, including the collection of King Charles I. No self-portraits were listed on Rembrandt's studio inventory at the time of his death.

Self-portraiture played an important role during Rembrandt's formative years as an artist. Following an apprenticeship in his home town of Leiden, Rembrandt set up his own painting workshop around 1625. By the mid-1630s, Rembrandt had already produced more than half of his entire output of self-portraits. The reason for this flurry is partly practical. Many of Rembrandt's early self-portraits were exercises in facial expression and emotion, with successful motifs and ideas often incorporated into subsequent historical and religious scenes. In the small-scale etchings of 1630, we find the artist striking poses in front of a mirror: pouting, grimacing, snarling and laughing. The etching needle dashes across the picture surface with expressive agility, capturing the rough texture of a shaggy old coat, a bulbous nose, the creative wilderness of Rembrandt's unkempt hair. There is a heightened sense of drama: some areas are shrouded in a darkness so intense that eyes and whole areas of the face become obscured. The artist appears as an outsider, a brooding character, a creative mind. Even in these small 'studies', Rembrandt was projecting himself as a significant figure long before his reputation was fully established.

Rembrandt van Rijn
Self-portrait open mouthed shouting, 1630
Etching,
7.3 x 6.2cm (2⅞ x 2½ in.)
Rijksmuseum,
Amsterdam

Rembrandt often used self-portraiture to test facial expressions ahead of their incorporation in future work. The tortured expression in this etching found its way onto the face of Jesus in Rembrandt's 1631 painting *Christ on the Cross*. This fusion of an artist's features with Christ's recalls Dürer's self-portrait of 1500 (see page 21). Rembrandt was an admirer of Dürer's work and collected his prints.

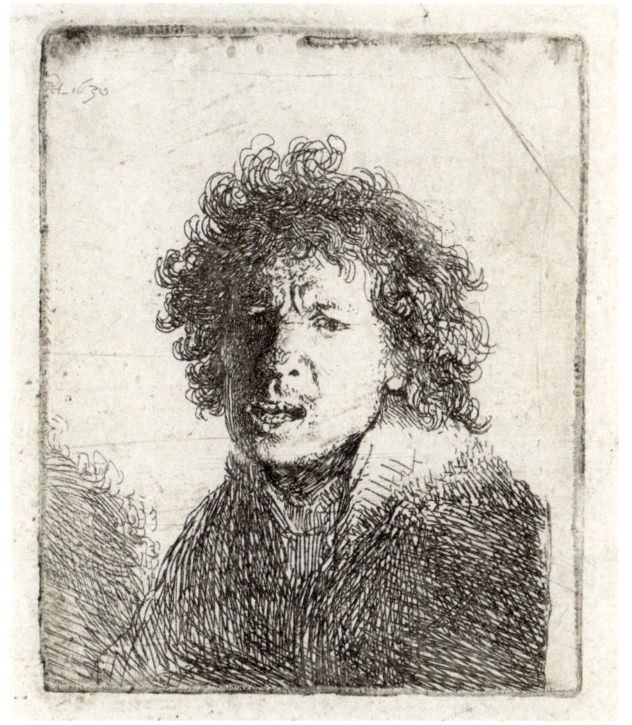

As Rembrandt's reputation grew, his self-portraits became
increasingly stately and static in pose. *Self-portrait at the
age of 34* (1640) reveals an artist at the top of his game. At
first glance, Rembrandt appears as a dignified and affluent
gentleman, all dressed up in fine silks, furs and a plumed hat.
On closer inspection it becomes clear that the artist has raided
the dressing-up box, for he is wearing early sixteenth-century
garments. His authoritative pose – billowing sleeve resting on a
horizontal ledge – marks a striking correspondence with Titian's
A Man with a Quilted Sleeve (1511, National Gallery, London, UK).
The rich tonal qualities of Rembrandt's hat and drapery also recall
Raphael's *Portrait of Baldassare Castiglione* (1514–15, Musée du
Louvre, Paris, France). Both of these Renaissance portraits had
passed through Amsterdam auction rooms some years earlier.
Rembrandt was a regular attendee, making sketches of classic
works before they slipped into private hands. In drawing a direct
connection between himself and his Renaissance forebears,
Rembrandt sought to bolster his reputation as a natural heir and
a true, great master.

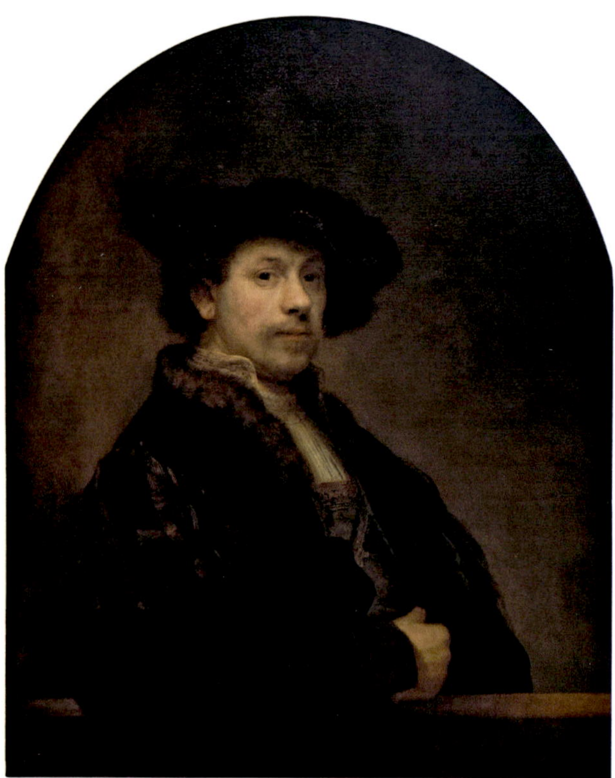

Rembrandt's late self-portraits are known for their loose handling, searing honesty and enigmatic grandeur. In 1656, the artist was declared bankrupt after many years of living beyond his means. His house and possessions were sold by auction. The commissions had dried up and his patrons had gone elsewhere. Given these challenges, it is no surprise to discover a devil-may-care attitude in much of Rembrandt's late work. No longer concerned with status symbols or attracting potential patrons, this world-weary artist can barely be bothered to get dressed. In his iconic *Self-Portrait* of c.1665, Rembrandt wears a shabby old cap and a painter's tabard. He holds his palette, brushes and maulstick, poised ready to paint. His facial expression appears sombre, tired, reflective. The paint is thick and dry, scraped across the surface or daubed in encrusted clumps. There is an honest appraisal of advancing age. Skin sags and slumps, forming deep, sculptural crevices and furrows. The overall effect is majestic and liberated. Against all odds, the artist continues to work, searching for deeper truths.

Rembrandt van Rijn
Self-Portrait at the age of 34, 1640
Oil on canvas,
102 x 80 cm
(40⅛ x 31½ in.)
National Gallery, London

Rembrandt's self-portraiture has provided a huge source of inspiration to successive generations of artists. His oeuvre acts as a catalogue of ideas for poses and role-playing opportunities, tonal and chiaroscuro handling, compositional devices and potential routes for introspection.

Rembrandt van Rijn
Self-Portrait, c.1665
Oil on canvas,
114.3 x 93 cm
(45 x 36⅝ in.)
Kenwood House, London,
English Heritage

There has been much speculation as to the meaning of the two circles sketched on the canvas behind the artist. Some scholars believe the circles represent two unfinished world maps. Others point to the legendary story of Giotto who drew two perfect freehand circles to prove his exceptional skills. Rembrandt was perhaps, therefore, aligning himself with Renaissance greatness.

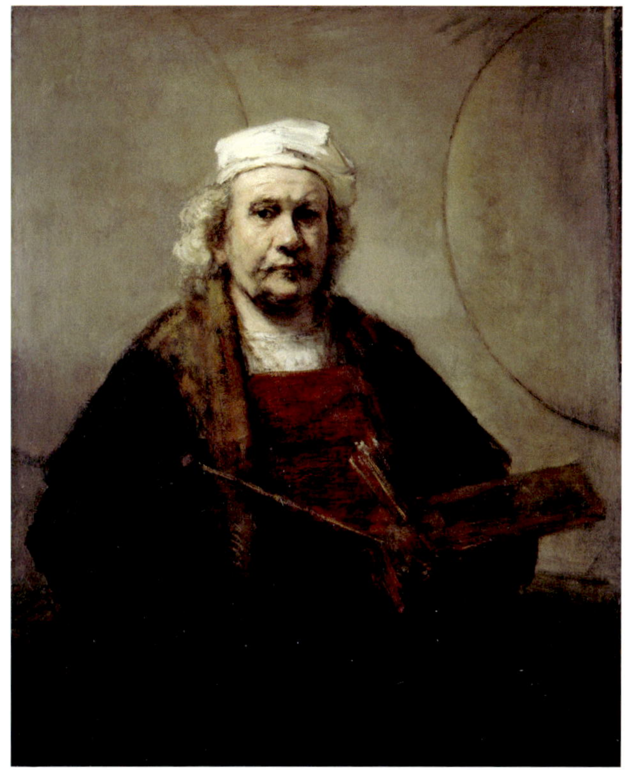

OTHER KEY WORKS

Self-Portrait as a Young Man, c.1628, Rijksmuseum, Amsterdam,
　Netherlands
Self-Portrait as Zeuxis Laughing, 1662, Wallraf-Richartz-Museum,
　Cologne, Germany

KEY FEATURES

Prolific and sustained interest in self-portraiture across a range
　of media
Adoption of the genre for a variety of reasons, including
　assistenza self-portraiture, ideas testing and autonomous
　self-portraiture
Interest in role-playing, posturing and costume
Insertion of motifs borrowed from Renaissance portraiture to
　elevate status
Dramatic use of chiaroscuro and tonal handling
Gestural use of impasto in his late self-portraiture

DIEGO VELÁZQUEZ
1599–1660

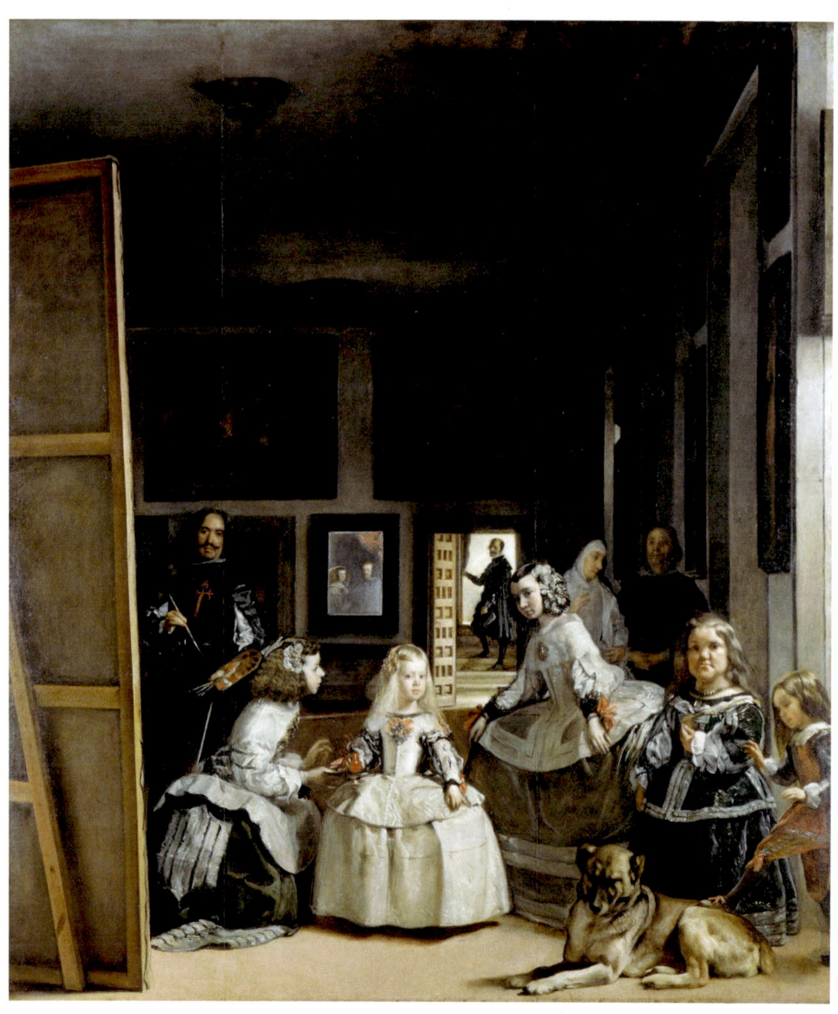

Diego Velázquez
Las Meninas, 1656
Oil on canvas,
318 x 276 cm
(125¼ x 108⅝ in.)
Museo Nacional del
Prado, Madrid

**The mirror on the back
wall of this work recalls
the convex mirror in Jan
Van Eyck's *Portrait of
Giovanni(?) Arnolfini and
His Wife* (see page 12).
Both artists used mirrors
to channel miniature
portraits into other parts
of the picture plane. In
Las Meninas, Velázquez
uses the device to enable
the royal couple to
occupy the foreground
and the background
simultaneously.**

Diego Velázquez was the preferred court painter of the Spanish
King Philip IV and his second wife, Queen Mariana. The royal family
loved to visit his large studio in the royal apartments to watch him
work. *Las Meninas*, 'Ladies in Waiting', appears to capture one such
moment. Velázquez occupies the shadowy left-hand corner of the
image, dressed in fine courtier's garments, hard at work on a huge
canvas. Margarita, the five-year-old daughter of the King and Queen,
takes the centre ground. She is all shimmering skirts, silken hair and
perky inquisitiveness. Surrounded by maids, Margarita is entertained
by court dwarfs and guarded by the family dog. The artist, the
princess and various other protagonists stare back at the viewer with
expressions of awe and reverence, as if pausing to take a breath. The
source of their respect can be found reflected in the mirror behind
them: the King and Queen are standing in front of them, occupying
the space of the viewer. Have the royal couple just dropped by to see
Velázquez at work or are they posing to have their portrait painted,
themselves a vision of magnificence?

It is hard to find a more ambitious portrait of an artist at work
than this. Many artists enjoyed close relations with royalty, but none
had dared place themselves within a royal portrait. Assuming greater
prominence than the monarchs themselves, Velázquez looks at ease,
like one of the family. He takes full control of the scene, mastering
a highly complex composition and choosing the epic scale of history
painting to depict a fleeting moment. He reduces the size of the
figures to merely players on a stage, containing them within the
lower half of the painting with their exits and entrances. The upper
echelons of this space are reserved exclusively for art, for in the eyes
of Velázquez, art is king.

KEY FEATURES

Daring and innovative approach to court portraiture, capturing
   informal moments rather than stiff, static poses
Direct insertion of a self-portrait into a royal portrait, elevating
   the status of the artist
Baroque interest in chiaroscuro and the theatrical potential of
   human interaction
Unusual focus on support staff, including jesters and maids
Innovative use of mirrors to project miniature portraits into
   surprising areas of the canvas
Loose handling of paint to capture a range of surfaces and textures
Large, ambitious scale

MARY BEALE
1633–99

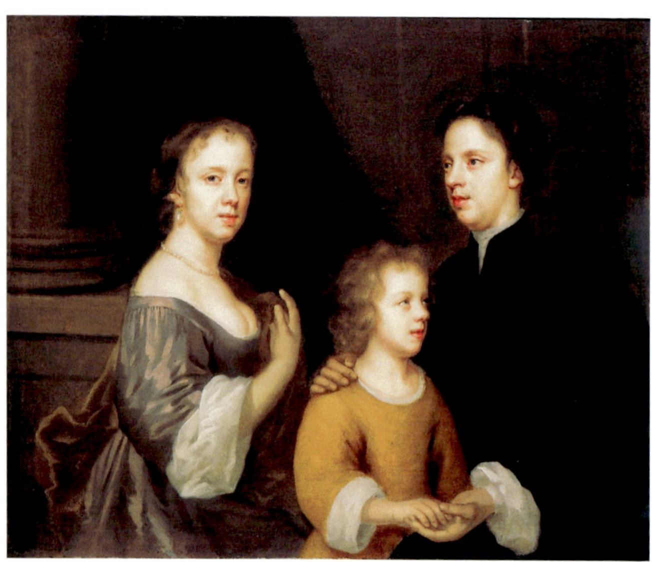

Mary Beale was one of the first female professional painters in England. She ran a successful portrait studio in London's Pall Mall and was the main breadwinner of the household. Her husband Charles, a former City worker, spent many years supporting her business: managing the accounts, preparing the paints and welcoming the sitters. Mary and Charles also raised two sons together. The Beales could be described as a very modern couple.

Charles asserted that his 'dearest heart' painted herself 'for study and improvement'. This was nothing radical; many artists had used self-portraiture to hone their skills. Beale did, however, introduce a new motif: she was the first artist to use self-portraiture to identify herself as a working parent. *Self-Portrait with her Husband Charles and Son Bartholomew* (c.1663–4) directly acknowledges the support she received from her family. Charles maintains affectionate contact with his son and gazes adoringly across to his wife. Beale stands close to them both, but she also maintains some autonomy, turning to face the viewer with an expression of confidence and pride. She raises her right finger to point to herself, indicating her position as the figurehead of the family.

Mary Beale
Self-Portrait with her Husband Charles and Son Bartholomew, c.1663–4
Oil on canvas,
63.5 x 76.2 cm
(25 x 30 in.)
Museum of the Home,
London

There was a growing market for portraiture in seventeenth-century Britain. Many artists were able to sustain successful careers as portraitists, although as a female painter Beale was a rarity. To earn enough money to support a family, however, a portraitist would need a successful formula, a consistent stream of clients and a willingness to work very hard.

Just over a year later, Beale revisited her coexisting roles of artist and parent in her *Self-Portrait Holding Portraits of her Sons* (c.1665). She assumed a stately seated pose for this work. Every inch the matriarch, she is draped in fine clothing and wears her hair in a fashionable style. This self-portrait not only idealizes Beale as a most gracious and respectable lady, but it also serves as a fine advertisement of her skill in capturing a likeness for potential sitters. The clean palette hanging on the wall indicates Beale's professional standing. And there, in the bottom left-hand corner, are her two boys, depicted on a canvas, rendered and supported by the artist's own fair hand.

KEY FEATURES

Use of self-portraiture to explore the coexisting roles of
  professional painter and parent
Family group self-portraiture
Confident and strong representations of women
Idealization of the human face and body
Baroque theatricality of pose and drapery
Use of self-portraiture to practise technique and composition
Reflects a growing market for portraiture in Britain

Mary Beale
Self-Portrait Holding Portraits of her Sons,
c.1665
Oil on canvas,
109.2 x 87.6 cm
(43 x 34½ in.)
National Portrait Gallery,
London

Beale was a friend of Sir Peter Lely (1618–80), the court portraitist to Charles I. Both artists sought to elevate their sitters into idealized, statuesque figures draped in great plumes of fabric, as evidenced in this self-portrait. Although fashions changed and business slowed towards the end of her life, Beale continued to work right up until her death in 1699.

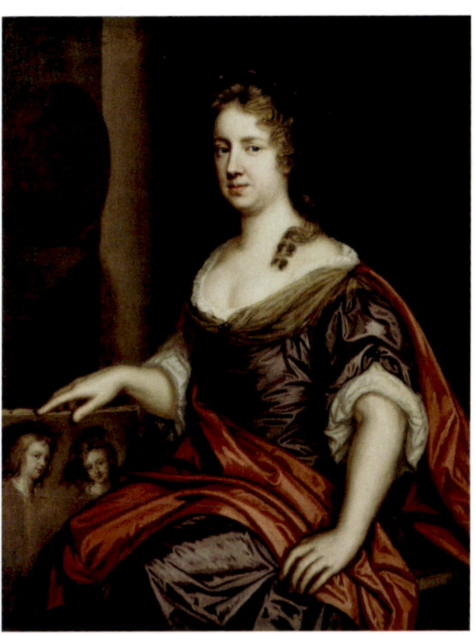

ANNE SEYMOUR DAMER
1748–1828

*'Mrs Damer, daughter of General Conway, has chosen a walk
more difficult and far more uncommon than painting. The annals
of statuary record few artists of the fair sex, and not one that
I recollect of any celebrity.'*
Horace Walpole, 1780

Negotiating the macho world of sculpture was a very difficult
thing for a woman to do in eighteenth-century England. The
British amateur sculptor Anne Seymour Damer had the talent,
financial means and perseverance needed to break new ground.
Her aristocratic parents supported her unusual interest, investing in
specialist carving, modelling and anatomical tuition. After removing
herself from an unhappy marriage (her ex-husband later committed
suicide), Damer found the freedom and focus to pursue her practice
as a sculptor. She gained recognition for neoclassical bust portraits
of various notable figures including politicians and actors, and for
her animal sculptures. Damer was the source of much society
gossip, not just because of her unconventional pursuit of sculpture,
but also as a result of her close relationships with women and her
preference for masculine clothing.

Damer's *Self-Portrait* of 1778 is a rare work. There are few
sculpted self-portraits in eighteenth-century art, fewer still made by
women. Damer assumes a composed and contemplative full-frontal
pose, her downward gaze avoiding eye contact with the viewer, as if
focusing on deeper intellectual concerns. Unlike many of her female
contemporaries, Damer chose not to wear the latest fashions for
her self-portrait, preferring to adorn her body with the gender-
neutral folds of Greek drapery. Her hair is natural and not 'done'.
The symmetrical handling of the face shows the direct influence
of classical ideals of balance and poise. There is no risk of the sitter
going unidentified: Damer carved her name into the work at the
front and at the back. The Greek inscription translates as 'Anne
Seymour Damer from Britain, made herself'. The choice of Greek
adds a further classical reference and also highlights the artist's
extensive education.

Anne Seymour Damer
Self-Portrait, 1778
Marble,
height 60 cm (23⅝ in.)
Uffizi Gallery, Florence

**This unusual self-portrait
is the only sculpture to be
represented in the Uffizi
Gallery's impressive
collection of over 1,600
self-portraits. Established
by Cardinal Leopoldo
de' Medici in 1664, this
collection was originally
displayed in the Vasari
corridor connecting the
Uffizi with the Palazzo
Pitti in Florence. Many
artists have donated
their self-portraits to the
collection, aware of its
longstanding significance.**

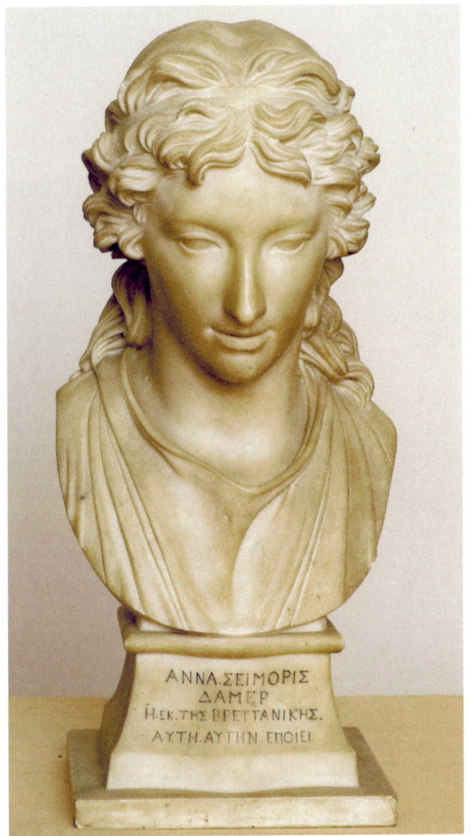

OTHER KEY WORKS

Joshua Reynolds, *Portrait of Anne Seymour Damer*, 1773,
 Yale Center for British Art, Paul Mellon Fund, USA

KEY FEATURES

Rare example of an eighteenth-century sculpted self-portrait
Carved marble bust assuming an unusual full-frontal profile
Neoclassical style: strong influence of Ancient Greek and
 Roman sculpture
Choice of classical drapery and styling rather than contemporary
 fashions
Refusal to engage in frivolity or flirtation
Gender-neutral detailing
Carved inscription to preserve the identity of the sitter

ELISABETH LOUISE VIGÉE LE BRUN
1755–1842

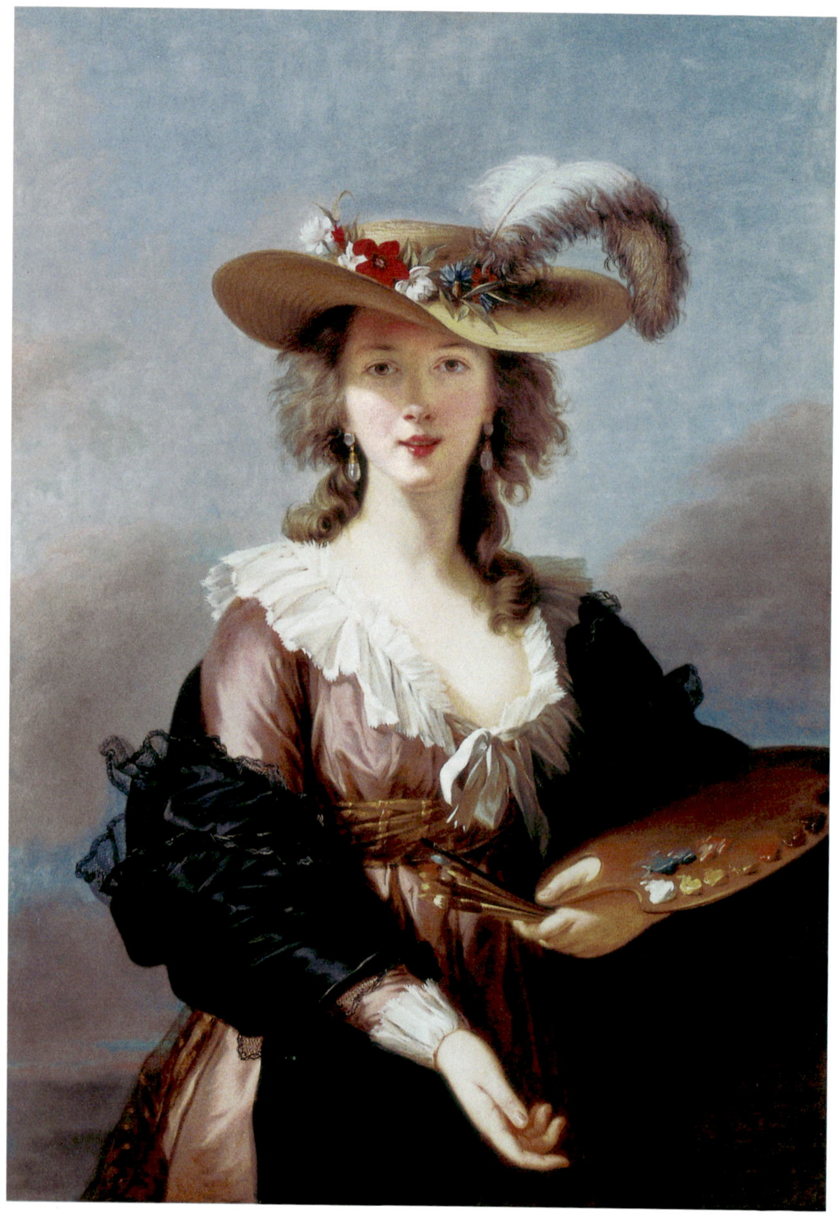

**Elisabeth Louise Vigée
Le Brun**
*Self-Portrait in a Straw
Hat*, after 1782
Oil on canvas,
97.8 x 70.5 cm
(38½ x 27¾ in.)
National Gallery, London

**Vigée Le Brun's
reputation as an artist
remains conflicted. Some
feminist critics have taken
a dim view, considering
her work to be too
entrenched in narcissism,
prettification and a need
for male approval. Others
discern a strategic and
canny influencer able
to operate within the
highest social circles
and to sustain a hugely
successful career in a
male-dominated field.**

The French portraitist Elisabeth Louise Vigée Le Brun knew
exactly what women wanted. Through a gentle process of flattery
and accentuation, she could always find a sitter's best angle or
redeeming feature. The daughter of a portraitist, Vigée Le Brun
raided her father's contacts book to rise through the ranks,
eventually reaching the highest echelons of society. In 1778, Vigée
Le Brun was introduced to Marie Antoinette, the Queen of France,
who was immediately smitten by her breezy and endearing style.
Vigée Le Brun became her favourite painter and made over twenty
portraits of the monarch and her children.

Despite her meteoric rise to fame, Vigée Le Brun knew
her place within the wider artistic fraternity. Women were not
allowed to enter the French Royal Academy unless in exceptional
circumstances. Vigée Le Brun was granted access only because
of the express wish of the King. Academy training programmes
were equally restrictive. Women were forbidden from studying the
nude, thus hampering their ability to contribute to the genre of
history painting, which was considered to be the highest form of
art. Vigée Le Brun decided to dedicate her professional life to the
less esteemed genre of portraiture. She specialized in depictions of
women, but often referenced the paintings of the old masters to
justify and elevate her work.

Vigée Le Brun produced approximately twenty self-portraits
during her lifetime, most of which reflect the artist's wider interest
in expressing style, beauty and grace. *Self-Portrait in a Straw Hat*
(after 1782) directly acknowledges Peter Paul Rubens' *Portrait of
Susanna Lunden* (1622–5, National Gallery, London), commonly
nicknamed 'Le Chapeau de Paille' or 'The Straw Hat'. Vigée Le
Brun first saw this work on a trip to the Netherlands in 1782 and
recalled in her memoirs how its 'great power lies in the subtle
representation of two different light sources, simple daylight and
the bright light of the sun'.

Vigée Le Brun borrowed Rubens' vision of an attractive woman
basking in daylight. Both Vigée Le Brun and Lunden wear low-cut
stylish clothing, keeping the sun off their faces with flamboyant
hats. However, the similarities end here, for Vigée Le Brun drops
the submissive flirtation in favour of a more assertive stance:
shoulders back, direct gaze and right hand forward as if to engage
us in thoughtful discourse. Many of Vigée Le Brun's influential
fashion choices are also evident. She preferred a natural hairstyle to
an elaborate, powdered 'do', and favoured a flowing outline without
recourse to trussed-up corsetry. The inclusion of the artist's palette
asserts Vigée Le Brun's status as an attractive woman *and* an artist.

This self-portrait was exhibited in 1783 at the Salon, a major art exhibition held every two years in Paris. The critics marvelled at the work, exclaiming, 'Have you seen Madame Le Brun? What do you think of Madame Le Brun?'

Equally admired were Vigée Le Brun's self-portraits with her daughter, Julie. Again, the artist referenced old master paintings to elevate through association. *Self-Portrait with her Daughter, Julie* (1786) bears a striking resemblance to Raphael's Madonna and Child paintings, particularly *Madonna della Sedia* (c.1514, Palazzo Pitti, Florence). Although the artist and her daughter appear at ease, reclining in neoclassical drapery to engage in a tender embrace, Vigée Le Brun was under close scrutiny at the time of making this work. Not only was her lavish and frivolous lifestyle beginning to raise eyebrows, but there were rumours of an extramarital affair with the finance minister, Charles Alexandre de Calonne. What better way to signal her innocence and virtue than this, a perfect image of motherhood depicting a woman's 'proper' place at the heart of the family? The close union of a mother and daughter made sacred through religious association. Vigée Le Brun used self-portraiture to engage in a strategic, if dangerous, game of public relations management. In 1789, Vigée Le Brun fled revolutionary France due to her close connections with the monarchy. Four years later, Queen Marie Antoinette was executed.

**Elisabeth Louise
Vigée Le Brun**
*Self-Portrait with her
Daughter, Julie*, 1786
Oil on canvas,
105 x 84 cm
(41⅜ x 33 in.)
Musée du Louvre, Paris

The enduring appeal of Vigée Le Brun's art is evidenced by its reproduction on all manner of goods from tea towels to chocolate boxes. Her work is noted for its relaxed informality, with sitters often leaning casually, lips parted ready to speak. A sense of ease infuses this saccharine scene, with the artist's doe-eyed daughter adding a further injection of sweetness.

OTHER KEY WORKS

Self-Portrait with Daughter, after 1787, Musée du Louvre,
  Paris, France
Self-Portrait, 1790, Uffizi Gallery, Florence, Italy

KEY FEATURES

Use of self-portraiture to forge an identity as a woman and a
  successful artist
Production of 'mother and child' self-portraiture to reinforce
  myths of virtue and propriety
Confident and attractive representations of women
Idealization of the human face and body
Inclusion of neoclassical references and 'old master' motifs to
  elevate her work
Self-conscious fashioning and trendsetting
Deliberate presentation of relaxed informality and ease

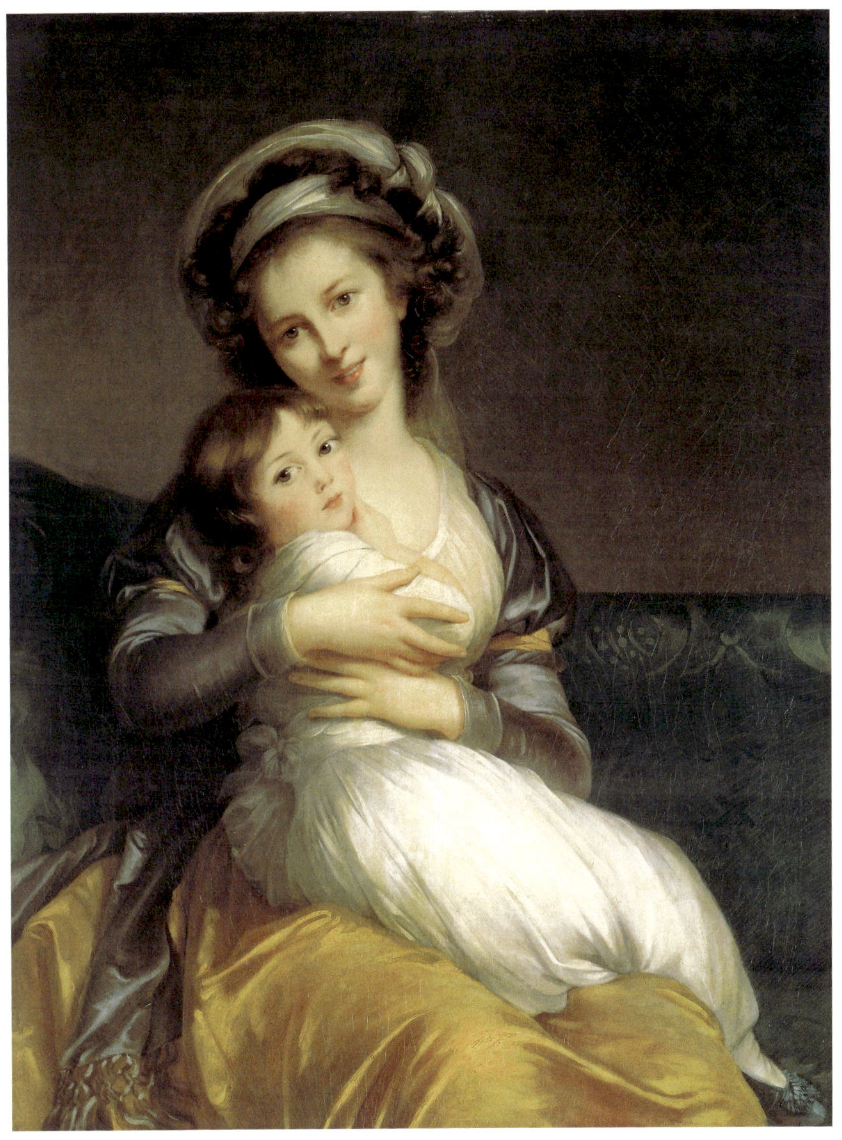

FRANCISCO GOYA
1746–1828

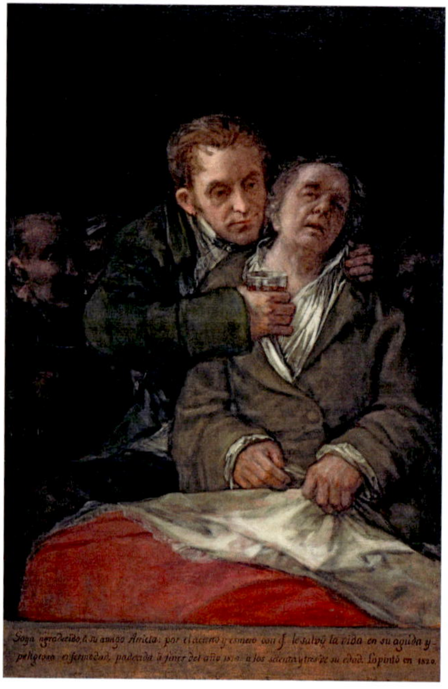

In many respects, the work of Francisco Goya could be said to occupy a conceptual crossroads. His brooding paintings and graphic works combine the skills and techniques of an 'old master' with a psychological intensity associated with the Romantic movement. This prolific and versatile Spanish artist enjoyed huge success during his lifetime as a portraitist and as a court painter. His graphic work was printed and circulated widely, conveying darker visions, a strong narrative impulse and satirical commentary. Goya chose an intriguing self-portrait to provide the frontispiece for his 1799 book of prints, *Los Caprichos* ('The Whims'). This collection of eighty aquatint etchings chronicles various acts of human violence, horror and destruction. The frontispiece features a surly character who slumps into his self-portrait with reluctant disdain. He expresses little desire to turn and engage with the viewer, choosing instead to cast a shifty sideways glance from the sharpest corner of his eye.

Goya's art grew even darker towards the end of his life and he gradually withdrew from public engagement altogether. Around 1792, Goya succumbed to a mysterious malaise which left him deaf

Francisco Goya
Self-Portrait with Dr Arrieta, 1820
Oil on canvas,
114.6 x 76.5 cm
(45⅛ x 30⅛ in.)
Minneapolis Institute of Art, Minneapolis

Goya's interest in narrative is revealed in this unusual composition which pays homage to a favourite doctor. The lengthy inscription running across the bottom of the work praises Dr Arrieta for his 'compassion and care with which he saved his life during the acute and dangerous illness he suffered'.

and incapacitated. He endured another severe illness in 1819, which left him close to death. In his final self-portrait of 1820, Goya pays homage to the compassion and skill of his physician, Dr Eugenio García Arrieta. This painting depicts the artist propped up in bed, tugging at his sheet perhaps for comfort or in an attempt to squeeze away the pain. The attentive doctor supports Goya's body with tenderness whilst offering a glass of water. Together, the two figures recall a pietà – a dramatic Christian scene depicting Mary cradling the dead Christ in her arms. Goya would later give this unusual portrait to Dr Arrieta as a mark of gratitude for saving his life.

OTHER KEY WORKS

Self-Portrait, 1795–7, Metropolitan Museum of Art, New York, USA
Self-Portrait, 1815, Museo Nacional del Prado, Madrid, Spain

KEY FEATURES

Unidealized representations of the ageing self
Interest in darker psychological states, anxiety and unease
Strong use of chiaroscuro effects
Expressive handling of painted surfaces and etched lines
Use of unusual compositions, body language and expression
   to establish barriers
Dramatic presentation of a moment of crisis
Strong narrative impulse

Francisco Goya
Francisco Goya y Lucientes (Self-Portrait), Plate 1 of Los Caprichos, 1799
Etching, aquatint, drypoint and burin on paper, 21.7 x 15 cm (8½ x 5⅞ in.)
Metropolitan Museum of Art, New York

Goya was influenced by Rembrandt's atmospheric use of chiaroscuro. In this print, Goya creates looming shadows and dark recesses to build a sense of tension and reserve. The body language and the disgruntled sideways glance act as barriers to intimacy.

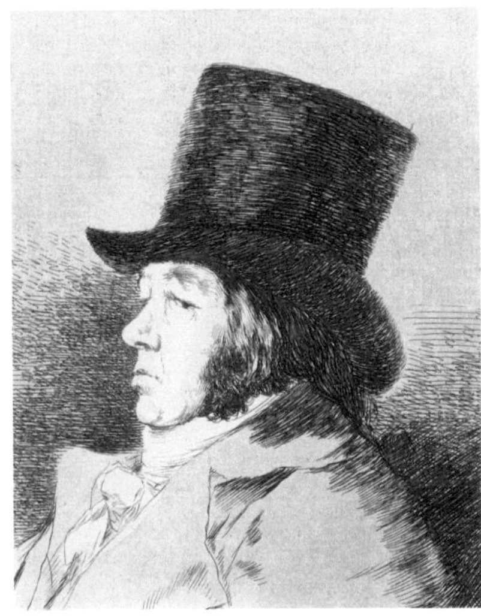

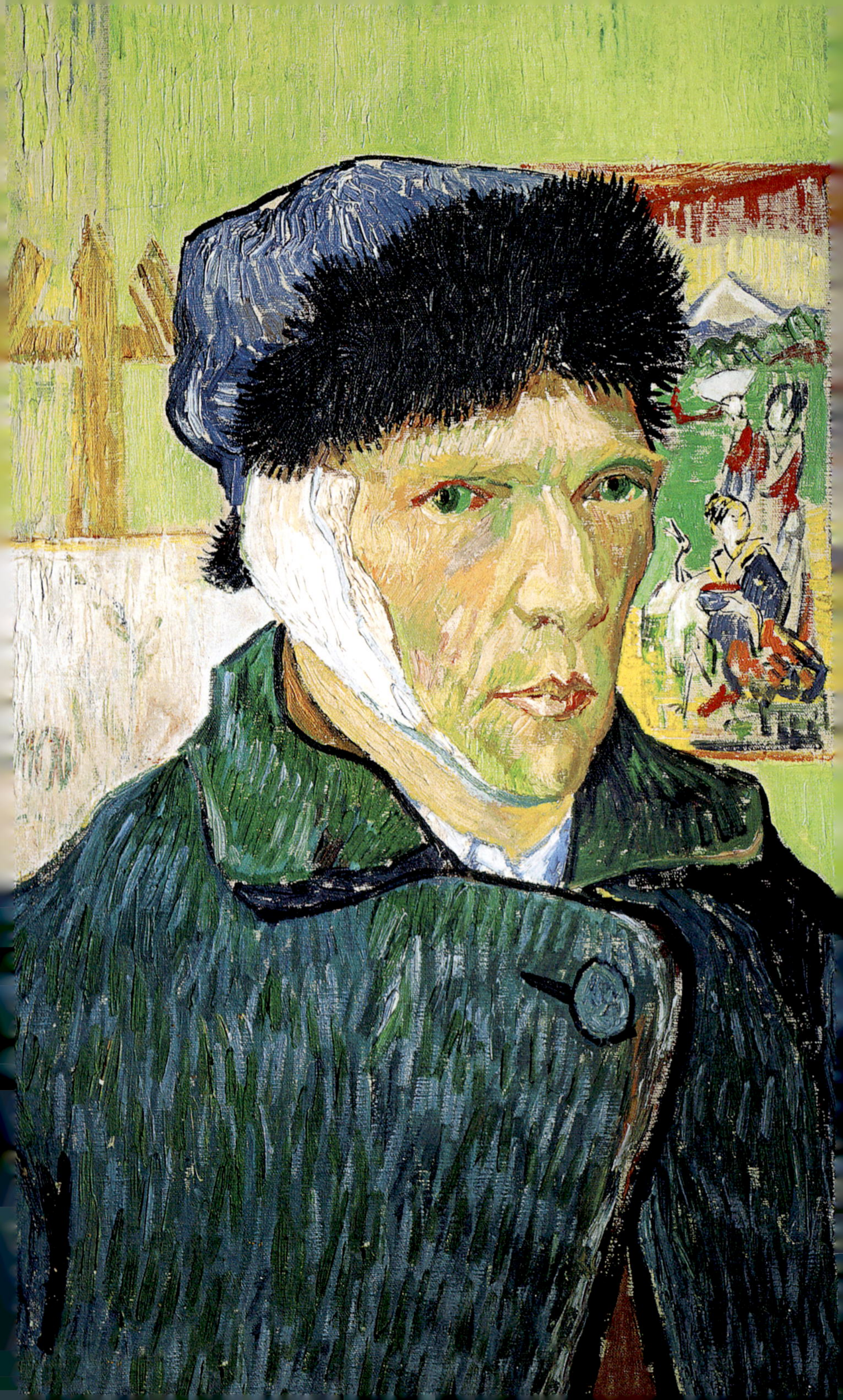

SOUL SEARCHING

-

... painted portraits have a life of their own
that comes from deep in the soul of the painter
and where the machine can't go.

-

Vincent van Gogh, 1885

GUSTAVE COURBET
1819–77

The image of the bohemian artist has lingered long in the public imagination. According to the myth, this penniless genius stalks the shadows, ostracized from bourgeois society. He haunts dimly lit streets, dingy café bars, his freezing garret, or he abandons the city altogether, preferring the intense solitude of a desolate landscape. The bohemian artist is tall, dark and handsome. He has tousled, unkempt hair and a bold stare illuminated by ideas. This melancholic figure dominated the art and literature of the Romantic period.

The French artist Gustave Courbet sustained his bohemian image with remarkable consistency and imagination right up until the end of his life. Born in a rural corner of eastern France, he moved to Paris at the age of twenty. He quickly settled into the bohemian lifestyle, holding court in bars and cafés and racking up huge tabs. Courbet spoke in a loud regional dialect. His words, often slurred with alcohol, called for a new, earthy realism in art. A media-savvy self-publicist, he was also a prolific self-portraitist, and a very willing subject of countless photographs and caricatures. Courbet was notoriously vain. Even in old age, when his turgid body was ravaged by the effects of excessive drinking, the figures in his self-portraits remain eternally svelte.

Despite his purported love of realism, Courbet's self-portraits operate as works of fiction with the artist playing the starring role.

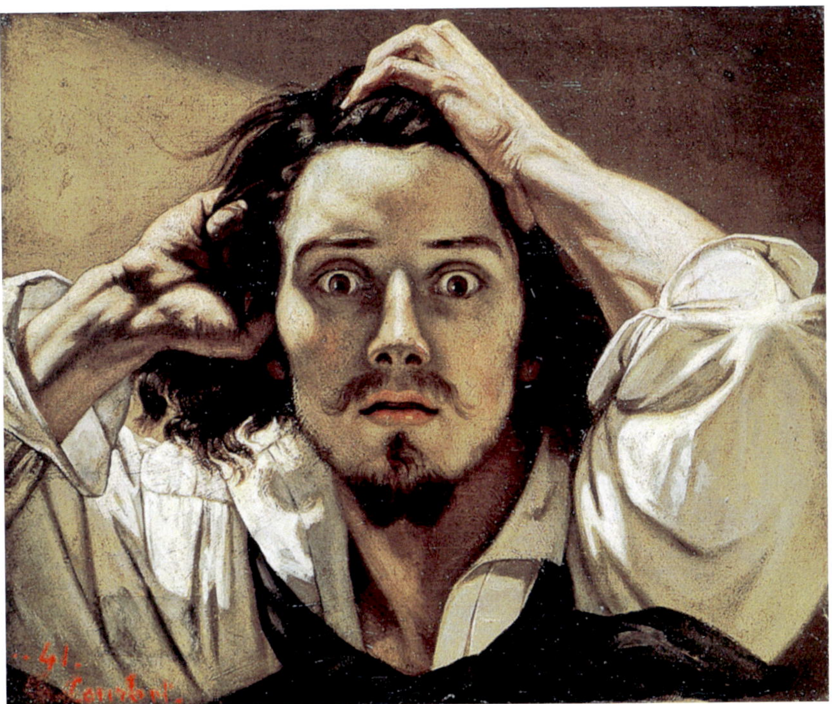

Gustave Courbet
*Self-Portrait: The
Desperate Man*, 1841
Oil on canvas,
45 x 55cm (17¾ x 21⅝ in.)
Private collection

**In this dramatic work,
Courbet lurches into
the viewer's space, as
if bursting out of the
picture plane. Expressive
hands hold back the
artist's hair to reveal
his fine features and
trademark beard. The
expression of an artist
on the verge of sanity
supports the myth of the
bohemian as an eccentric
and vulnerable figure.**

We find him playing a cello with soul-searching sensuosity (even though he couldn't play a note), or drooling with exhaustion having carved a masterpiece into a rockface (he was never a sculptor). Courbet's hands are often tactile and active, his body often draped or propped at ground level. These sensuous gestures indicate an artist in touch with himself, with nature and with the earth. Locations are often rural and unoccupied: Courbet presents himself as an outsider, far removed from his bourgeois critics in Paris. He asserts wilful independence.

Courbet was very sensitive to criticism. In 1855, he submitted a number of works to the Universal Exhibition at the Palais des Beaux-Arts in Paris. On discovering that two of his paintings had been rejected by the selection committee, he became enraged and decided to take direct action. He built a temporary structure, 'The Pavilion of Realism', on land directly opposite the venue, and used the space to stage his own solo exhibition, which featured many self-portraits. Much to his personal embarrassment, the exhibition was a total flop, with very poor attendance prompting a slashing of the entrance fee. Nevertheless, the concept of making an alternative exhibition to counter institutional tastes would influence subsequent generations of artists. The *Salon des Refusés* exhibition of 1863, for example, featured a diverse range of Impressionist art rejected by the academy.

The notion of the artist as an outcast finds further expression in Courbet's famous painting, *The Meeting* (1854). This work depicts the travelling artist bumping into his patron, Alfred Bruyas, and his servant, Calas. The chance encounter takes place at a crossroads outside Montpellier. The edgeland setting offers an opportunity for Courbet to express his exceptional talents as a landscape painter; the scene is bathed in radiant sunlight. Once again, Courbet keeps his distance: he appears friendly and amenable, yet he marks his independence with the assertive placement of his rugged wooden staff. He carries his life upon his back, indicating his position as a wanderer, a nomad. Intriguingly, Courbet is the only figure to cast a shadow, indicating a godlike ability to block the sun.

Courbet died from alcoholism in 1877 at the age of fifty-eight, following a spell in prison for his allegiance to radical politics. Broke and broken, he remained a rebel and a revolutionary until the very end.

Gustave Courbet
The Wounded Man,
1844–54
Oil on canvas,
81.5 x 97.5 cm
(32⅛ x 38⅜ in.)
Musée d'Orsay, Paris

Courbet often used self-portraiture to explore notions of victimhood. In this work he appears slumped against a tree, apparently mortally wounded. The close-up perspective draws the viewer into the heart of the drama. Nevertheless, despite the suggestion of a severe chest wound, the scene is ultimately unconvincing: the artist appears to have nodded off after a heavy night's drinking.

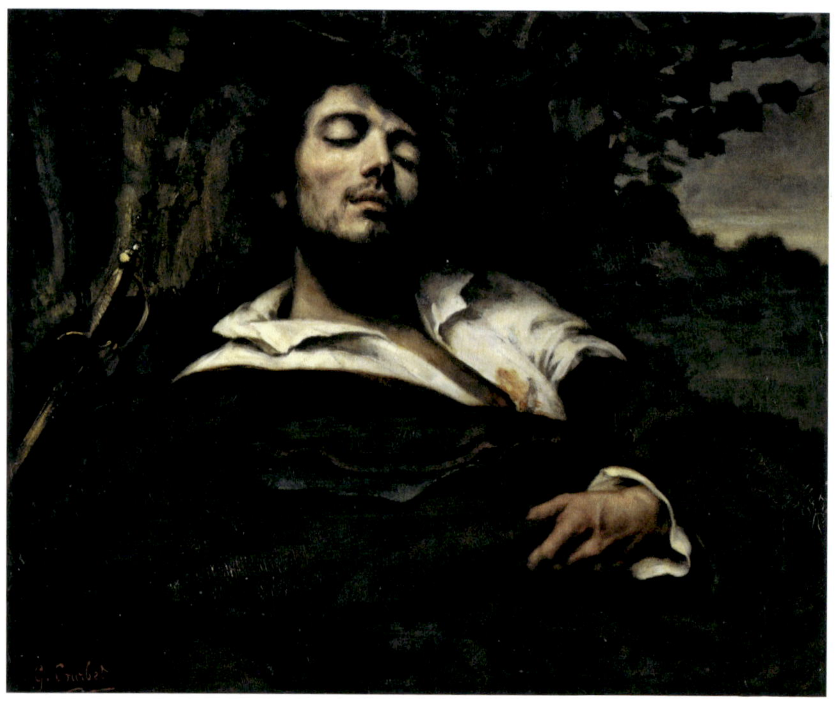

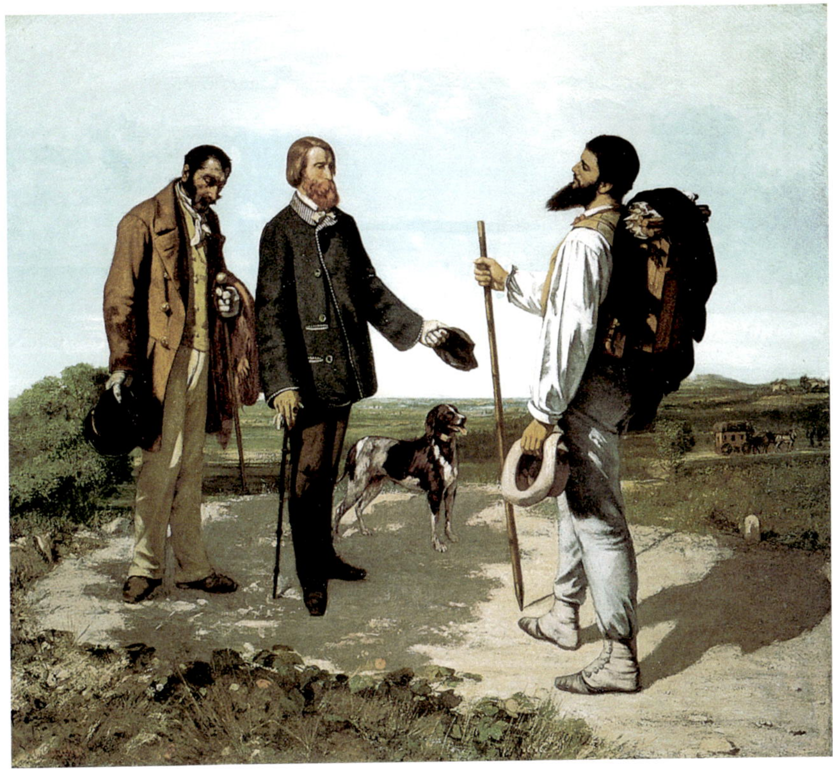

Gustave Courbet
*The Meeting ('Bonjour
Monsieur Courbet')*, 1854
Oil on canvas,
129 x 149cm
(50¾ x 58⅝ in.)
Musée Fabre, Montpellier

This work reveals the
productive cooperation
between an artist and
his patron. Courbet
appreciated the support
of Alfred Bruyas, an art
collector and writer. In
1854, Courbet wrote
to Bruyas to outline his
intentions for this work:
'There remains one more
[self-portrait] for me to
do, that is a man firm in
his principles: the free
man.'

OTHER KEY WORKS

Man with a Pipe, c.1846, Musée Fabre, Montpellier, France
The Painter's Studio, c.1854–5, Musée d'Orsay, Paris, France

KEY FEATURES

Intense and sustained self-interest
Idealization of the figure and the face
Deliberate mythmaking and self-aggrandizement including
    the perpetuation of bohemian myths
Use of self-portraiture to act out different narratives and
    identities
Preoccupation with freedom, independence and individualism
Use of the close-up view to increase impact

VINCENT VAN GOGH
1853–90

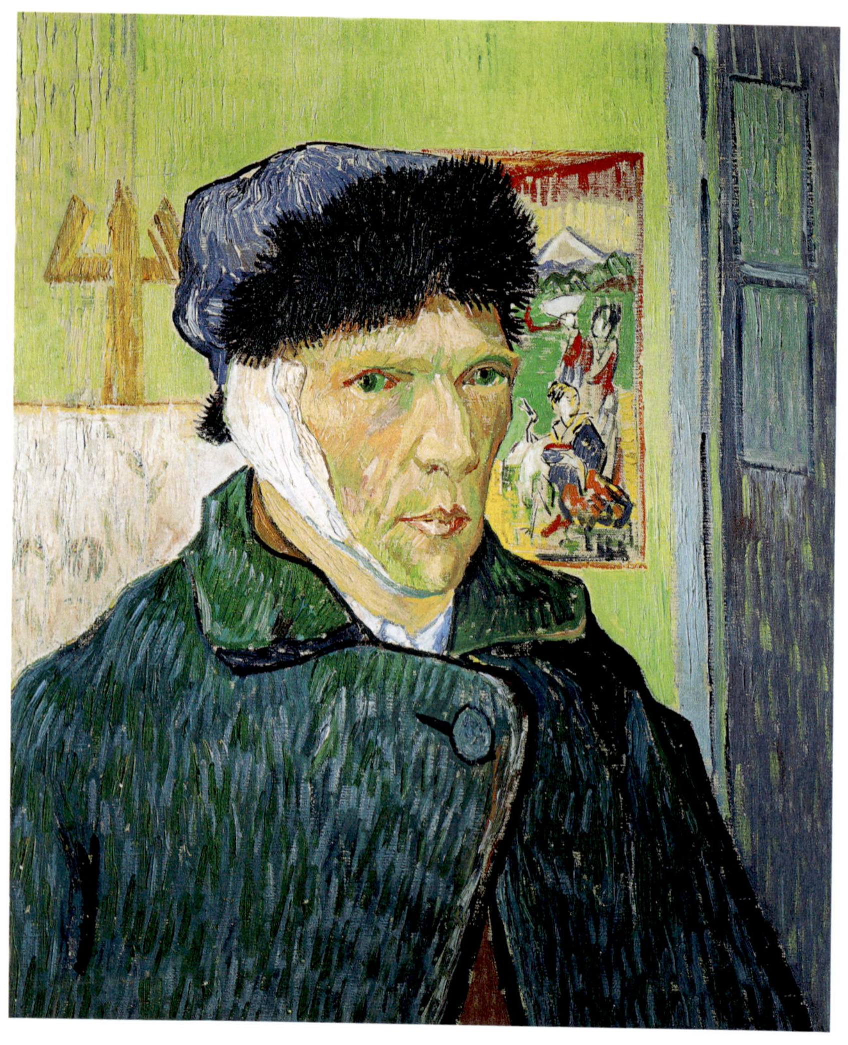

Vincent van Gogh
*Self-Portrait with
Bandaged Ear*, 1889
Oil on canvas,
60 x 49 cm
(23⅝ x 19¼ in.)
Courtauld Gallery,
London

**Van Gogh decorated
his home in bright
colours, often pinning
inspirational source
material to the walls.
A Japanese woodblock
print can be seen in
the background of this
self-portrait, indicating
Van Gogh's interest in
the flowing forms and
enchanting hues of these
influential nineteenth-
century prints.**

In 1885, the Dutch painter Vincent van Gogh described how 'painted portraits have a life of their own that comes from deep in the soul of the painter and where the machine can't go'. With the medium of photography increasingly able to capture external appearances, opportunities arose for artists to extend the expressive potential of paint. Van Gogh's melancholic self-portraits are some of the most famous paintings in western art history. Mostly head and shoulders in format, these works reveal Van Gogh's exceptional originality as a painter and a colourist. Bright dashes of contrasting colour jostle against one another on the picture surface to create an overriding feeling of emotional intensity and anxiety. Equally well known is the sad story of Van Gogh's tortuous life: a classic tale of genius, vulnerability and mental illness, one that hurtles towards an inevitable tragic end.

Van Gogh struggled to achieve recognition during his lifetime. He could barely afford the costs of employing life models and so he turned to the cheapest, most readily available model he could find: himself. Between 1886 and 1888, he lived with his art-dealer brother in the Montmartre district of Paris. Here he embarked on a rapid flurry of approximately twenty self-portraits. Despite this creative surge, Van Gogh disliked Paris intensely and longed for a rural, spiritual life. In 1888 he moved to Arles, in the south of France, to rejoice in God's work as evidenced in nature and to establish a new artistic community. His vision was to forge a brotherhood of like-minded artists keen to surpass realism in search of deeper, spiritual visions.

The Post-Impressionist painter Paul Gauguin was intrigued by his friend's vision of a 'Studio of the South' and made speedy plans to travel from his home in Brittany to stay with Van Gogh at his house in Arles. A series of frustrating delays prompted the two artists to engage in an unusual kind of pen-friendship, exchanging letters and self-portraits to maintain creative momentum. Gauguin finally arrived in November 1888. Van Gogh had spent considerable time in anticipation, making adjustments to his home to ensure his friend's comfort. This homemaking impulse is revealed in a pair of paintings that Van Gogh initiated after his friend's arrival, documenting each artist's designated chair. Chairs provide spaces for bodies. Although these paintings are devoid of figures, they convey a strong individual presence and point to deeper psychological states. Gauguin's upholstered chair has a menacing, spectral quality, its legs splaying like tentacles, pointing to growing discontent between the artists. Van Gogh's rush-weave seat appears more self-contained, painfully isolated and inhibited. Sadly, the

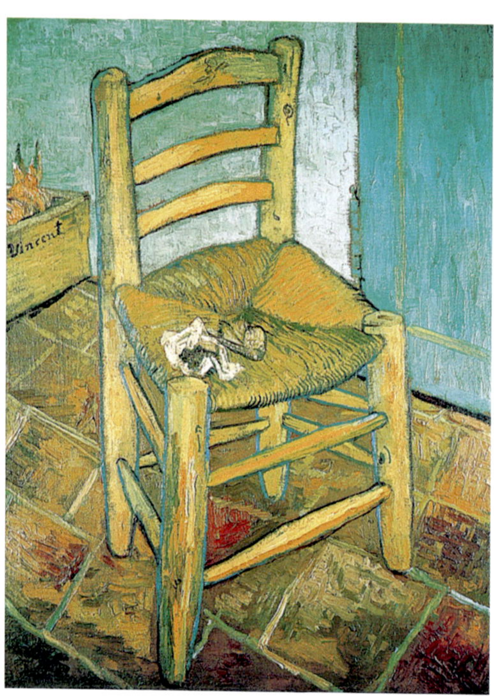

Vincent van Gogh
Van Gogh's Chair, 1888
Oil on canvas,
91.8 x 73cm
(36⅛ x 28¾ in.)
National Gallery, London

**Van Gogh yearned for
a simple, rural life as
reflected in his choice of
simple, rustic furnishings,
such as this rush-weave
seat, the bare tiled flooring
and the simple box of
onions in the corner. The
poignancy of this work
rests in the pervading
sense of isolation and
loneliness. The only
faithful friends ready to
greet Van Gogh are his
pipe and his tobacco.**

brotherhood was very short-lived. On 23 December 1888, Van
Gogh suffered a severe psychotic episode. After threatening
Gauguin with a razor, he dashed into the centre of Arles, slicing off
part of his own ear and presenting it to a passing sex worker with the
request that she 'keep it safe'. Police later found Van Gogh alone in
his house, suffering from acute blood loss.

For both artists, the process of recovering from this traumatic
episode involved the creation of new self-portraits. Van Gogh's *Self-
Portrait with Bandaged Ear* (1889) seeks to normalize the incident.
He sits upright as always, wearing fluffy winter headwear that at first
glance looks like a trapper hat fastened beneath the chin. Only on
closer inspection does the ear covering register as the bandage used
to protect his wound. Van Gogh appears remarkably composed,
stoical, steadfast. His skills as a painter remain unscathed for this is a
masterpiece in colour, a blaze of brilliant vermillion reds, acid greens,
midday blues. Gauguin pursued an entirely different direction,
reworking the incident in three dimensions. *Jug in the Form of a Head,
Self-Portrait* (1889) finds Gauguin in a state of decapitation, head
tilted back, eyes dead shut. This is post-traumatic stress pottery.
The vessel lacks ears. The blood-red glaze flows in all directions.

OTHER KEY WORKS

Self-Portrait Dedicated to Gauguin, 1888, Harvard Art Museums,
  Harvard, USA
Paul Gauguin, *Self-Portrait with Portrait of Émile Bernard (Les
  misérables)*, 1888, Van Gogh Museum, Amsterdam, Netherlands
Gauguin's Chair, November 1888, 1888, Van Gogh Museum,
  Amsterdam, Netherlands

KEY FEATURES

Repeated use of self-portraiture to explore psychological
  states
Intense bursts of creativity, often working across several
  self-portraits concurrently
Expressive use of colour and brushwork
Projection of individual identities onto everyday objects
Exchange of self-portraiture to intensify a friendship and
  to pay homage
Representation of the artist as an outsider
Therapeutic use of self-portraiture to reflect on trauma

Paul Gauguin
*Jug in the Form of a Head,
Self-Portrait*, 1889
Glazed stoneware,
height 19.3 cm (7⅝ in.)
Kunstindustrimuseet,
Copenhagen, Denmark

Gauguin's interest in self-portraiture increased as a result of his friendship with Van Gogh. His decision to represent himself as a domestic object was perhaps made in response to Van Gogh's paintings of chairs. The representation of a severed head may also reference Caravaggio's influential painting *David with the Head of Goliath*, 1609–10 (see page 30).

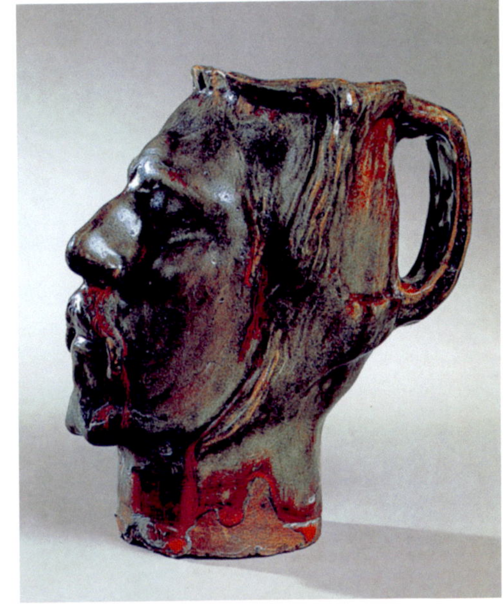

JAMES ENSOR
1860–1949

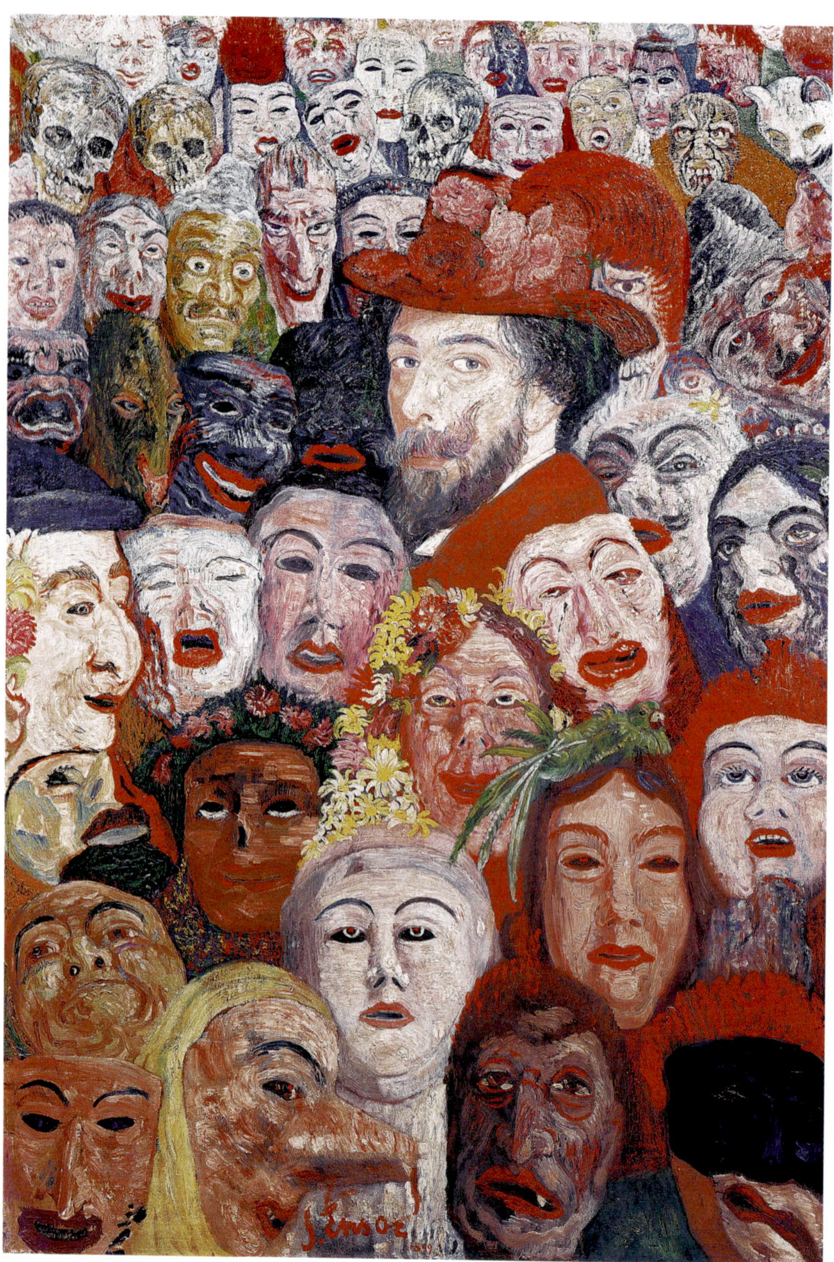

James Ensor
Self-Portrait with Masks,
1899
Oil on canvas,
117 x 82 cm (46 x 32¼ in.)
Menard Art Museum,
Komaki, Japan

**Ensor's unique vision
has provided a source
of inspiration to many
artists. The strong use
of colour, the playful
distortion of space and
the menacing imagery
anticipate German
Expressionism, Surrealism
and French Symbolist
painting. His work has
also influenced various
contemporary artists
including the Belgian
painter Luc Tuymans.**

The Belgian painter James Ensor was fascinated by the creative potential of masks. His mother sold a terrifying selection in her novelty souvenir shop in their home town of Ostend. In Ensor's extraordinary *Self-Portrait with Masks*, 1899, we find the artist peeking out from a grotesque jumble of blank faces: death masks, dolls, skulls, ethnographic masks, jesters and goblins. The painted surface is equally claustrophobic – a riot of putrid colour daubed in thick impressionistic clumps. It is hard to tell if Ensor considers himself the proud owner of his grotesque collection, the ringmaster of a macabre performance or at risk of being gobbled up by the malevolent crowd, for Ensor assumes a mask of his own – a fixed, impenetrable stare giving nothing away. He wears a flamboyant hat filled with flowers and casts a nonchalant glance over his shoulder, recalling the swagger of Anthony van Dyck's self-portraiture (see pages 40–41). In fashioning himself as an eccentric historical figure, Ensor highlights his wariness of modern life. He appears to distance himself from society, seeking shelter in his own fictional world.

Ensor was a true outsider, rarely leaving Ostend during his lifetime. Ignoring the repeated scorn of his critics, he retreated to the privacy of the family attic to create increasingly dark and macabre scenes. He would dress model skeletons in fancy outfits, manipulating the figures into disturbing scenarios which he would then represent in paint. Another novel strategy involved the overpainting of his earlier realist canvases, applying gruesome new faces. This process of masking and concealment led to the revelation of disturbing new narratives. As Ensor explained, the mask provided a source of freedom and opportunity: 'For me the mask stands for freshness of tone, exaggeration of expression, splendour of decor, grand unexpected gesture, uninhibited movement, exquisite turbulence.'

OTHER KEY WORKS

Me and My Circle, 1939, private collection

KEY FEATURES

Prolific self-portraitist, producing over 100 images of himself
Unconventional 'outsider' approach
Disturbing and satirical subject matter
Distrust of modern life and bourgeois society
Impressionistic application of thick, brightly coloured paint
Use of overpainting to develop layers of narrative
Interest in the mask as a source of concealment and revelation

EDVARD MUNCH
1863–1944

An all-encompassing darkness encircles the work of the Norwegian
artist Edvard Munch, even scenes set in bright sunshine. His works
convey an undercurrent of imminent threat and danger. The
characters in his paintings appear to be on the brink of mental or
physical demise. Munch's personal life was equally beset by periods
of melancholy and crisis. His childhood was scarred by the loss of
several close family members and by the sustained disapproval of his
pious father. As a young man, Munch deliberately pursued the path
of the outsider, inspired by the nihilistic company of his bohemian
friends in Kristiana (now Oslo). He would later spend time in Paris,
drawing inspiration from the Post-Impressionist painters Vincent
van Gogh (see pages 66–9) and Paul Gauguin, particularly their
emotive use of colour.

Self-portraiture provided an ideal genre for Munch's unique
exploration of anxiety and estrangement. He produced over seventy
painted self-portraits across his long career, plus over 100 works on
paper, including prints, watercolours and drawings. His dysfunctional
and tempestuous relationships with women provided an ongoing
source of inspiration. Munch was wary of women, fearing they might
suck his creativity with vampiric zeal. In 1902, he split with the
heiress Tulla Larsen after four turbulent years of keeping her at arm's
length. The affair ended violently, with Munch incurring damage to
his hand following gunshots. *Self-Portrait in Hell* (1903) reveals the
persistence of raw emotions one year after the breakup. Munch
stands naked in front of a fiery backdrop; the looming shadow in the
background appears ready to eat him alive. The brush marks used
for the face are particularly gestural, leading to grotesque distortion
and a sense of disembodiment. Although Munch's expression is hard
to read, his assertive pose suggests that he is in control of the dark
forces that envelop his body and occupy his inner thoughts.

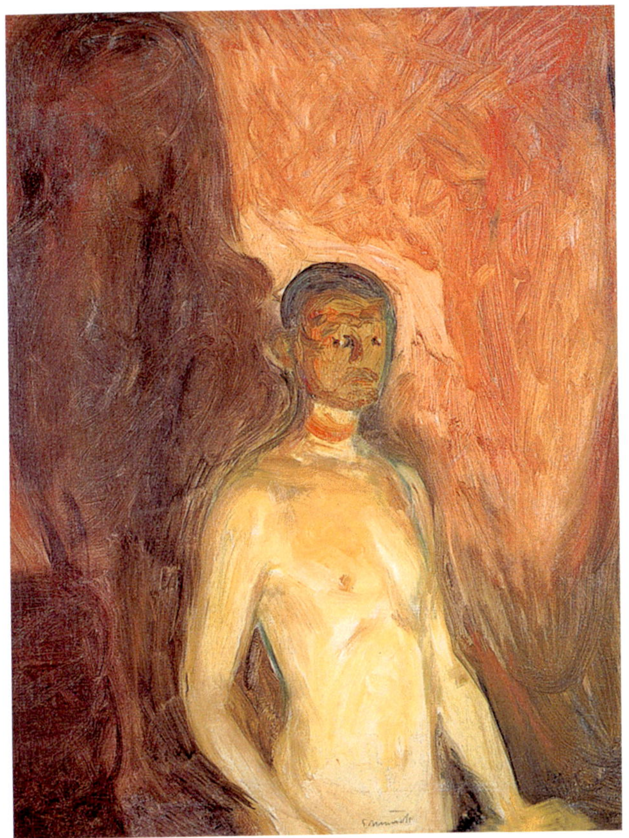

Edvard Munch
Self-Portrait in Hell, 1903
Oil on canvas,
82 x 66 cm (32¼ x 26 in.)
Munch Museum, Oslo,
Norway

Much of Munch's work reveals a strong narrative drive, which at times verges on melodrama. This impulse perhaps derives from the artist's childhood. Munch's father would entertain his children by recounting gruesome ghost stories and narrating the dark fiction of the American writer Edgar Allan Poe.

OTHER KEY WORKS

Self-Portrait with Burning Cigarette, 1895, National Museum
   of Art, Architecture and Design, Oslo, Norway
Self-Portrait Between the Clock and the Bed, 1940–43, Munch
   Museum, Oslo, Norway

KEY FEATURES

Prolific self-portraitist working across a variety of media
Identification with the bohemian myths of the outsider and
   the victim
Use of self-portraiture to explore trauma and anxiety
Emotional and expressive use of colour and mark making
Dramatic deployment of shadows and looming backgrounds
Interest in disembodiment and engulfment

KÄTHE KOLLWITZ
1867–1945

Käthe Kollwitz is best known for her searing and expressionistic drawings and prints documenting the impact of poverty and war on disadvantaged communities. She lived in an impoverished area of Berlin with her doctor husband, Karl, who ran a surgery from their small apartment. The steady stream of needy clients provided Kollwitz with a daily reminder of the plight of the poor. Kollwitz battled with anxiety and depression throughout her life. She experienced the death of her siblings as a child, and in October 1914 her son Peter was killed in action in the First World War. Much of her work is tinged with personal sadness and autobiographical allusions. Her etching *Woman with Dead Child* (1903), for example, is achingly reflective and prophetic: Kollwitz had employed Peter as the model for this devastating image.

In addition to her socially conscious graphic work, Kollwitz was also a prolific self-portraitist. She produced over 100 drawn and etched images of herself, plus two sculpted portrait busts. Many of these works depict a world-weary figure, ravaged by her responsibilities as witness and chronicler. Even the self-portraits she produced in her thirties appear to represent a much older woman. There is no desire to prettify or idealize. Instead she addresses the viewer with a set jaw and a guarded stare; her haunted eyes appear to have seen too much. Quite often she supports her head with her hand in a further gesture of weariness. The lack of colour in her drawings and prints adds to the oppressive atmosphere, with Kollwitz building up dark areas of shadow, reminiscent of Rembrandt's chiaroscuro handling. Lines dig deep into the picture surface, reflecting the crevices of the artist's ageing skin. This is unflinchingly honest self-portraiture, undercut with anxiety and despair.

Käthe Kollwitz
Frontal Self-Portrait,
1922–3
Woodcut,
15 x 15.6 cm (5⅞ x 6⅛ in.)
Museum of Modern Art,
New York

This woodcut incorporates many of the characteristics of Kollwitz's approach to self-portraiture: the exclusive focus on the face, the full-frontal composition and the intense gaze. Kollwitz's choice of woodcut gives her lines a sculptural quality, gouged from the block with expressive force. Her choice of black ink adds to the oppressive atmosphere.

OTHER KEY WORKS

Woman with Dead Child, 1903, etching, Barber Institute of Fine
 Arts, Birmingham, UK

Self-Portrait, 1926–36, bronze, Los Angeles County Museum of
 Art, Los Angeles, USA

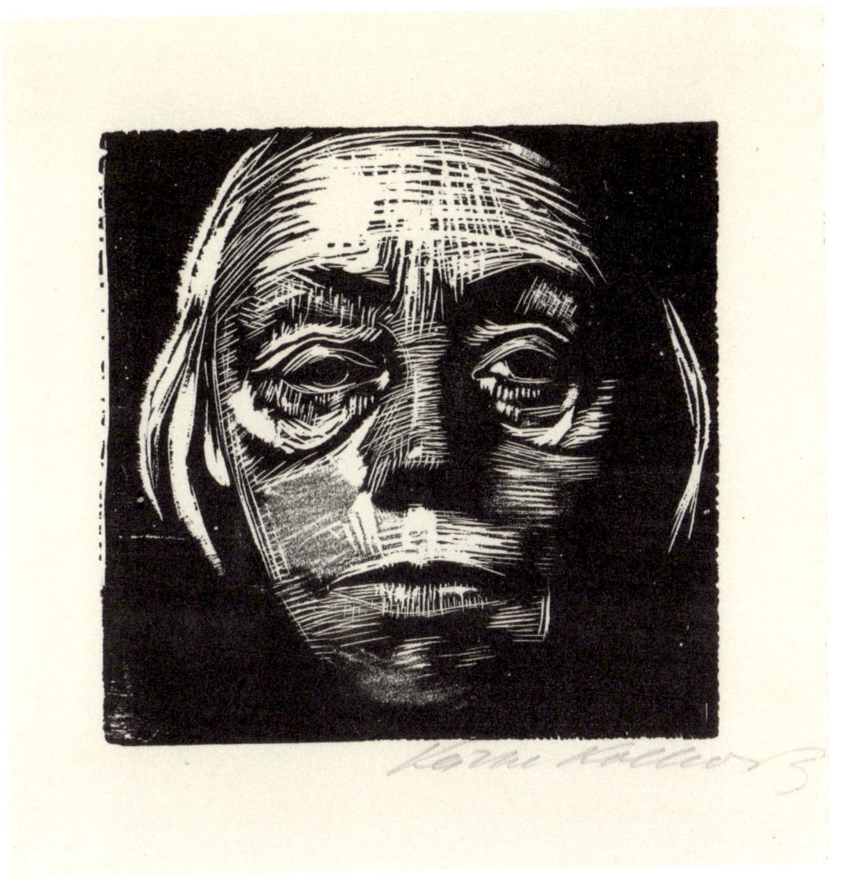

KEY FEATURES

Socially conscious self-portraiture spanning drawing,
  printmaking and sculpture

Predominant focus on the full-frontal face

Intense self-scrutiny

Unidealized representation of ageing

Expressionistic use of line

Monochromatic palette and bold handling of chiaroscuro
  tonalities and shadows

DOROTHEA TANNING
1910–2012

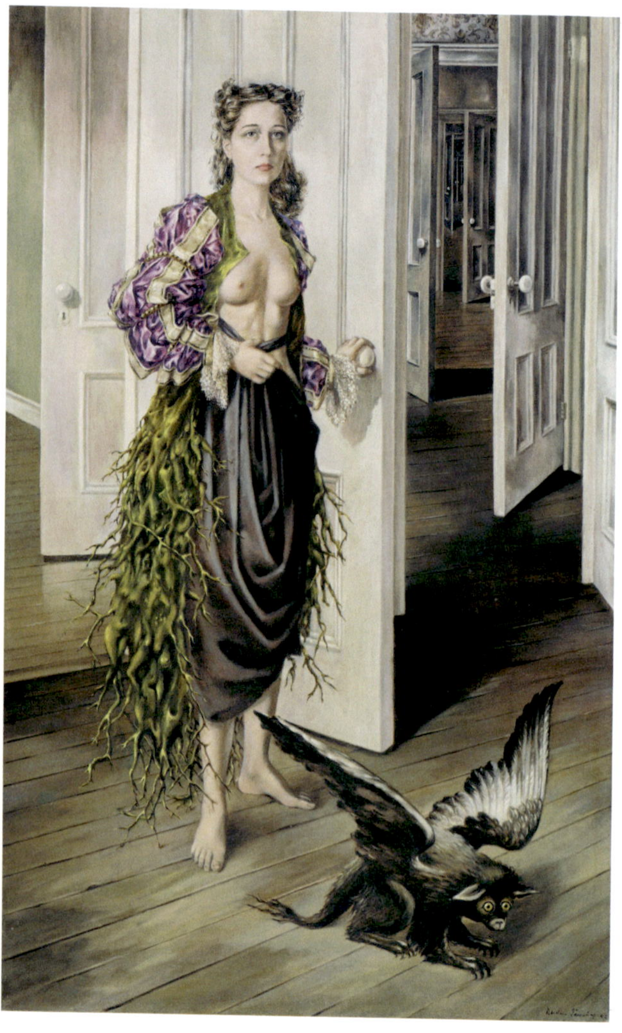

Surrealism first emerged in the 1920s and spanned art, philosophy
and literature. Drawing on Freudian psychoanalysis, Surrealist
artists explored irrational and unconscious states and processes in
search of deeper truths. The American artist and writer Dorothea
Tanning first encountered Surrealist art in 1936 when she visited the
landmark exhibition *Fantastic Art, Dada & Surrealism* at the Museum

Dorothea Tanning
Birthday, 1942
Oil on canvas,
102 x 65 cm
(40⅛ x 25⅝ in.)
Philadelphia Museum
of Art, Philadelphia

**The intense realism
evident here in Tanning's
early work would later
subside, giving way to
suggestive, abstract
paintings, soft stitched
sculptures and immersive
installations. She also
produced a rich body
of fiction and poetry.
Tanning's long and
successful career spanned
seven decades. She died
in 2012 at the age of 102.**

of Modern Art in New York. Reflecting on its seismic impact, she stated, 'Here in the museum is the real explosion, rocking me on my run-over heels. Here is the infinitely faceted world I must have been waiting for.' With little formal art education, Tanning immediately launched into the formulation of her own surreal language.

Tanning's intriguing self-portrait *Birthday* (1942) heralds her arrival on the international Surrealist circuit. Like many of her early paintings, this work features a female protagonist occupying a dreamlike, architectural setting. Tanning opens the door to reveal a succession of further routes and ways forward. We are spoilt for choice; there are many possibilities here. Standing tall on the balls of her feet, the thirty-two-year-old artist appears in control not just of her future, but also of her sexual identity. Her naked torso is framed by fantastical garments including an entrancing green skirt, its tassels unravelling into writhing human forms. A gruesome winged gremlin sits at Tanning's feet – the perfect pet for a Surrealist encounter of this kind.

At the end of 1942, fellow Surrealist artist Max Ernst visited Tanning's cramped studio in Greenwich Village. He was undertaking research for his forthcoming *Exhibition by 31 Women* to be staged at the Art of This Century Gallery in New York, owned by his first wife, Peggy Guggenheim. Ernst was struck by Tanning's entrancing self-portrait and suggested the title *Birthday* to highlight her awakening to Surrealist ideas. His visit also marked the dawn of a new relationship. Ernst and Tanning were married in 1946 and their creative partnership would continue until Ernst's death thirty years later.

OTHER KEY WORKS

Self-Portrait, 1944, San Francisco Museum of Modern Art, San Francisco, USA

KEY FEATURES

Construction of Surrealist personalities and characters
Realistic rendering of dreamlike scenarios
Interest in uncanny interior spaces and architecture
Flamboyant clothing and styling
Assertive, unselfconscious pose
Strong narrative impulse

FRIDA KAHLO
1907–54

At the heart of Frida Kahlo's work lies a spirit of resilience in the face of trauma. Born in the Coyoacán district of Mexico City, Kahlo contracted polio at the age of six, which led to lameness in her right leg. Misfortune returned in her teens when the bus she was travelling on crashed. Kahlo suffered severe spinal and pelvic damage. Despite countless operations, the extent of her injuries prevented her from carrying a baby to term. Kahlo's personal relationships were equally unsettled. She married fellow Mexican painter Diego Rivera twice, with both parties engaging in frequent extramarital affairs.

Kahlo once mused: 'Some are born under a lucky star, and others are out in the dark…. I'm one of those for whom it looks pitch black.' Despite her many personal afflictions, Kahlo's symbolic and deeply autobiographical work is surprisingly optimistic. The majority of her oeuvre comprises self-portraiture, modest in scale yet universal in reach. In many of these works, Kahlo subjects herself to excruciating processes: her body appears cut, pinned, dissected and transfused. She conceals her pain with a set, stoic expression. Her steady gaze, guarded by her trademark brow, gives nothing away. Kahlo was drawn to Sigmund Freud's theory of psychoanalysis and the notion of delving beneath the surface to find greater self-awareness. She was, however, very wary of Surrealist labels, saying, 'I have never painted dreams. What I represented was my own reality.'

Kahlo engaged with developments in European art yet remained committed to Mexican culture and politics. She collected indigenous clothing and deliberately maintained a powerful identity as a Mexican woman. Many of her paintings reveal the strong influence of Mexican *ex voto* or *retablo* art. Others are bathed in radiant light or set in a jungle context with lush flora and fauna. All are fantastical and intoxicating yet at the same time deeply vivid and authentic.

OTHER KEY WORKS

The Two Fridas, 1939, Museo de Arte Moderno, Mexico City, Mexico
Self-Portrait with Cropped Hair, 1940, Museum of Modern Art,
  New York, USA
The Broken Column, 1944, Museo Dolores Olmedo, Mexico City,
  Mexico

Frida Kahlo
Self-Portrait with Thorn Necklace and Hummingbird, 1940
Oil on canvas,
61.2 x 47 cm
(24 x 18½ in.)
Harry Ransom Center,
Austin, Texas

Diego Rivera once gave Kahlo a pet monkey. In this painting, made soon after their divorce, the mischievous creature tugs at Kahlo's sharp thorn necklace, causing her to bleed. The hummingbird is a popular symbol of luck in love, but could also represent Huitzilopochtli, the Aztec god of war. The hovering dragonflies perhaps suggest notions of resurrection and recovery.

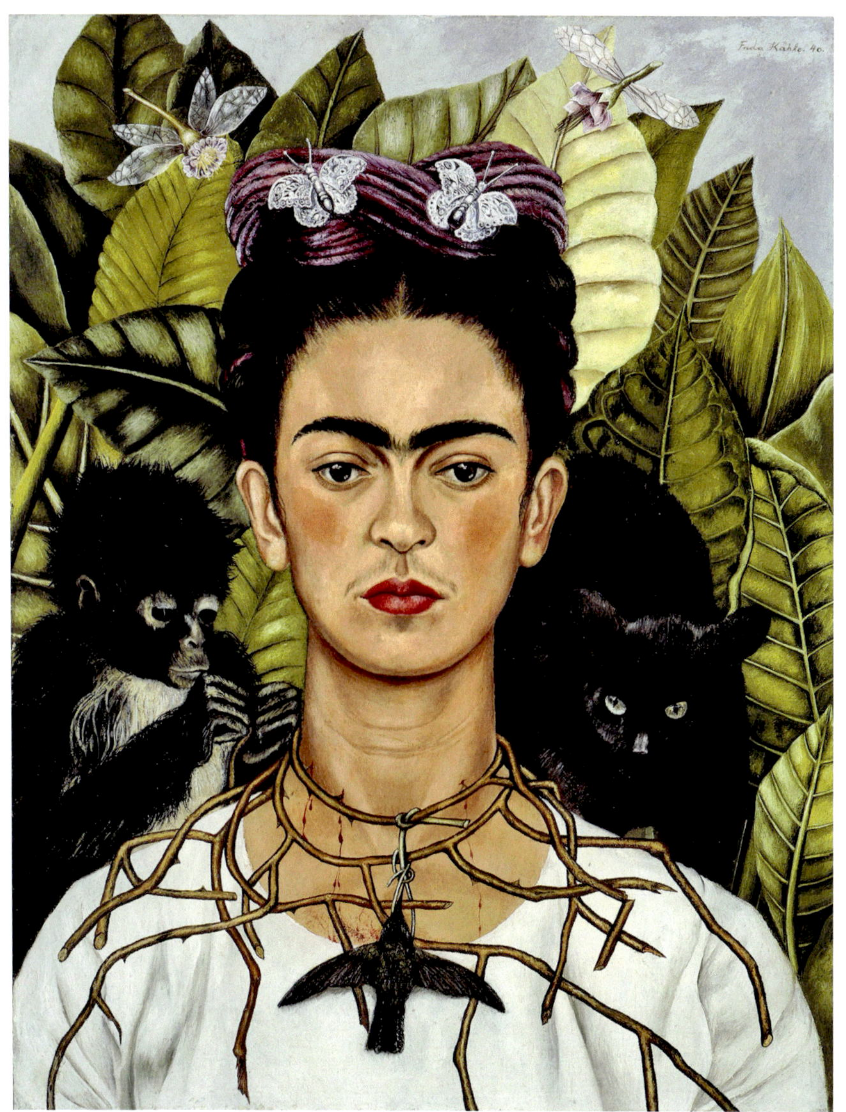

KEY FEATURES

Stoic visions of pain and suffering
Strong interest in autobiography
Use of metaphor and symbolism to intensify reality
Interest in psychoanalysis and unconscious states
Construction of a strong visual identity in her life and art
Influence of Mexican art, culture and fashions

CHARLOTTE SALOMON

1917–43

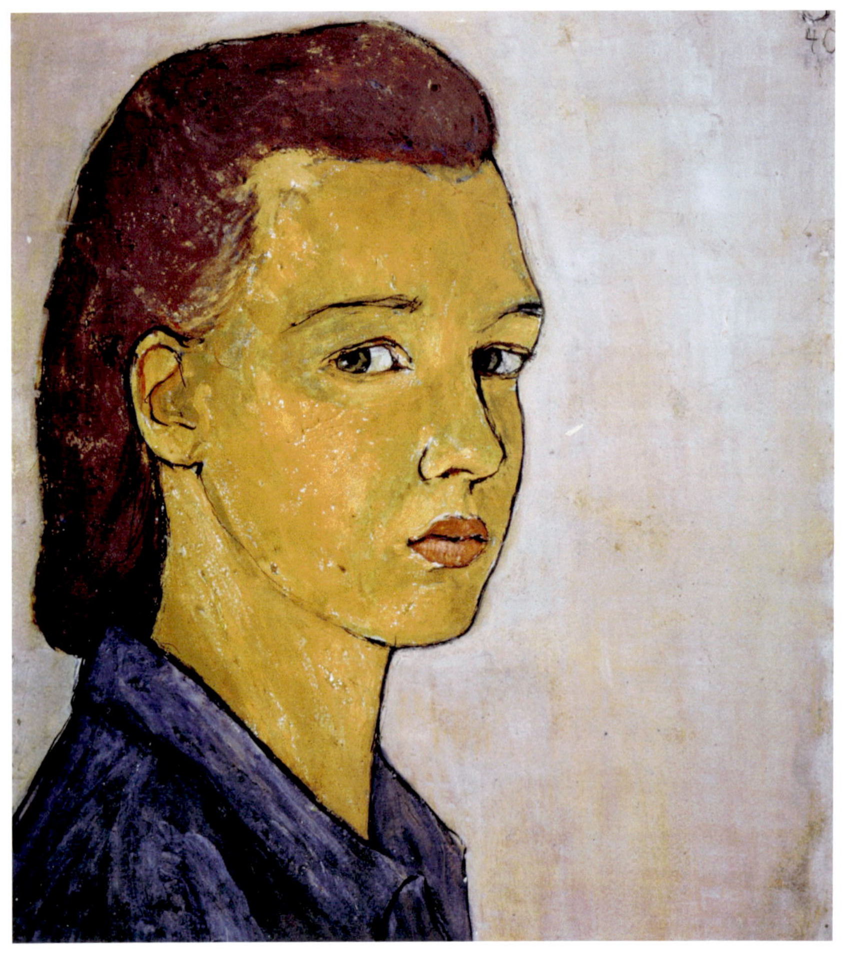

Charlotte Salomon
Self-Portrait, 1940
Gouache paint
on cardboard,
54 x 49 cm
(21⅜ x 19⅜ in.)
Collection Jewish
Historical Museum,
Amsterdam

This rare self-portrait highlights Salomon's quiet intensity. She turns to face the viewer with guarded reserve, and it is hard not to interpret a deep sadness in her plaintive gaze. Salomon's face and neck are delineated with neat dark lines – perhaps symbolizing her natural self-containment, but also reflecting her graphic, almost 'comic-book' approach to painting.

Many artists have returned to self-portraiture throughout their lives, creating a kind of diary tracking personal and artistic transformations. The German artist Charlotte Salomon sensed from an early age that time was not on her side. As a consequence, her work is filled with a sense of urgency and a desire for immediate comprehensiveness.

Salomon was born into a prosperous Jewish family in Berlin. She was named after her mother's sister, who had committed suicide at the age of eighteen. Her mother took her own life when Salomon was just nine years old; she was told that her mother had died of influenza. The rise of Nazism during Salomon's formative years added an additional layer of anxiety. In this tense, anti-Semitic context, she was fortunate to secure a place at the United State Schools for Applied Arts in 1936. Very few Jewish students were admitted to university at this time, however Salomon's reserved nature was deemed suitably unthreatening. In 1938 she was forced to abandon her studies and her home in Berlin. Life under Nazi rule had become too dangerous.

Salomon joined her grandparents at a safe haven at Villa L'Ermitage near Nice, France. Its affluent American owner, Ottilie Moore, had opened her doors to refugees. But this was no rural idyll: the risk of German invasion and being captured by the Nazis remained high. Her grandparents kept a stock of lethal drugs in case the time came. Just months after Salomon's arrival, her grandmother succeeded in committing suicide following a previous failed attempt. Only then did her grandfather reveal the truth that her mother and her aunt had taken their own lives. Devastated by this news, Salomon considered following in their footsteps, but she quickly affirmed that she must persevere: 'How beautiful life is. I believe in life! I will live for them all!'

Salomon decided to make a book with words, pictures and suggestions for music. She wanted to capture her life on paper: her experiences, her relationships, the unfurling social and political picture, all bound together in one ambitious tome. Her vision was to produce an epic work, an opus. It was a nod to Richard Wagner's concept of the *Gesamtkunstwerk*, a 'total work of art' embracing art, poetry and music. However, rather than adopt Wagner's unwavering celebration of German culture, Salomon revolutionized the form by exploring her fragile position as a young, persecuted Jewish girl, alienated from society. Between 1941 and 1943 she worked tirelessly from her small room to produce a unique volume, *Life? Or Theatre?*. The final work features 769 gouache paintings. Many of these images are overlaid with transparent papers featuring narratives and poems.

Life? Or Theatre? embraces a broad spectrum of Salomon's life, from her childhood and family relationships to her obsessive love affair with her stepmother's music teacher, Alfred Wolfsohn, all played out against a worsening social and political context. Salomon used thinly veiled pseudonyms to protect identities, calling herself 'Charlotte Hann'. She hummed while she worked, envisaging her book as a 'Singspiel' – a play with songs. She even suggested appropriate accompanying music, including works by Mozart and Schubert, and Nazi marching tunes. As the book progresses, her handling of paint becomes increasingly expressionistic and urgent, as if working at breakneck speed to ensure completion.

In 1943, Salomon handed the finished work to a local doctor, urging him, 'Keep this safe, it is my whole life.' The Nazis arrived in October. Salomon and her husband, Alexander Nagler, were forcibly removed from their home and sent to Auschwitz. It is thought that Salomon was gassed soon after her arrival; she was five months pregnant. Nagler died at the camp the following year.

An intriguing postscript to Salomon's tragic life emerged in 2015 with the discovery of a long, confessional letter written by the

Charlotte Salomon
Illustrations from *Life? Or Theatre?*, 1941–2
Gouache,
32.5 x 25 cm
(12⅞ x 9⅞ in.)
Collection Jewish Historical Museum, Amsterdam

One scene from Salomon's *Life? Or Theatre?* (opposite) features the artist as a child in bed, embracing her deceased mother, Franziska. Her mother promises to return as an angel to deliver a letter to tell her more wonderful things about heaven. The dreamlike quality of this innovative composition recalls the work of the Russian artist Marc Chagall, who admired Salomon's imagery.

As Salomon's book progresses her use of paint becomes looser and more expressive. Together, the book illustrations convey a fresh, contemporary quality, like comics or storyboarding sequences for a film.

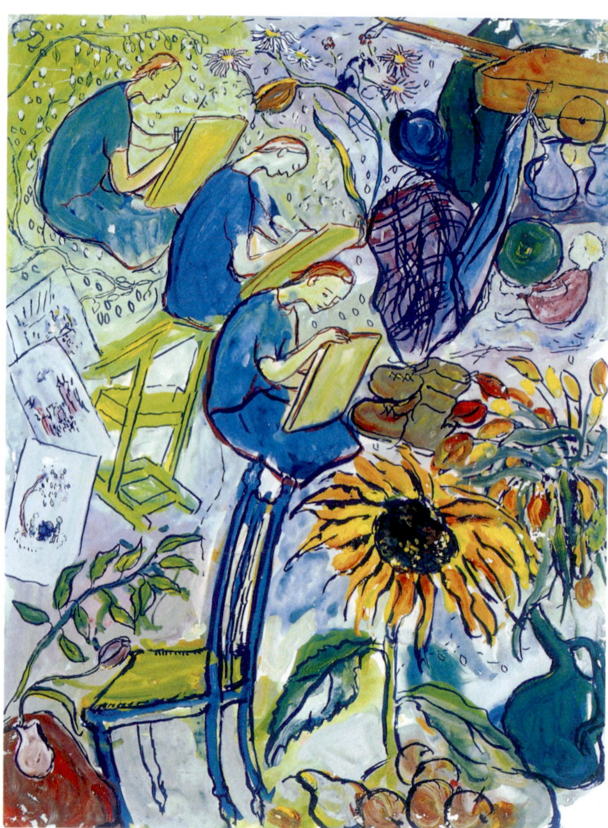

artist. The letter details how she murdered her grandfather in 1942 by preparing a drug-laced omelette for his breakfast. Was this a mercy killing? Or an act of revenge in response to her grandfather's sustained sexual abuse of several female members of her family? Perhaps it was pure fiction and her grandfather died of natural causes. Life or theatre? We will never know for sure.

KEY FEATURES

Presentation of autobiographical content across painting,
  literature and music
Use of pseudonyms
Lyrical and expressive handling of gouache
Graphic use of line and creative interplay of imagery and text
Dreamlike representation of deceased characters
Expressive urgency and intensity

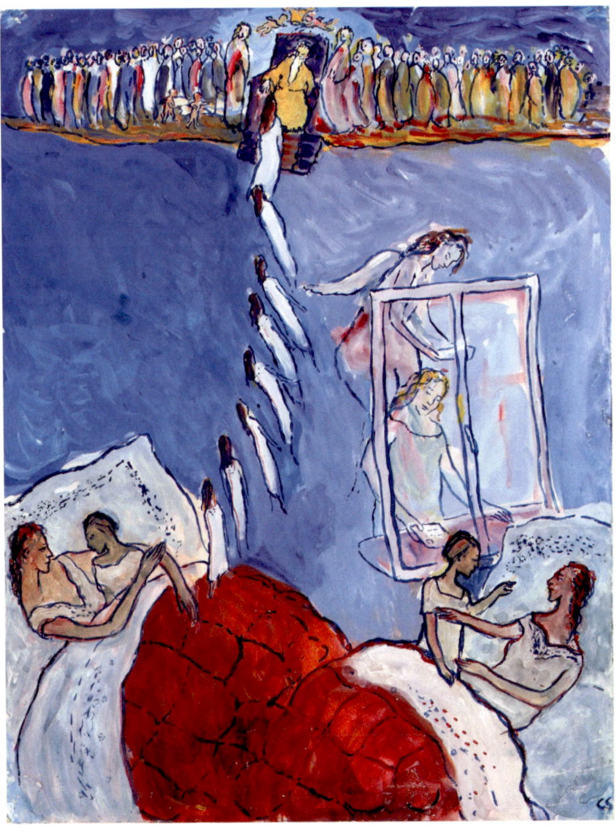

HELENE SCHJERFBECK

1862–1946

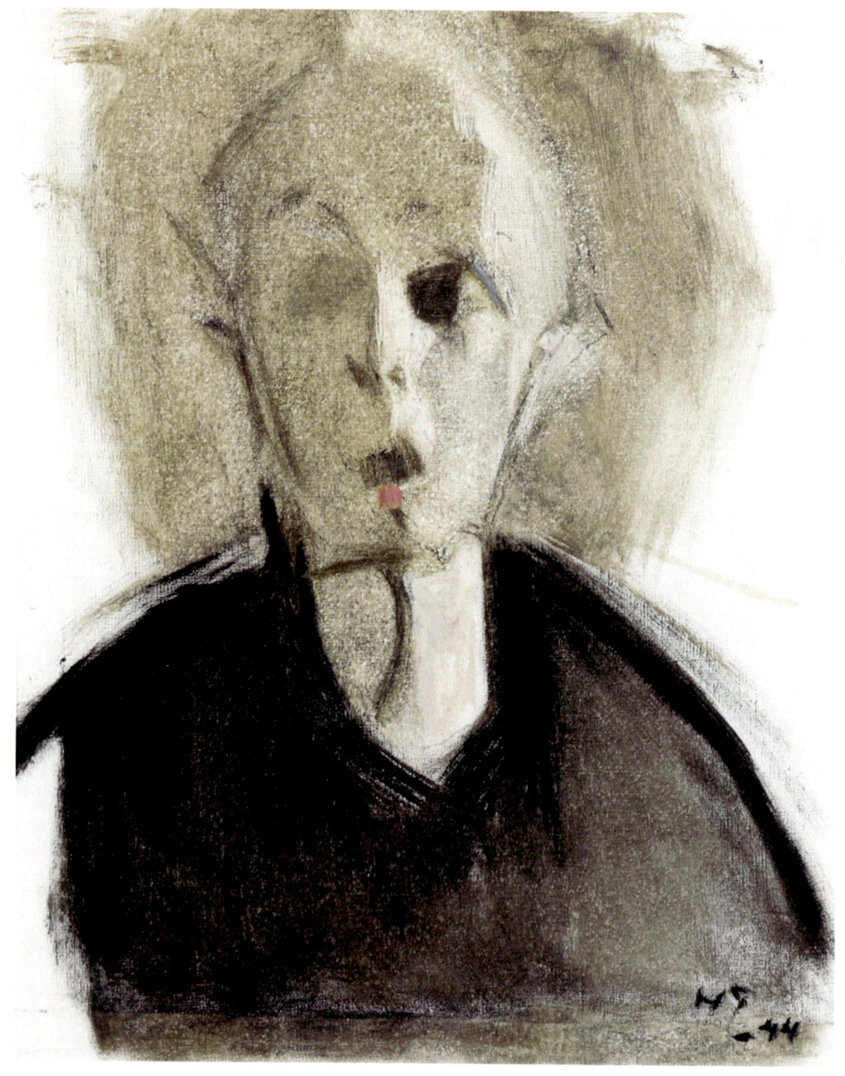

Helene Schjerfbeck
*Self-Portrait with Red
Spot*, 1944
Oil on canvas,
45 x 37 cm
(17¾ x 14½ in.)
Ateneum Art Museum,
Helsinki

**This self-portrait reveals
a clear interest in
abstraction. Schjerfbeck's
free and gestural use
of paint anticipates the
distortive treatment of
the face later pursued by
artists including Frank
Auerbach and Francis
Bacon.**

Helene Schjerfbeck enjoyed considerable artistic success in her home country of Finland during her lifetime, becoming well known for her expressive and painterly portraits, landscapes and genre scenes. She experimented with self-portraiture throughout her career, shifting from early realist representations to increasing stylization as her personal aesthetic developed. Schjerfbeck's most startling self-portraits were produced in her eighties. She created over twenty paintings and drawings of herself in the final two years of her life. Her substantial end-of-life enquiry was perhaps inspired by Rembrandt's late flowering of self-portraiture. It also resolved the issue of having few remaining sitters. She said, 'The model is always available, although it isn't always pleasant to see oneself.'

Schjerfbeck's searing self-analysis avoids theatricality and melodrama. She chose to explore the impact of old age on her head and shoulders, tracking her physical and psychological decline with a quiet and determined objectivity. The resulting images convey the gradual deterioration of a particular individual while touching on universal processes of ageing. There is also a strong spirit of freedom, as highlighted by Schjerfbeck in a letter to her friend, the writer Einar Reuter, in 1926: 'The exhaustion of old age is something completely different – liberating, too, because you can let things go their own way, and are left with nothing but the sensitivity of the brush.'

In *Self-Portrait with Red Spot* (1944), paint is applied, smeared and scraped off the surface, leaving a ghostly mask: part person, part skull. Whole areas of her face dissolve into an amorphous grey cloud. Her left eye recedes into the gloom. Her right eye is enlarged, wide open with a terrifying, haunted expression. Despite her physical frailty, Schjerfbeck's artistic interests are irrepressible. Her shift towards gestural abstraction is evident in the loose brushwork and the startling red dot on her bottom lip. It occupies the centre of the canvas with a spirit of defiance, a spark of life.

KEY FEATURES

Late flowering of self-portraiture in old age
Sustained documentation of psychological and physical
  deterioration
Gestural and expressive use of paint
Dissolving of physical features
Unflattering and honest depiction of ageing
Mask-like treatment of facial features

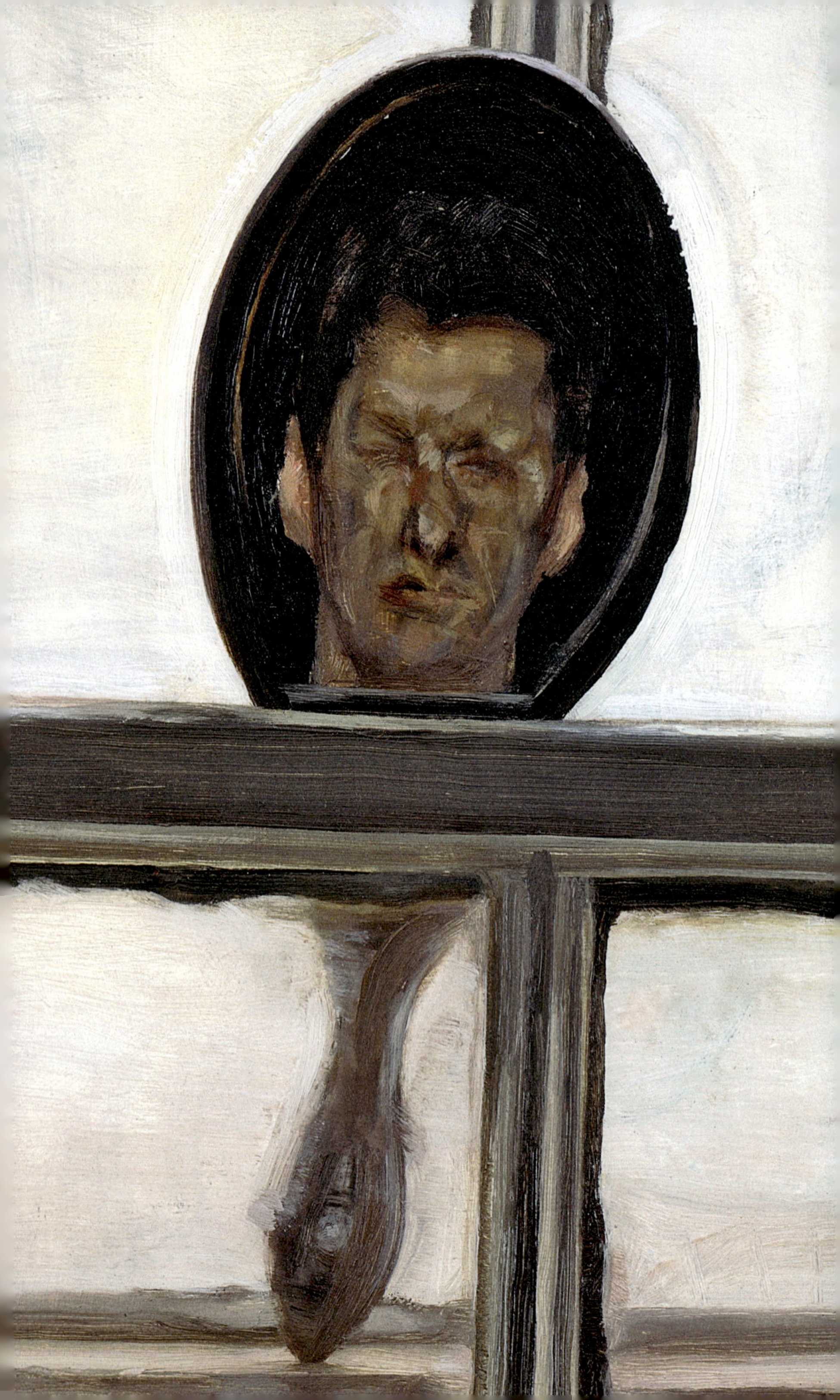

UP CLOSE AND PERSONAL

-

I want paint to *work as flesh* ... my portraits
to be *of* the people, not *like* them... As far
as I am concerned the paint *is* the person.
I want it to work for me just as flesh does.

-

Lucian Freud, 1982

PAULA MODERSOHN-BECKER
1876–1907

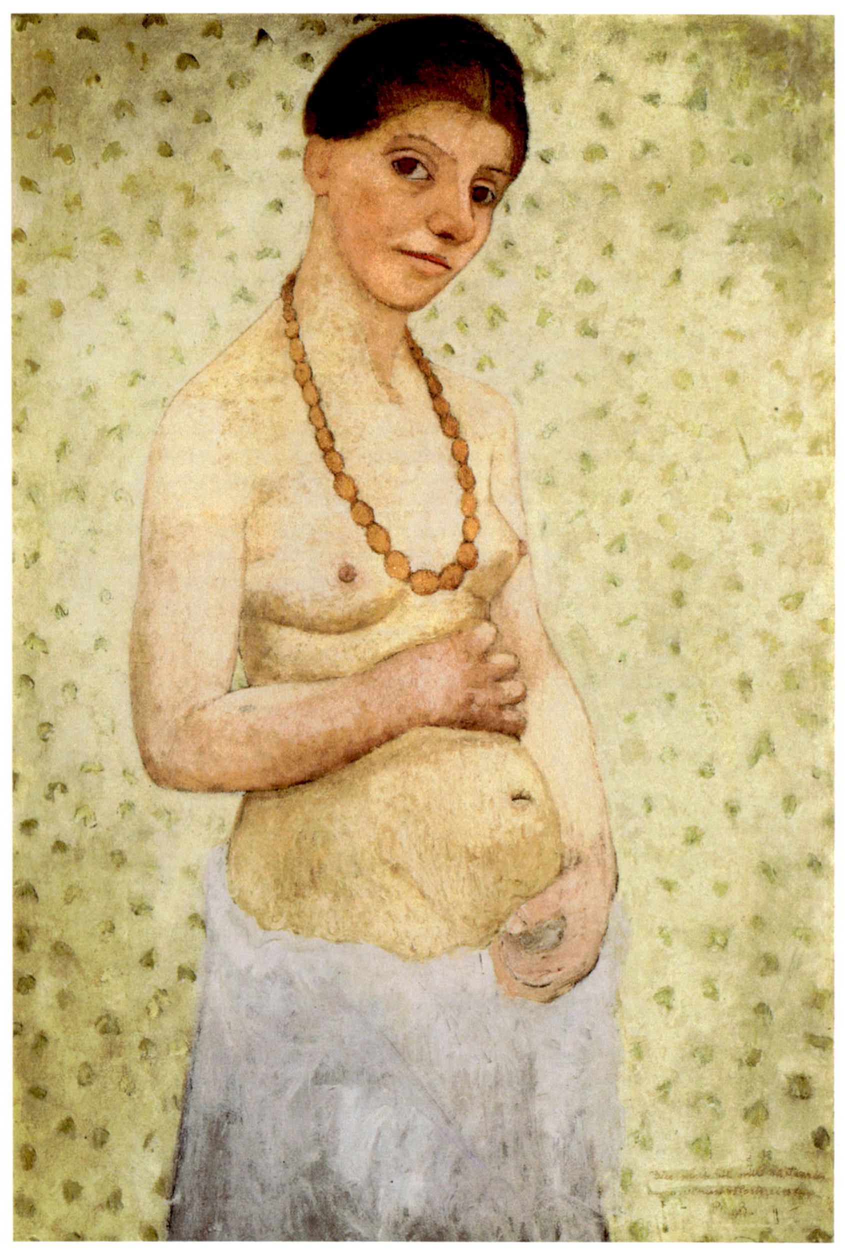

Paula Modersohn-Becker
*Self-Portrait on Her Sixth
Wedding Anniversary,*
1906
Tempera on canvas,
101.8 x 70 cm
(40⅛ x 27½ in.)
Paula Modersohn-Becker
Museum, Bremen

**A year after this painting
was made, Modersohn-
Becker resumed her
life in Worpswede,
still torn between her
family responsibilities
and her urge for artistic
independence. She
gave birth to a baby
girl, Mathilde, in
November 1907 but sadly
died a couple of weeks
later from a pulmonary
embolism.**

The long-held notion of the sexually driven artist commanding the attention of his submissive female (and often naked) muse resonates across art history. Many women struggled to assert their identity within this entrenched myth. Paula Modersohn-Becker invented a new way of representing female creativity. In 1906, she decided to take leave from her husband and her home in Worpswede, Germany. She set out for Paris to push her practice as a painter. Taking inspiration from Paul Cézanne, Vincent van Gogh (see pages 66–9) and the haunting Egyptian mummy paintings in the Louvre, she developed a unique figurative style involving the application of thick lozenges of pastel-coloured paint onto the picture surface. During the same year, she made the radical decision to paint herself naked to the waist.

Self-Portrait on Her Sixth Wedding Anniversary (1906) is one of the first naked female self-portraits in western art history. The artist assumes an almost sculptural solidity, standing with confidence and poise. She addresses her audience with a clear and steady gaze, gently embracing her rounded belly. Although Modersohn-Becker was not thought to be pregnant at the time of making this work, she was under considerable pressure to return to Worpswede to start a family. She appears to be deep in thought in this painting, as if musing on her future. Her swollen abdomen signifies a maternal direction; however, it also points to the inherent productivity of the female body. In presenting herself as naked and pregnant, Modersohn-Becker acknowledges her ability to operate as a generator of new forms, both physically and artistically. This self-portrait therefore acts as a kind of manifesto, confirming her creative intent and her legitimacy as a woman and an artist. In 1906 she wrote, 'I am – ME – and hope to become ME more and more.'

OTHER KEY WORKS

Self-Portrait with Amber Necklace, 1906, Paula Modersohn-Becker
  Museum, Bremen, Germany
Mother and Child Lying Nude, 1907, Paula Modersohn-Becker
  Museum, Bremen, Germany

KEY FEATURES

An early example of naked female self-portraiture
Use of the female body to challenge patriarchal myths
Simultaneous presentation of the self as artist and muse
Interest in maternity and mother and child subjects
Use of thick impasto paint and unusual colour tonalities

ERNST LUDWIG KIRCHNER
1880–1938

In 1905, the Dresden-based artist Ernst Ludwig Kirchner co-founded a new collective of like-minded artists. *Die Brücke*, or The Bridge group, sought to forge a point of connection between their spiritual forebears, Albrecht Dürer (see pages 18–21) and Lucas Cranach, and the latest developments in Fauvist and Post-Impressionist painting. Their paintings combined strong colour and exaggerated forms to convey heightened emotions, an approach later named German Expressionism. Kirchner and his circle believed in the complete fusion of art and life: living, working and loving together. Kirchner's studio was the initial meeting place for *Die Brücke* group painting sessions, parties and sexual encounters. They later moved into a larger space on the Berliner Straße in Dresden, which Kirchner decorated with brightly painted wall-hangings to enhance this shared utopia.

Self-Portrait with Model (1910) presents Kirchner as the ultimate bohemian artist, embodying genius and virility. He swaggers onto the scene, wearing an exotic, brightly coloured dressing gown covering his otherwise naked body. His pipe slumps nonchalantly to one side of his mouth. His paintbrush, loaded with vermillion, rests next to his groin. Kirchner is poised and ready for action. An anonymous young woman wearing a floaty sky-blue dress occupies the background, seated on a red pouffe. Perhaps a lover, a model, or both, she appears ready and available if somewhat guarded: she clutches her right knee with her left hand, effectively closing her body. Their ambiguous relationship adds to an already claustrophobic scene jam-packed with a heady mix of intoxicating colour and jostling brushstrokes.

The dominant sexuality expressed in this painting was short-lived. After 1915, Kirchner's self-portraiture repeatedly channelled the 'artist as victim' myth. In his famous *Self-Portrait as a Soldier* (1915), Kirchner holds aloft the stump of his right arm, his hand presumably lost in imaginary action. Kirchner's brief experience of service in the First World War contributed to the gradual decline of his mental health. He committed suicide in 1938.

Ernst Ludwig Kirchner
Self-Portrait with Model,
1910 (revised 1926)
Oil on canvas,
150.4 x 100 cm
(59¼ x 39⅜ in.)
Hamburger Kunsthalle,
Hamburg

This painting reveals Kirchner's extraordinary skills as a colourist. Royal blues collide with acid oranges, baby pinks and jet blacks. Strong stripes and hanging fabrics give further licence to explore clashing colour combinations. In this context, facial expressions appear to recede in importance, reduced to vacant, hollow eyes and ambiguous mask-like features.

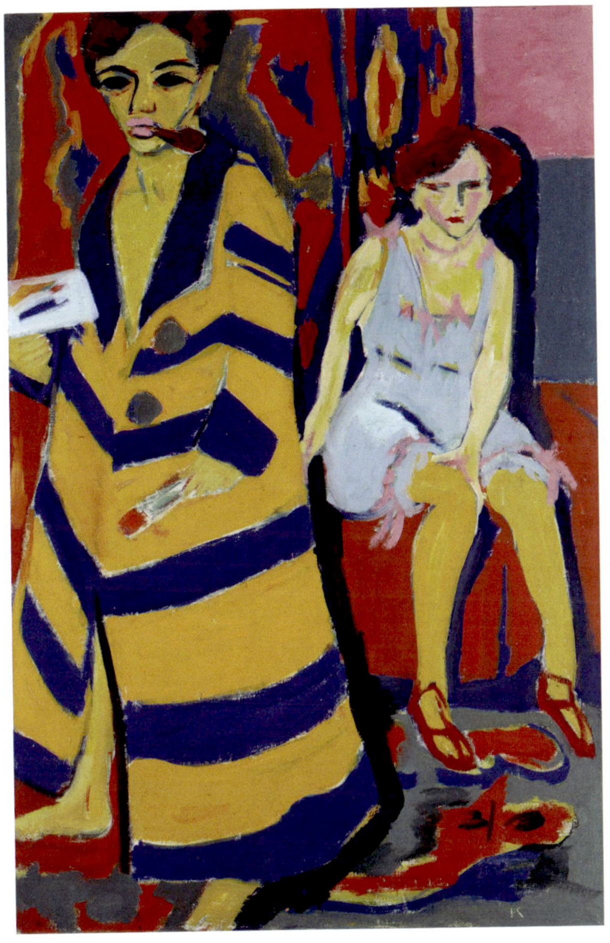

OTHER KEY WORKS

Self-Portrait as a Soldier, 1915, Allen Memorial Art Museum,
Oberlin, USA

KEY FEATURES

Expressionist self-portraiture
Interest in the myth of the promiscuous, sexually driven artist
Exploration of the 'artist with model' trope
Strong implication of sexual relations and narratives
Intense juxtaposition of contrasting colours and patterns
Gestural and expressive brushstrokes
Influence of Fauvism and Post-Impressionism

ZINAIDA SEREBRIAKOVA
1884–1967

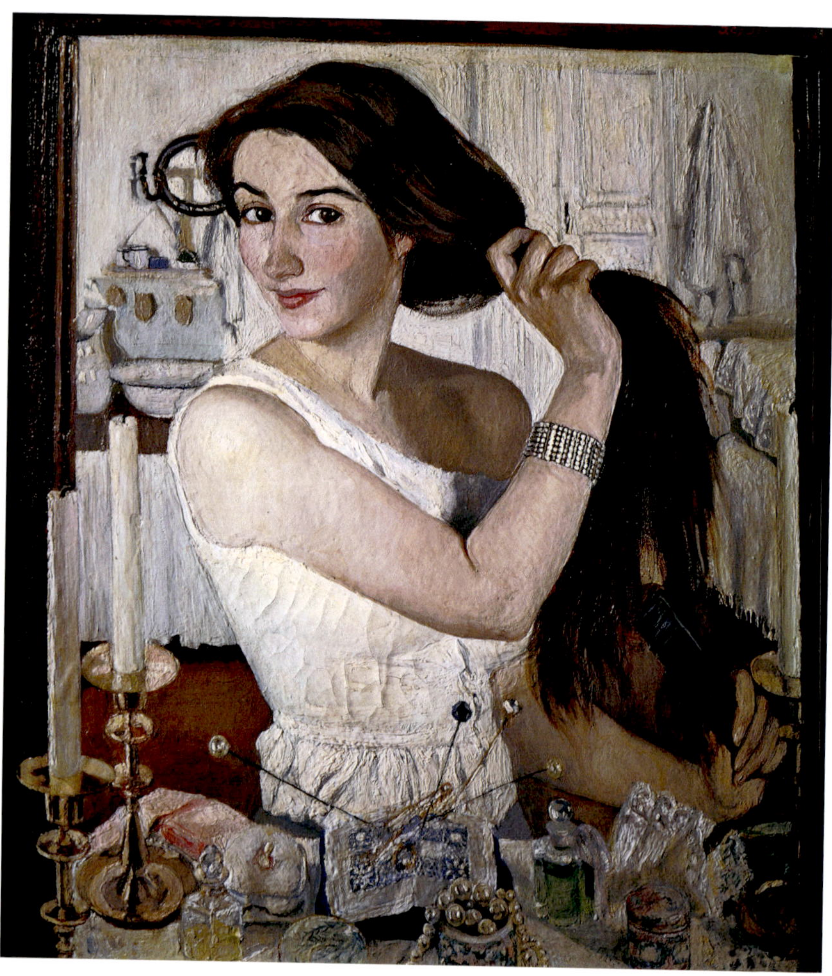

There are few self-portraits of women in a state of undress in early
twentieth-century western art. Compared with Paula Modersohn-
Becker's contemplative nudity (see page 88) or Gwen John's
tentative naked self-images, Zinaida Serebriakova's *At the Dressing
Table* (1909) positively brims with self-confidence. This painting was
made in winter. It was snowing outside and so Serebriakova stayed

Zinaida Serebriakova
At the Dressing Table,
1909
Oil on canvas,
75 x 65 cm
(29½ x 25⅝ in.)
Tretyakov Gallery,
Moscow

**This self-portrait
endorses the spirit of
living in the moment
and appreciating the
small things, from
hair pins and perfume
bottles to pearls and
knick-knacks. Sadly,
the Russian Revolution
shattered Serebriakova's
happiness. Her husband
was imprisoned and died
of typhus in 1919 and
she was left to fend for
her four children and
her sick mother with
limited resources.**

home, enjoying the warmth of her bedroom and appraising herself in the mirror. She stands close to get a better view, filling the picture plane with her radiant presence. The mother of four young children, Serebriakova appears to relish this rare moment of personal space. She is dressed in her underclothes; her chemise drops casually from her shoulder, revealing a strong, athletic physique. She gazes directly at the viewer; her impish smile is more than a little coquettish. This young Russian artist is aware of her beauty and grasps every opportunity to celebrate her happiness, one year into her marriage.

Serebriakova's self-portrait was first exhibited in 1910. It featured in the seventh Union of Russian Artists exhibition in St Petersburg and was immediately admired by many, including the Russian portrait painter Valentin Serov, who deemed it 'a very cute and fresh thing'. During the following year, Serebriakova made another self-portrait, *Bather* (1911). This work features the artist naked, draped and posed with all the grace of a classical statue. Her confident figurative style reveals her knowledge of the paintings of Titian and Jean-Antoine Watteau, gleaned from her studies in Italy and France. In choosing a landscape backdrop, Serebriakova fulfils her desire to celebrate the beauty of the Russian countryside in her work. Her skill in capturing the monumentality and intimacy of the naked female form would find further expression in several other major works, including the epic group painting *Bathhouse* (1913).

OTHER KEY WORKS

Bather, 1911, State Russian Museum, St Petersburg, Russia
Self-Portrait as Pierrot, 1911, Odessa Art Museum, Odessa, Ukraine
Bathhouse, 1913, State Russian Museum, St Petersburg, Russia

KEY FEATURES

Assertive representations of female nudity and intimacy
Classical interest in the human body
Statuesque and heroic representations of women
Self-conscious and playful idealization
Interaction of figures with landscape or domestic contexts
Representation of different light effects including natural light

EGON SCHIELE
1890–1918

The Austrian Expressionist artist Egon Schiele was just twenty-eight years old when he succumbed to the pandemic influenza of 1918. During his short life he produced approximately a hundred self-portrait drawings and watercolours. These extraordinary works on paper still hold the power to shock, even a century after they were made. Schiele frequently presented himself naked. He appears to grimace and scowl, pushing his emaciated body into jaunty, animalistic poses or engaging in masturbation. Certainly, there is a strong desire to distort and exaggerate: limbs are elongated or amputated, fingers splay open to make strange fan-like forms and skin is mottled with purples and greens conveying a deathly pallor. Schiele's inimitable use of line is tight and taut, etching into the paper with clarity and purpose as if he is desperate to capture this outpouring of potent sexuality. It is hard to deny the suggestion of self-conscious performativity. The existence of numerous black-and-white photographs confirms that the artist undertook preparatory pose-work in front of a mirror or lens.

Born in Tulln, Lower Austria, Schiele studied in Vienna, where he caught the attention of the leading Secessionist artist Gustav Klimt, well known for his languorous and decorative figuration. Although Schiele maintained an independent stance throughout his short career, Klimt shared models and opportunities with the younger artist and provided a foothold into Vienna's rich cultural scene. Sigmund Freud's theories of psychoanalysis and sexual deviancy were a source of much discussion during these years. Schiele's self-portraiture displays an awareness of developing ideas concerning the relationship between the ego and subconscious drives. His posturing also reinforces long-held romantic myths of the artist as an outsider, occupying the fringes of society. Schiele's art and lifestyle was certainly misunderstood outside of art circles. In 1912, he endured a short spell in prison on grounds of sexual immorality, for displaying his work in his studio when children were present.

Egon Schiele
Self-Portrait with Splayed Fingers, 1911
Pencil and gouache, heightened with white, on paper,
28 x 52.5 cm
(11 x 20⅝ in.)
Leopold Museum, Vienna

This is a fine example of Schiele's approach to self-portraiture between 1910 and 1912. The artist assumes a defensive posture, recoiling behind his left shoulder, his fingers characteristically splayed. The pencil work is agile and tense, the skin mottled and grotesque. Schiele surrounds his body with white paint, creating a special halo, an additional exclusion zone emphasizing his outsider status.

OTHER KEY WORKS

Kneeling Nude with Raised Hands (Self-Portrait), 1910, Leopold Museum, Vienna, Austria

Self-Portrait with Chinese Lantern Plant, 1912, Leopold Museum, Vienna, Austria

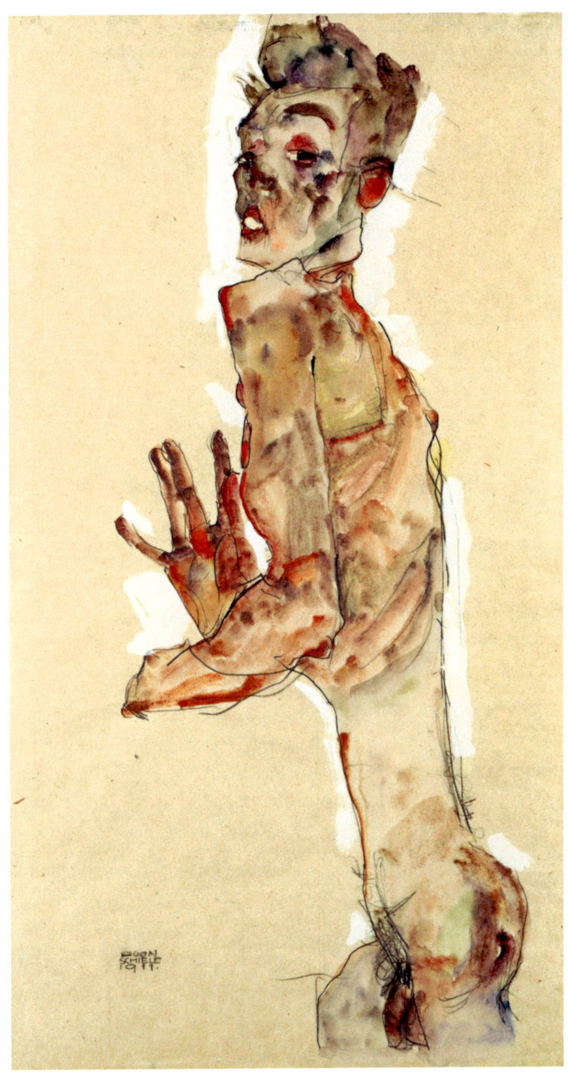

KEY FEATURES

Prolific self-portraitist

Interest in the creative potential of uninhibited sexuality

Exploration of the romantic myth of the artist as outsider

Extreme distortion and disfiguration

Strong suggestion of performance and posturing

Growing awareness of subconscious states

Interest in the expressive potential of drawing

AMRITA SHER-GIL
1913–41

The daughter of an aristocratic Sikh father and a Hungarian opera-singer mother, Amrita Sher-Gil spent her childhood in Hungary and India, travelling extensively. At the age of sixteen she arrived in Paris with her mother to commence her art education. She studied at L'Ecole des Beaux Arts and achieved early recognition for figurative paintings depicting women on their own or in groups. Sher-Gil made nineteen self-portraits during her short life. These works explore a range of moods and identities highlighting her cultural heritage and her position as a biracial, openly bisexual woman. Sher-Gil experimented with various fashions and poses. In some works she assumes a bohemian look, in others she sports a chic Parisian bob and western clothing, and elsewhere she wears a full sari. Together, these self-portraits provide a playful set of investigations testing notions of belonging.

In 1933, Sher-Gil became 'haunted by an intense longing to return to India, feeling in some strange inexplicable way that there lay my destiny as a painter'. *Self-Portrait as Tahitian* (1934) was one of the last paintings she made before returning to India and it reveals her ongoing exploration of different cultural and artistic identities. This work makes direct reference to Paul Gauguin's famous paintings of young Tahitian women: extraordinary images, rich in colour and form, yet undercut by a colonial, sexualizing male gaze. In assuming the identity of a Tahitian woman, Sher-Gil indicates her desire to find an empathic and empowering approach to the representation of gender and race. In a further twist, she presents a range of Japanese woodcuts in the background of the painting, recalling Vincent van Gogh's incorporation of Japanese prints into his self-portraiture (see page 66). This insistence on a fusion of styles reflects Sher-Gil's own complex position. She was, herself, an outsider, an aristocrat versed in European Post-Impressionism, intending to represent indigenous communities within her new modern Indian art.

Amrita Sher-Gil
Self Portrait as Tahitian,
1934
Oil on canvas,
90 x 56 cm
(35⅜ x 22 in.)
Collection of Navina
and Vivan Sundaram

Sher-Gil assumes an assertive three-quarter stance in this painting. She looks into the distance, aware of her sexuality yet refusing the ownership of the viewer's gaze. Some have commented on the dark presence behind the artist: is this her own shadow, or does it represent the looming male figure often visible in representations of the female nude?

OTHER KEY WORKS

Young Girls, 1932, National Gallery of Modern Art, New Delhi, India

Self-Portrait in Blue Sari, 1937, Kiran Nadar Museum of Art, Noida, India

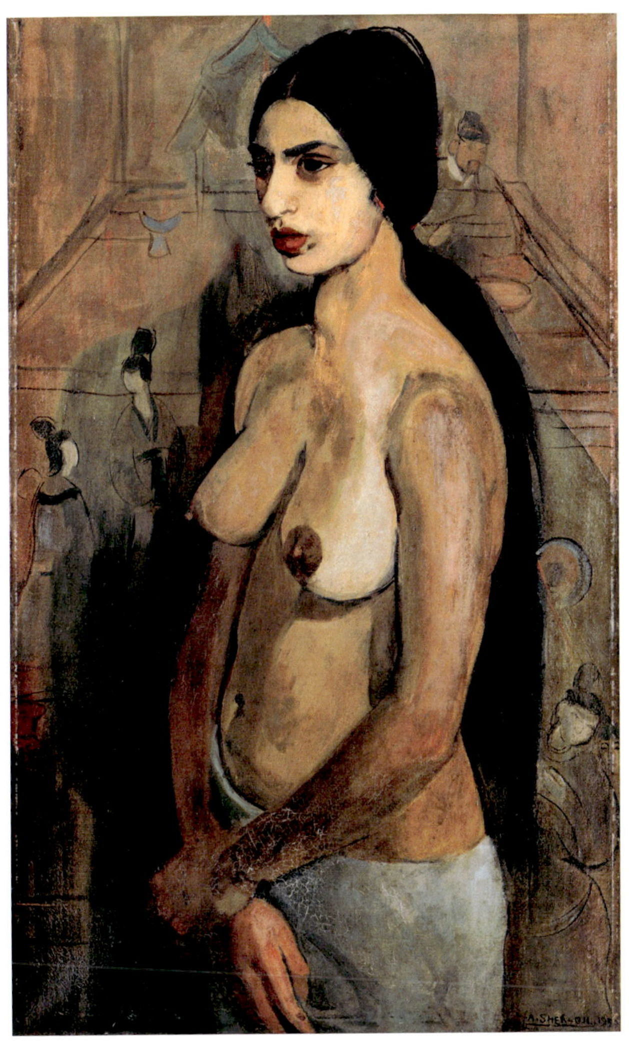

KEY FEATURES

Use of self-portraiture to explore intersectional identities

Playful use of costume and styling

Fusion of a global range of cultural and art-historical references

Influence of Post-Impressionist painting and references

Exploration of sensuality from a female perspective

LUCIAN FREUD
1922–2011

Lucian Freud was a reclusive figure, a man of few words. This renowned figurative painter chose his sitters with great care, preferring to paint those he knew well: friends, family or close associates. Freud explained, 'It's about myself and my surroundings. I work from the people that interest me and that I care about.' Freud expressed a strong preference for representing naked bodies, using paint to capture every dimple, slump and fold. He said, 'As far as I am concerned, the paint *is* the person.' Enjoying his intimate and familiar studio surroundings, he positioned his sitters in complicated poses, demanding they hold still for many hours. His sitters often sprawl on beds or sofas, apparently sleeping or looking unwell. Freud's best work emerged from the intense scrutiny of a reclining individual, behind closed doors – a strikingly similar process to that undertaken by his grandfather, Sigmund Freud, during his psychoanalytic investigations.

Freud returned to self-portraiture again and again throughout his life, from early crayon and pencil drawings capturing smooth, youthful features, to gnarled impasted representations interrogating the imperfections of old age. Freud never worked from photographs. He made paintings of others by working directly from the model, however his approach to self-portraiture involved the intervention of a mirror. To acknowledge its presence, Freud often incorporated the mirror into his self-portraits, or he included the word 'Reflection' in the titles.

In *Interior with Hand Mirror* (1967) the small mirror is wedged into the gap between the two panels of a sash window. Freud's somewhat ghoulish disembodied head fills the oval-shaped glass. He squints and grimaces, seemingly desperate to capture a sense of himself despite the startling glare of daylight shooting through the window pane. Closer inspection of this small jewel-like painting reveals a highly wrought process, with the artist applying, scraping back and reapplying the oil paint over and over again. The final image appears hard won, wrestled into existence. It serves as a reminder of the enduring complexities and challenges associated with painting the self.

Lucian Freud
Interior with Hand Mirror (Self-Portrait), 1967
Oil on canvas,
25.5 x 17.8 cm (10 x 7 in.)
Private collection

It is difficult to tell if the view from the window in this painting represents a cloudy sky or a light-drenched wall. Freud's manipulation of different lighting effects is also intriguing. Although the overall image is bathed in bright daylight, the mirror reveals the more subdued light infusing the recesses of his studio.

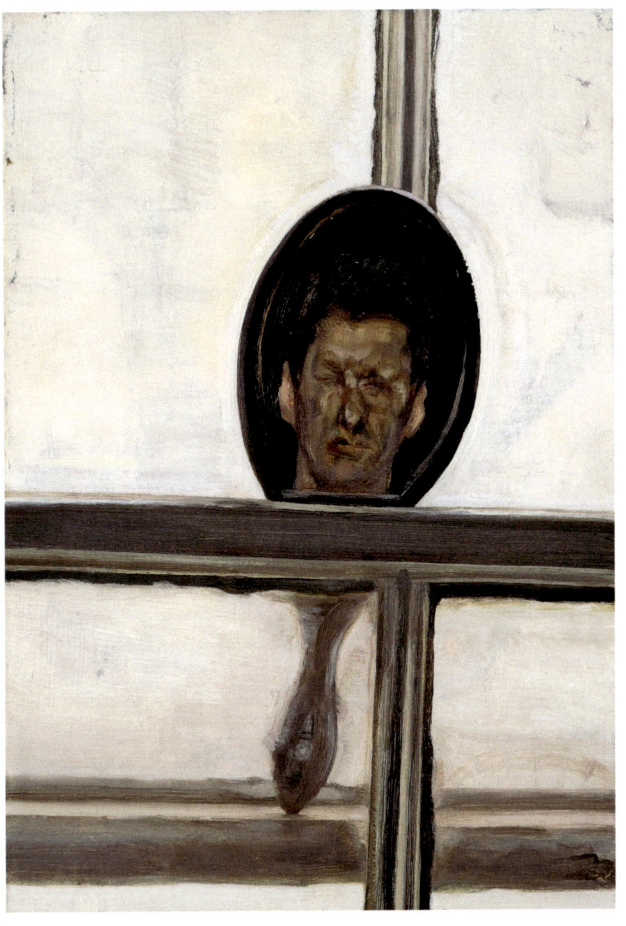

OTHER KEY WORKS

Reflection with Two Children (Self-Portrait), 1965,
  Museo Thyssen-Bornemisza, Madrid, Spain
Painter Working, Reflection, 1993, private collection

KEY FEATURES

Intense and prolonged interrogation of the self and others
'Warts-and-all' representation of the naked body
Use of a range of compositions, from glimpses in small
  mirrors to full-length, full-frontal self-portraiture
Private, studio-based practice
Incorporation of different light sources and effects

CHUCK CLOSE
b.1940

In 1967, the American painter Chuck Close resolved the issue of what to paint by turning the camera on himself. He took a head and shoulders selfie, overlaying the image with an intricate grid. He then commenced the painstaking and time-consuming task of upscaling the image onto a very large canvas. Using acrylic paint, he built the painting sequentially, square by square, working from top to bottom.

The bare-chested figure in *Big Self-Portrait* (1967–8) towers over the viewer with beatnik nonchalance. He wears thick-rimmed glasses and his hair is a mess; a cigarette balances precariously between his lips. We see everything: the stubble, the cigarette smoke. Even the areas of blur and surface imperfection created by the photographic process are faithfully airbrushed to breathtaking effect. Despite the extreme proximity and the strong physical likeness, there is no invitation to delve deeper. Close is not concerned with conveying emotional or psychological depth, nor is he interested in providing any contextual breadth. He is up close but not personal. This painting is fundamentally concerned with systems, sequences and surface relations. If we soften our focus on the figure we discover a formal, abstract painting.

Close has made paintings of himself and his friends for over five decades, returning to the same head and shoulders compositions over and over again in a quest to find 'everyman' and 'everywoman', yet no one in particular. Gradually his systems have expanded to include colour and looser pixelated units, leading to greater pictorial texture and optical complexity. Despite this relentless quest for the impersonal, it is hard to deny the grandstanding and personal ambition driving this early work. The enduring power of *Big Self-Portrait* resides in its clamorous affirmations. I am an artist. I look like an artist. Look at me.

Chuck Close
Big Self-Portrait, 1967–8
Acrylic on canvas,
273.1 x 212.1 cm
(107½ x 83½ in.)
Walker Art Center,
Minneapolis

Close has compared the process of viewing his enormous paintings with the experience of the tiny Lilliputians clamouring over Gulliver's face in Jonathan Swift's book *Gulliver's Travels* (1726). He also enjoys the way in which the image clicks in and out of view depending on the viewer's position in relation to the canvas.

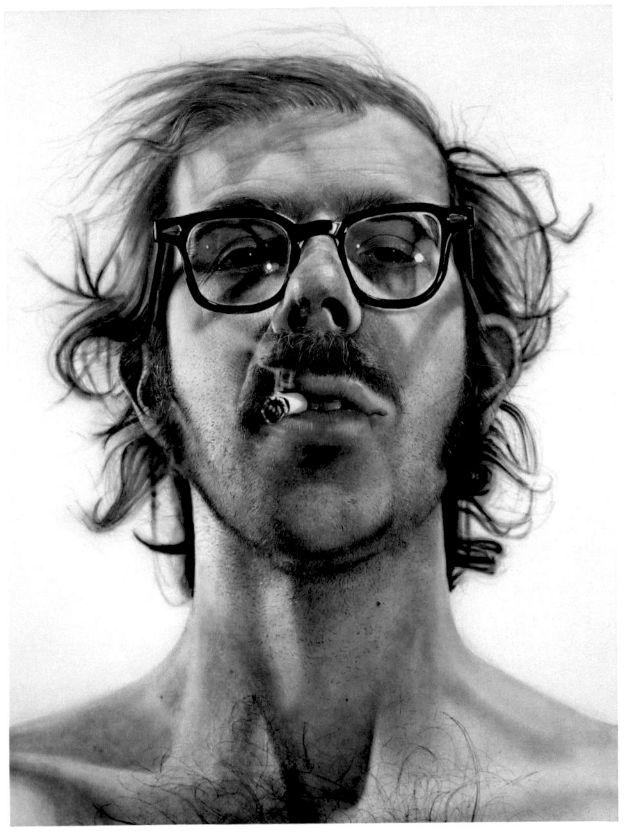

OTHER KEY WORKS

Self-Portrait, 1997, Museum of Modern Art, New York, USA

KEY FEATURES

Prolific self-portraitist

Large-scale paintings of himself and his friends

Close-up, full-frontal pose showing preoccupation with the head
and shoulders

Lack of interest in psychological insight or wider context

Close reference to photographic source material

Use of extreme figurative realism to interrogate formal concerns

Labour-intensive process, building up of the picture surface
section by section

MARINA ABRAMOVIĆ
b.1946

By the middle of the 1970s, feminist efforts to dislodge notions of the female body as a passive art object for male appreciation were well under way. Performance art provided an accessible and unrestricted space in which women could drive the narrative and the action, often using their bodies in challenging ways. Having initially studied painting, the Serbian-born artist Marina Abramović turned to using her own body in the early 1970s. Her early performances were physically and mentally demanding, involving risky and sometimes life-threatening actions, including taking psychoactive drugs or leaping through fire in front of an audience. In pushing herself to the extreme, Abramović hoped to find spiritual and intellectual enlightenment. She said, 'I test the limits of myself in order to transform myself, but I also take the energy from the audience and transform it…. A powerful performance will transform everyone in the room.'

In 1975, Abramović met the German artist Ulay (Frank Uwe Laysiepen). They became collaborators and partners, working together regularly until their separation in 1988. Much of their collaborative practice centred on issues of gender equality and on the politics and personal occupation of space. Their performance *Imponderabilia* took place at the Galleria Comunale d'Arte Moderna in Bologna, Italy, in 1977. The pair stripped naked and stood on either side of an entrance door to the gallery, turning inwards to face one another. Members of the public wishing to enter the space had to turn to one side to squeeze through, making a quick decision as to whether to share frontal bodily contact with a man or a woman. This simple if invasive physical intervention was designed to prompt reflection on gender, sexuality and otherness. In occupying a public entrance, Abramović and Ulay implicated their audience into becoming active participants and co-performers.

Marina Abramović and Ulay
Imponderabilia, 1977
Performance, 90 mins
Galleria Comunale d'Arte
Moderna, Bologna

In this work, Abramović and her partner Ulay collaborated to become a 'living door', offering only squeezed space for gallery visitors. A hidden camera documented visitors as they entered the space, projecting their reactions onto a nearby screen. The artists had intended to perform for three hours but the piece was stopped by police after ninety minutes.

OTHER KEY WORKS
Rhythm 0, 1974, performance, Studio Morra, Naples, Italy
Art Must Be Beautiful, Artist Must Be Beautiful, 1975, ZKM,
    Karlsruhe, Germany

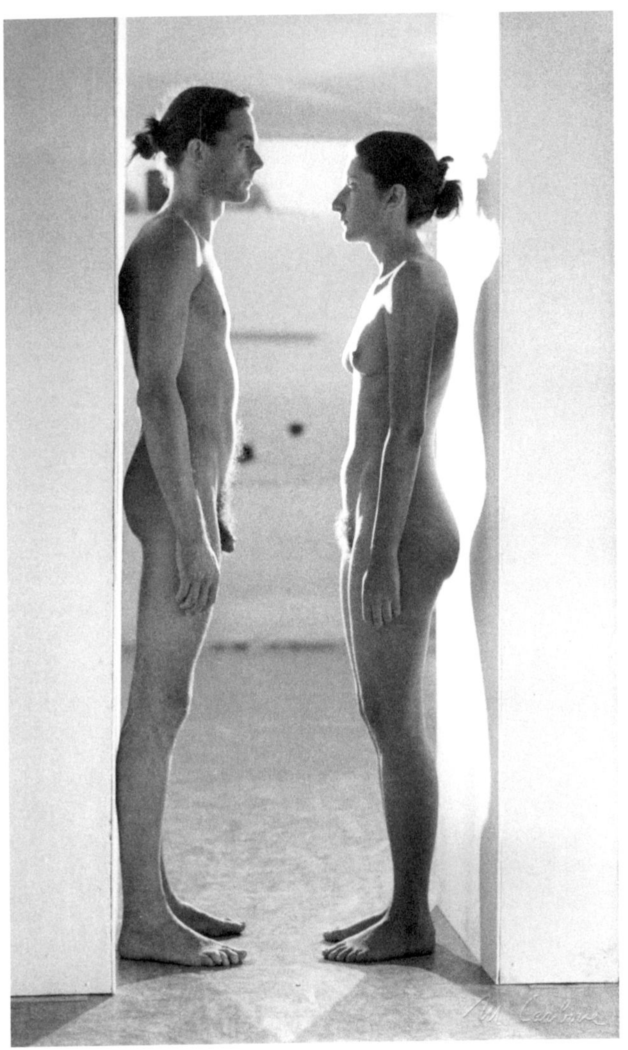

KEY FEATURES

Interest in the politics of gender, space and equality

Performance art requiring strength and endurance

Physical engagement in extreme, high-risk activities

Interest in repeated, ritualistic actions to achieve a state of
  enlightenment

Implicit requirement for audience involvement and engagement

Use of photography and video to document performances

ANA MENDIETA
1948–85

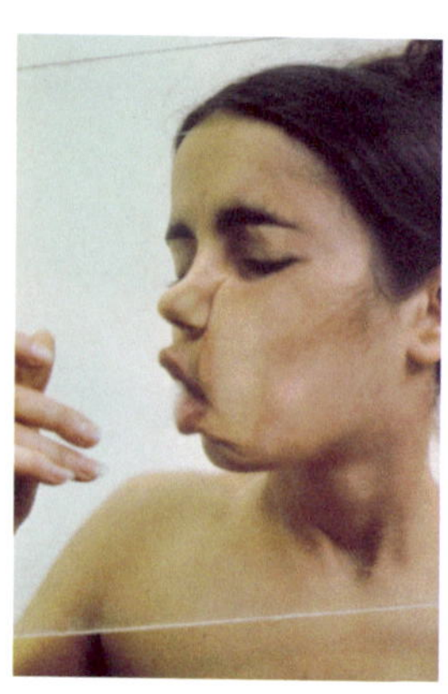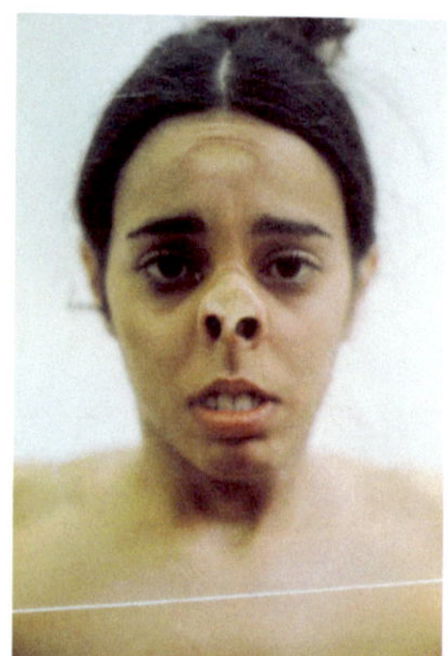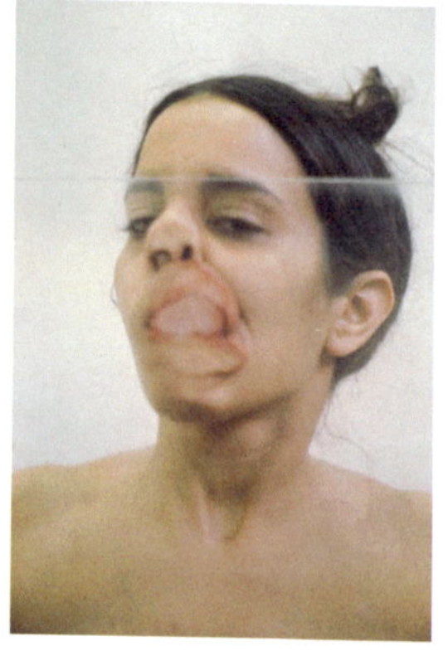

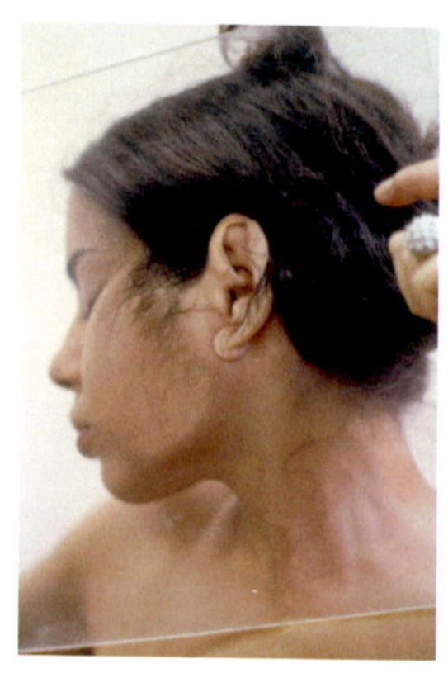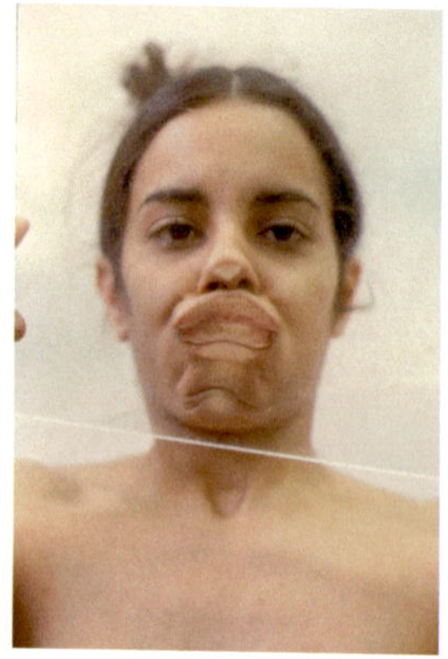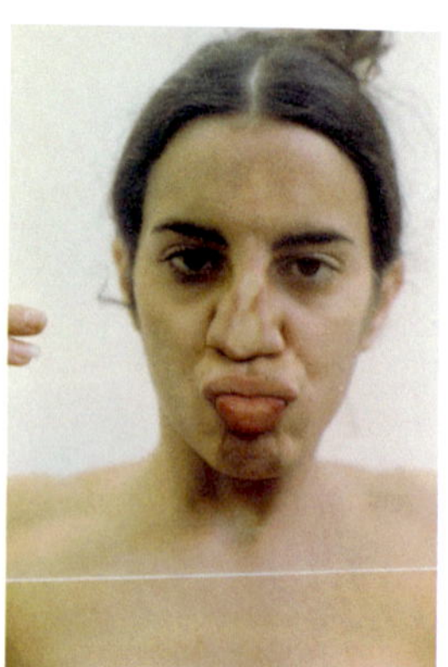

Ana Mendieta
Untitled (Glass on Face),
1972
Suite of six colour
photographs,
each 61 x 43.8 cm
(24 x 17¼ in.)
Institute of
Contemporary Art,
Miami

**These photographs
document Mendieta
pressing her face against
plexiglass to forge a
sequence of grotesque
distortions. There is an
implication of violence,
not just in the deliberate
uglification of the artist's
features but also in the
suggestion of impact
and compression. As
with much of Mendieta's
work, this piece provides
an eerie foretelling of
her fate.**

Ana Mendieta's childhood was fractured by displacement and exile.
Born in Cuba, she was one of 14,000 children sent to the USA as
part of 'Operation Pedro Pan'. This undercover exodus responded
to parental concerns regarding radical educational reforms
implemented by the Marxist–Leninist government. Separated from
their parents and younger brother, the twelve-year-old Ana and her
older sister Raquelín were sent to Iowa in 1961 to be looked after by
various foster agencies and institutions. Mendieta did not see her
family for five years and did not return to her homeland until 1980.

Mendieta studied at the University of Iowa, initially pursuing
painting but later enrolling to study in the Intermedia Department
led by the German-American artist Hans Breder. He encouraged
his students to pursue artist-centred practices, working across
performance, video and conceptual disciplines. Mendieta responded
readily to this approach, recalling how 'the turning point for me was
in 1972, when I realized that my paintings were not real enough for
what I want the image to convey, and by real I mean I wanted my
images to have power, to be magic'.

Mendieta's early experiments with performance and its
documentation resulted in a range of innovative short films and
photographic images capturing the artist in the act of physical
transformation. *Untitled (Facial Hair Transplants)* (1972) captures
Mendieta with a full beard, having carefully transplanted her friend's
facial hair onto her own jowls. This work provides a direct challenge
to binary definitions of gender and identity. Mendieta also manipulated
her facial features in various other radical ways, wearing stockings over
her head, donning wigs and make-up, or soaping up her long tresses
to create masks, spectacles and distortive protrusions. Informed by
emerging feminist discourses and spurred on by her own intersectional
experiences, Mendieta used her body to explore a range of identities
and positions, avoiding singular or fixed interpretations.

The implication of violence underscores much of Mendieta's
early practice. In an untitled series of photographs from 1972 we
find the artist pressed up against sheets of glass, causing the
significant distortion of her features. During the following year,
Mendieta documented herself with blood running down her face,
head tipped back to reveal her oozing nose. These disturbing and
confrontational works highlight Mendieta's attempts to force
attention onto the issue of violence towards women. Her interest in
blood also takes on a ritualistic significance, drawing on its symbolic
meaning as a force of life and renewal across many cultures and
belief systems, including Santería, the Afro-American religion
prevalent in Cuba.

In 1973, Mendieta embarked on the *Silueta* series of works, which would occupy her for seven years, resulting in over a hundred films and photographs taken on location at sites across Iowa and Mexico. In this series, Mendieta's body becomes increasingly obscured. We find its trace imprinted or silhouetted into a range of natural materials including mud, flowers, sand and leaves. Fusing ideas gleaned from performance, conceptual and land art, the *Silueta* works reveal Mendieta's increasingly ephemeral approach, which she termed 'earth-body art'. She acknowledged the biographical impulse behind her return to nature, saying, 'My exploration through my art of the relationship between myself and nature has been a clear result of my having been torn from my homeland during my adolescence. The making of my *silueta* in nature keeps (makes) the transition between my homeland and my new home. It is a way of reclaiming my roots and becoming one with nature.'

On 8 September 1985, Ana Mendieta's short life came to a sudden and violent end. Following reports of raised voices, she fell from the window of the thirty-fourth-floor apartment which she shared with her husband, the Minimalist sculptor Carl Andre. After a protracted and controversial trial, Andre was acquitted of her murder.

Ana Mendieta
Imagen de Yagul from the *Silueta* series, 1973–7
Silver dye-bleach print, 50.8 x 34 cm (20 x 13⅜ in.)
San Francisco Museum of Modern Art, San Francisco

This is one of Mendieta's first *Silueta* works, made just before her decision to eliminate her body from her work altogether. The performance took place in a Zapotec tomb in the architectural site of Yagul, Mexico, highlighting her interest in ancient cultures and rituals. Mendieta's motionless body is partially obscured by white wildflowers, providing a strong suggestion of death and renewal.

OTHER KEY WORKS

Untitled (Facial Hair Transplants), 1972, estate of the artist
Untitled (Facial Cosmetic Variations), 1972, Museum of Modern Art, New York, USA
Untitled (Self-Portrait with Blood), 1973, Tate collection, UK

KEY FEATURES

Performance-based practice evidenced through documentation
Exploration of intersectional experiences and identities
Use of the self to explore issues of violence and subjugation
Interest in physical absence, traces and ephemerality
Occupation of non-gallery sites and spaces
Embodiment of ancient cultures and rituals

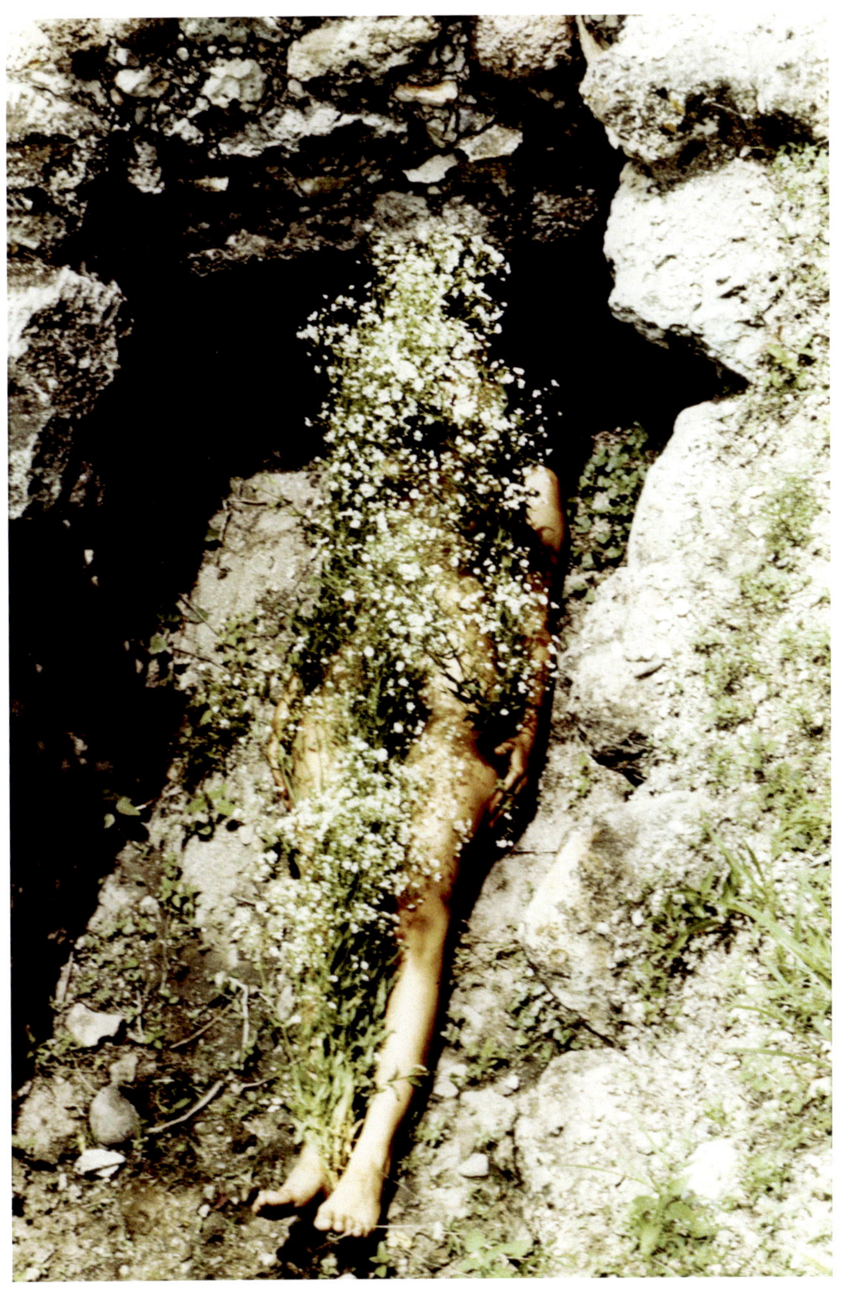

JEAN-MICHEL BASQUIAT
1960–88

Jean-Michel Basquiat was born in Brooklyn, New York City, to a Haitian father and Puerto Rican mother. As a child, Basquiat visited galleries frequently with his mother, developing a first-hand love of modern European and American art. He was also fascinated by comic books, poetry, music and the illustrations in *Gray's Anatomy*. Basquiat's teenage years were unstable: family unrest prompted him to drop out of school and run away from home. This precarious existence continued into young adulthood. With no fixed abode, he operated as a poet, musician and street artist, embellishing the urban fabric of Lower Manhattan using the tag SAMO©. During the early 1980s Basquiat made a rapid transition from street to gallery, from underground to mainstream, achieving international recognition for his stream-of-consciousness paintings fusing text, figures, gestures and political commentary. Basquiat died of a heroin overdose in 1988 at the age of twenty-seven.

Although Basquiat explored self-portraiture only intermittently during his brief yet prolific career, much of his art features autobiographical allusions. There are references to his identity as a black American artist and his experiences of operating within a predominantly white art world. He also used his art as a platform to acknowledge the contribution made by his musical and sporting heroes, including Charlie Parker and Muhammad Ali, and to comment on racial injustice and marginalization. Basquiat once reflected on the motivation driving his work: 'it's about 80% anger.'

Basquiat's self-portraiture is characteristically confrontational, intense and brutal. The head is often subjected to enlargement and contortion. Eyes become empty hollows, teeth are bared in painful grimaces. Basquiat's body appears powerful and heroic, arms extended with purpose, anatomy defined and delineated. The influence of Pablo Picasso and Robert Rauschenberg is discernible, so, too, an awareness of African art, cartoons and children's drawings. Basquiat's sophisticated fusion of sources invokes multiple dualities: past and present, life and death, heroism and vulnerability.

Jean-Michel Basquiat
Self-Portrait, 1986
Acrylic on canvas,
180 x 260.5 cm
(70⅞ x 102½ in.)
Museu d'Art
Contemporani de
Barcelona (MACBA),
Barcelona

Made towards the end of Basquiat's short life, this self-portrait assumes epic proportions. The artist occupies the centre of the painting and strikes an assertive, full-frontal pose. Surrounded by a range of symbolic objects, he stands naked, brandishing his tools, part victor, part Grim Reaper. It is hard to define whether the painting represents artistic freedom or intense anguish and isolation.

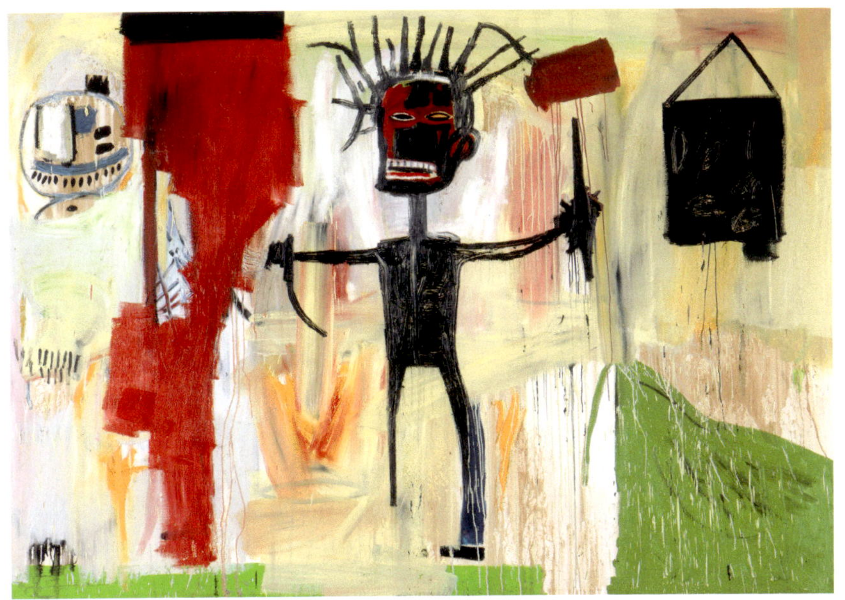

OTHER KEY WORKS

Self-Portrait as a Heel - Part Two, 1982, Collection of Stéphanie
  Janssen
Self-Portrait, 1984, Yoav Harlap Collection, USA

KEY FEATURES

Extensive autobiographical references and allusions
Exploration of black male identities and experiences
Representation of isolated, heroic figures
Preoccupation with the expressive potential of heads, skulls
  and masks
Vigorous and spontaneous Neo-Expressionist paint handling
Intricate layering of ideas and motifs sourced from art, music,
  comic books and street art

JENNY SAVILLE
b.1970

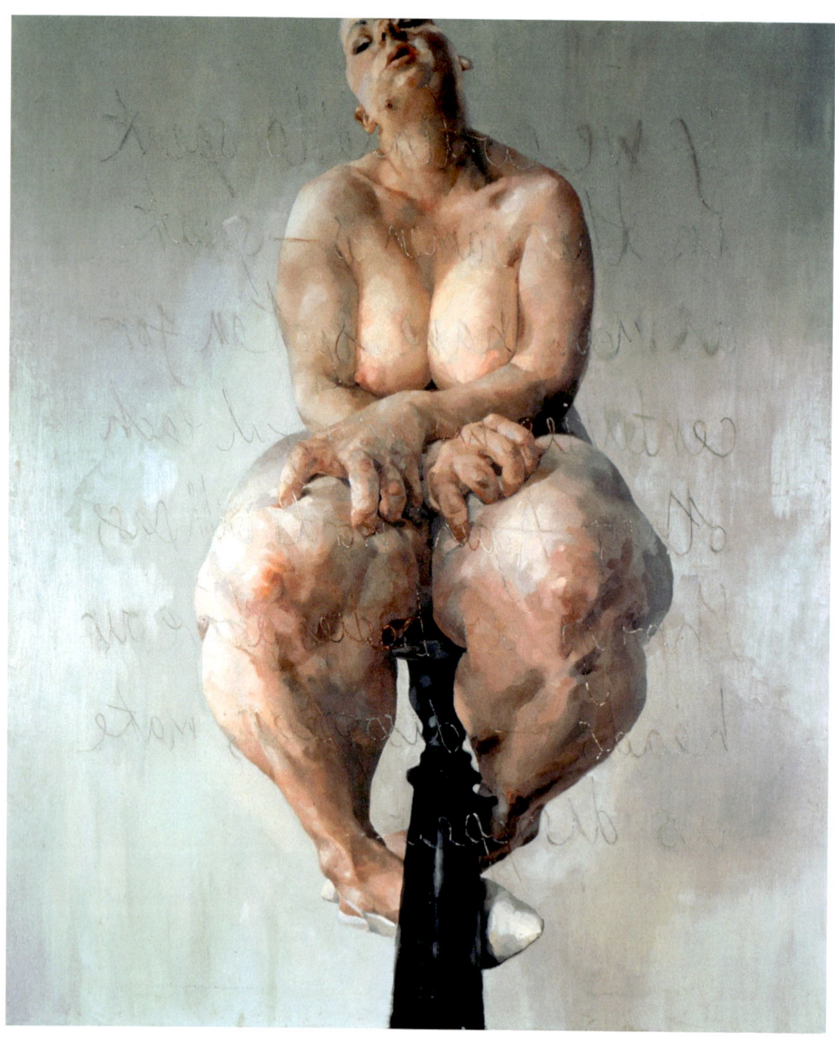

Jenny Saville's rise to fame can only be described as meteoric. The art collector Charles Saatchi invested in a number of her figurative paintings while she was still a student at the Glasgow School of Art, presenting them in two headline-grabbing exhibitions: *Young British Artists III* (1994) at the Saatchi Gallery and *Sensation* (1997) at the Royal Academy in London.

Jenny Saville
Propped, 1992
Oil on canvas,
213.5 x 183 cm
(84 x 72 in.)
Saatchi Collection,
London

This work features a passage of text by the feminist philosopher Luce Irigaray. In other paintings Saville has inscribed single significant words onto her flesh. She has also incorporated lines to trace the contours and gradients of her body, creating a mapping effect. This process recalls the notations made by a plastic surgeon prior to liposuction.

Many of Saville's early large-scale paintings featured the artist naked. She often chose a close-up, low-down perspective to create dramatic foreshortening and distortion of her body. Her substantial form fills each canvas. Gestural brushstrokes collide to recreate every bulge, blemish and bruise. Her little head perches atop these sculptural masses. She appears strangely distant, as if observing her obese frame with quiet acceptance. These unflattering self-portraits prompt the viewer to confront a body-type often deemed ugly or repulsive. Her work seeks to challenge idealized representations of the female body as evidenced throughout art history and in the media.

Saville's paintings nod to a wide range of influences, from classical sculpture to the fleshy figuration of Peter Paul Rubens, Lucian Freud (see pages 98–9) and Willem de Kooning. Working from enlarged photographs of her own body parts, Saville acknowledges the influence of confrontational feminist performance art of the 1970s. Her source material has also extended beyond the art world to include visceral images of surgical procedures, death, animals and meat.

Propped (1992) is a prime example of Saville's feminist approach to figuration. In this painting the artist sits on a tiny stool and gazes forward as if examining her reflection in a cloudy mirror. Her fingers claw into the soft folds of her thighs with tension and unease. The passage of text scratched onto the surface of the mirror references an essay by the feminist philosopher Luce Irigaray. It is written in reverse, like a secret message for the artist's eyes only.

OTHER KEY WORKS

Plan, 1993, Saatchi Collection, London, UK

KEY FEATURES

Feminist desire to challenge representations of women
Unidealized naked self-portraiture
Expressive brushstrokes and paint handling
Use of cropping and distortive viewpoints
Investigation of flaws and surface imperfections to challenge
   notions of beauty
Active poses and performative approach

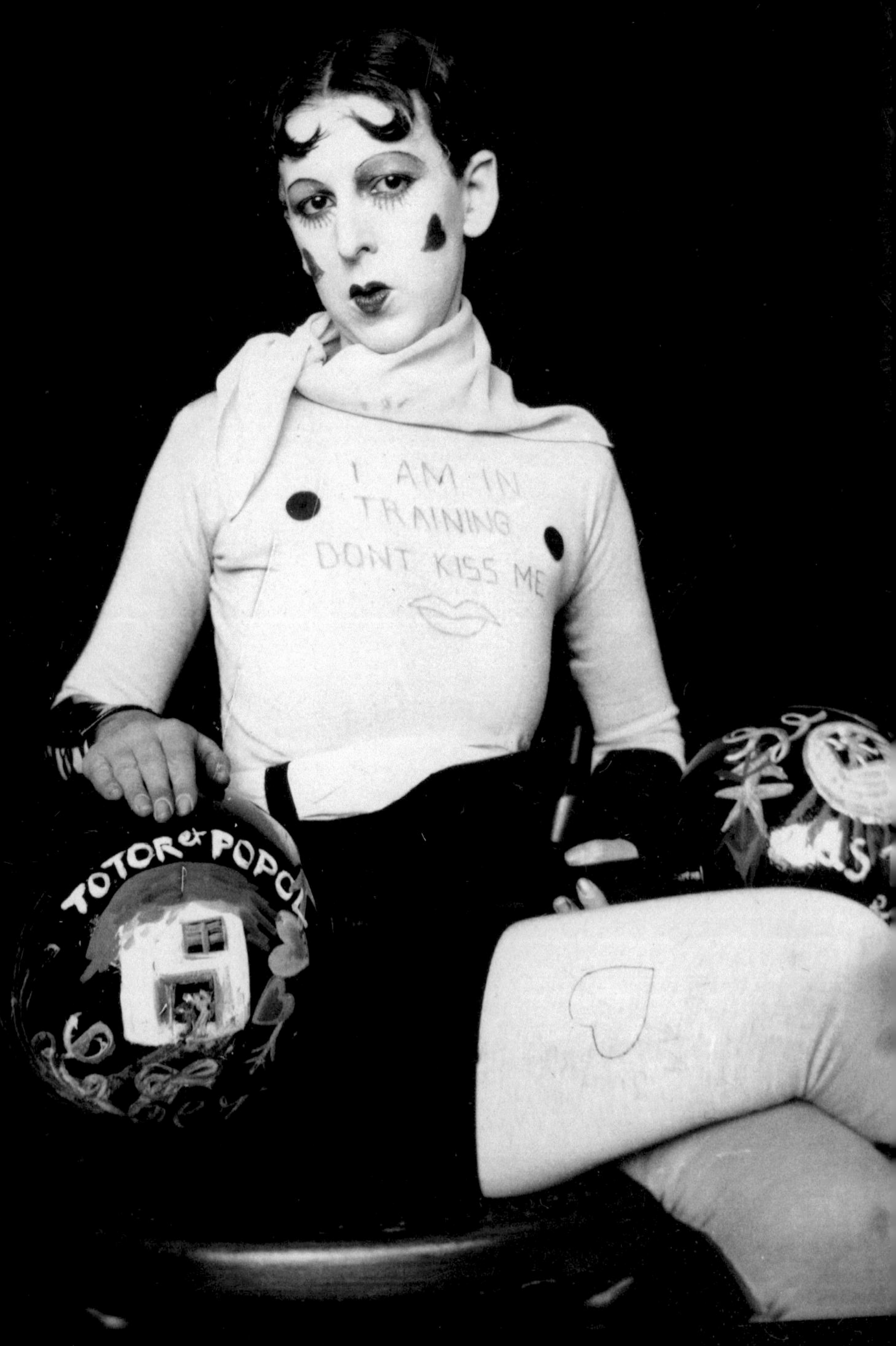

I AM IN
TRAINING
DONT KISS ME
TOTOR et POPOL

MAKING FACES

-

**Under this mask, another mask.
I will never finish removing all these faces.**

-

Claude Cahun, 1930

MARCEL DUCHAMP
1887–1968

'I don't believe in art. I believe in artists.'

In the early twentieth century, the French-American artist Marcel Duchamp posed big questions about art that remain relevant to this day. He became critical of art that appealed to the eye, deciding instead to make work that challenged the mind. In Duchamp's view, art was about ideas, language, interpretation and context. It had nothing to do with skilful technique or painterly brushstrokes. An early provocation involved him exhibiting a shop-bought bottle rack, claiming it as art. This new 'readymade' concept involved the investment of non-art objects with new meanings, overturning long-held assumptions about skill, expression and originality.

Duchamp's radical conceptual approach included a significant challenge to the conventions of portraiture. In 1919, he defaced a cheap reproduction of Leonardo da Vinci's *Mona Lisa*, adding a moustache and a goatee beard to the revered portrait and titling the piece *L.H.O.O.Q.* When spoken in fast French, the letters sound like *elle a chaud au cul* – she has a hot ass. Duchamp's playful intervention calls into question portraiture's ability to capture and fix the identity of a sitter. Taking this idea a stage further, in 1920 Duchamp created a new alter ego, Rose Sélavy. Her name plays on the French *Eros, c'est la vie*, meaning 'Love, that's life', highlighting Duchamp's ongoing fascination with droll wordplay. He worked collaboratively with the artist and fashion photographer Man Ray to create a series of black-and-white photographs of himself dressed as his intriguing female counterpart. He also signed various art works with Sélavy's name.

Duchamp's use of role-playing to challenge static definitions of gender and identity has influenced successive generations of artists. His enigmatic and unpredictable persona never slipped. In 1923, he announced his decision to stop making art so that he could dedicate his time to playing chess.

Marcel Duchamp and Man Ray
Rrose Sélavy (Marcel Duchamp), 1923
Gelatin silver print, 22.1 x 17.6 cm (8¾ x 7 in.)
J. Paul Getty Museum, Los Angeles

Duchamp and Man Ray collaborated on this series of photographs throughout the 1920s. For this image, Duchamp struck a pose and assumed his best sultry look. Man Ray increased the ambience through the use of soft lighting techniques gleaned from his work as a fashion photographer. In a further enigmatic twist, Duchamp added an extra R to Rose's name.

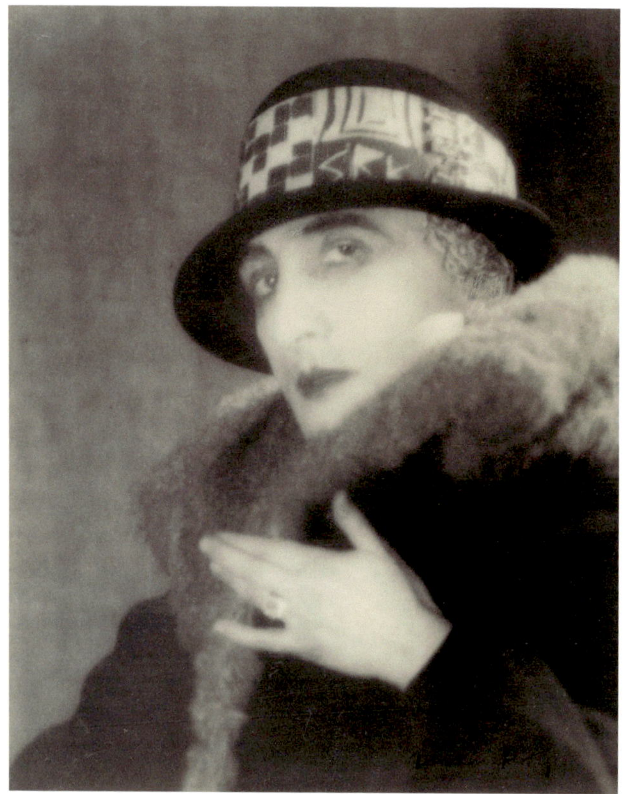

OTHER KEY WORKS

L.H.O.O.Q., 1919, private collection, Paris, France
Wanted, $2,000 Reward, 1923, Philadelphia Museum of Art,
  Philadelphia, USA
With My Tongue in My Cheek, 1959, Musée National d'Art Moderne,
  Paris, France

KEY FEATURES

Introduction of the notion that art can be anything
Employment of a wide range of materials, concepts and ideas
Creation of elusive and enigmatic personae
Interest in role-playing, masquerade and gesture
Avoidance of fixed interpretations of gender and identity
Collaborative, open-ended approach
Witty and ironic use of words, phrases and titles

CLAUDE CAHUN
1894–1954

Claude Cahun was a writer, a political activist and an artist. Christened Lucy Schwob, they were born into a prominent literary Jewish family based in Nantes, France. In 1909, the teenage Schwob fell in love with Suzanne Malherbe. They would become lifelong partners and collaborators. Several years later, Schwob and Malherbe made the joint decision to change their names. After experimenting with a number of different possibilities, Schwob became Claude Cahun – Claude being a gender-neutral name in France – and Malherbe used the pseudonym Marcel Moore. Together, they moved to Paris in the early 1920s, mixing in literary, artistic and theatrical circles and engaging with contemporary political debates including active opposition to fascism.

During the 1930s, Cahun was associated with Surrealism. Its co-founder, the writer and poet André Breton, described Cahun as 'one of the most curious spirits of our time'. The Surrealist interest in Freudian psychoanalysis, unconscious states, alter egos and suppressed sexual desires invigorated and intensified Cahun's writing. In their 1926 book *Carnaval en Chambre* (Carnival in the Bedroom), Cahun explored ideas of masking and multiple identities. In one passage, Cahun cautioned against wearing any one mask for too long for fear of it getting stuck: 'with horror you see that the flesh and its mask have become inseparable'. Although Cahun and Moore would leave Paris for Jersey in 1937, Surrealist ideas would underpin Cahun's practice for the rest of their life.

Alongside their outward-facing role as a writer and political activist, Cahun also created an extensive body of black-and-white photography, in which they assumed an astonishing range of roles and identities. Cahun often experimented with make-up, clothing, masks and wigs to intensify their visions, working in close collaboration with Marcel Moore throughout the process. Moore created many of the costumes and took an active role not just in contributing and developing ideas but also by taking many of the final

Claude Cahun
Photograph from the series *I am in training don't kiss me*, c.1927
Black-and-white photograph,
11.7 x 8.8 cm
(4⅝ x 3½ in.)
Jersey Heritage Collections, Jersey

Like Marcel Duchamp (see pages 114–15), Cahun considered photography to be the perfect medium for capturing shifting definitions of identity and gender. In this intriguing image, Cahun becomes a bodybuilder and assumes 'male' and 'female' characteristics. The dumbbells are decorated with the names of comic-book legends Totor and Popol, adding to the focus on powerful role models.

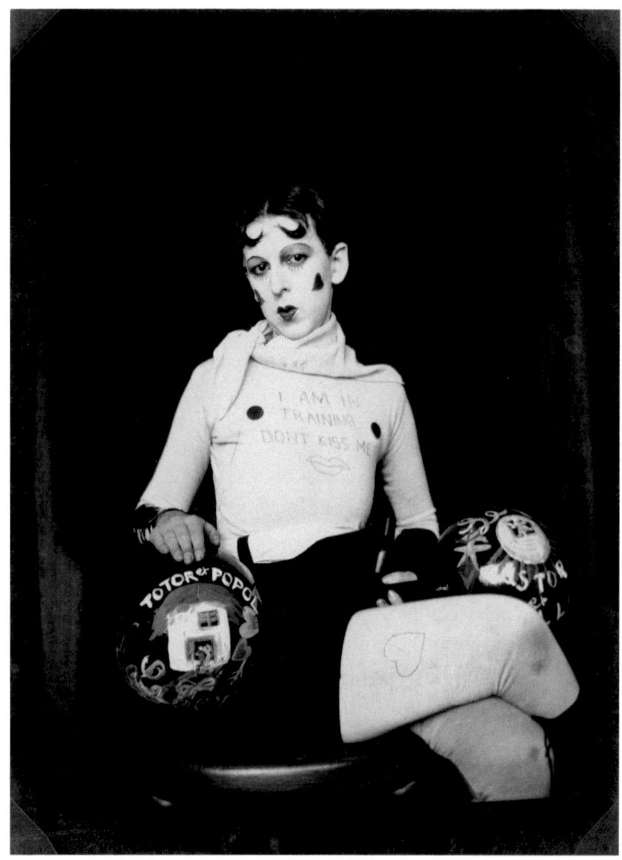

images. Only one self-portrait was published during Cahun's lifetime
and they rarely titled the photographs. Indeed, it is unclear if Cahun
ever intended to share these images publicly in any substantial way.

In Cahun's 1930 autobiographical book *Aveux non Avenus*
(Disavowals), the artist expressed their non-binary identity: 'Shuffle
the cards. Masculine? Feminine? It depends on the situation. Neuter
is the only gender that always suits me.' Many of their early images
present an androgynous figure, as in *What do you want from me?*
(1928) where the artist's trademark shaved head is disembodied and
duplicated. Sexual ambiguity recurs in the curious photograph *I am in
training don't kiss me*. Here we find Cahun in unusual attire: the tight
white body-stocking adorned with stitched-on nipples both flattens
and draws attention to the body. The use of white face paint creates
a mask-like visage, decorated with love-heart cheeks, exaggerated
lashes and an accentuated cupid's bow. Cahun's assured creation

of different identities even prompted them to travel back in time
to explore the experience of youth. In *Self-Portrait (in cupboard)*
(c.1932), the artist, now in their thirties, assumes a childlike
innocence, curled up as if sleeping in the laundry cupboard.

Eventually, Cahun and Moore's anti-fascist activity within
Nazi-occupied Jersey led to their arrest. They were imprisoned
and sentenced to death. With the liberation of the island in 1945,
Cahun and Moore were released. They were able to return to
their home, only to find that a large body of their work had been
destroyed by the Germans. Although Cahun continued to produce
self-portrait photographs until their death in 1954, they never fully
recovered from the experience of incarceration. Cahun's unique
oeuvre emerged from obscurity several decades later. Only now is
it fully recognized for its anticipation of many postmodern ideas
concerning collaboration and authorship, performance and identity.

Claude Cahun
*What do you want
from me?*, 1928
Gelatin silver print,
18 x 23 cm (7 x 9 in.)
Metropolitan Museum
of Art, New York

**In this curious
photograph, we find
two views of the artist's
head and shoulders, one
overlaid on top of the
other to create a surreal
twin or double image. The
head in profile appears
to be whispering into the
ear of its double. This
composition highlights
Cahun's interest in
challenging the notion of
a fixed, singular identity.**

OTHER KEY WORKS

Self-Portrait (double head image as Elle *in* Barbe Bleue*)*, c.1924,
   Jersey Heritage Collections, UK
Self-Portrait (full-length masked figure in cloak with masks),
   c.1928, Jersey Heritage Collections, UK

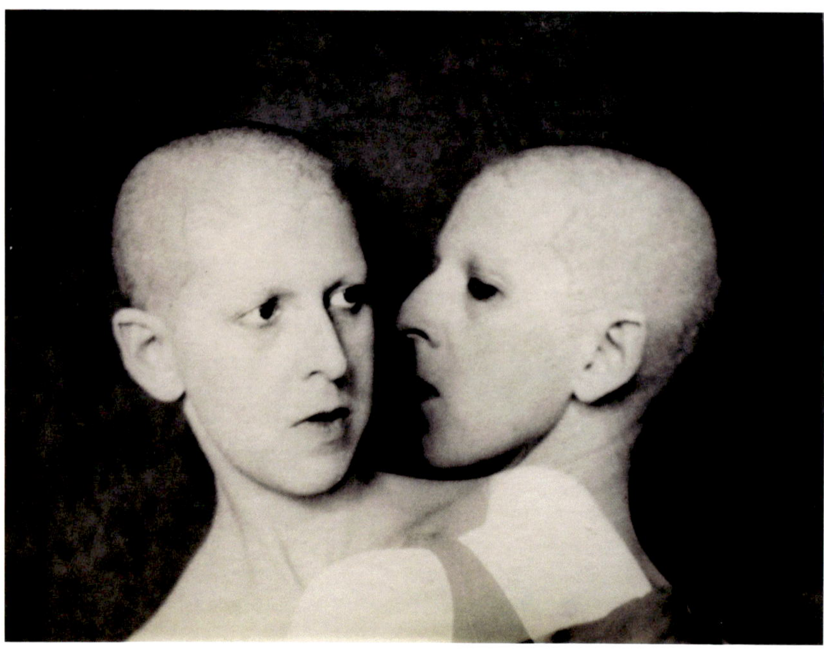

Claude Cahun
Self-Portrait (in cupboard),
c.1932
Black-and-white
photograph,
11.2 x 8.5 cm
(4⅜ x 3⅜ in.)
Jersey Heritage
Collections, Jersey

For this dreamlike image, Cahun dressed up in ankle socks and shorts, their hair set into blonde curls and finished with a fancy bow. There is more than a nod to Freud's theory of regression here. The implications of revelation and concealment are also reinforced by the opening and closing of drawers and doors.

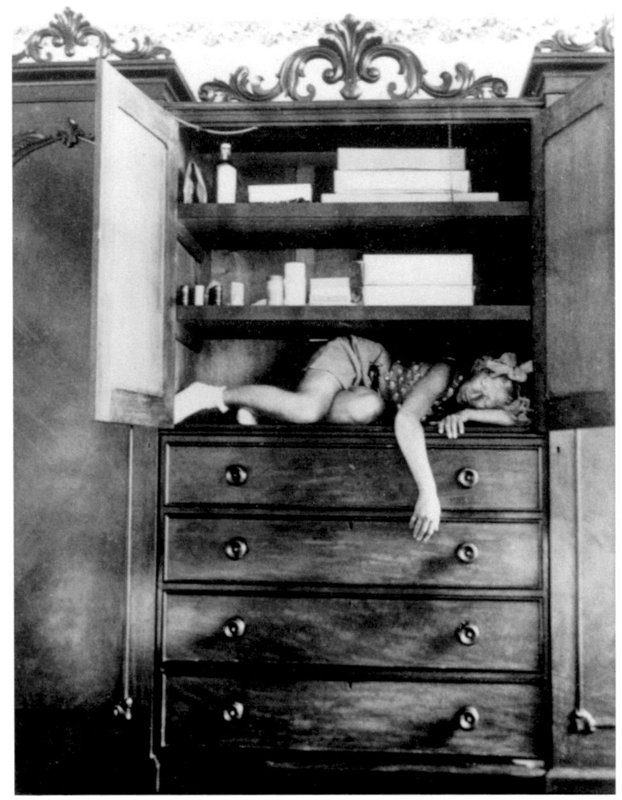

KEY FEATURES

Collaborative photographic practice

Exploration of multiple non-binary identities

Strong interest in performance, theatricality and role-playing

Use of styling, costumes and props

Surrealist exploration of alter egos

Investigation of dreamlike narratives and states

MARISOL
1930–2016

Maria Sol Escobar was born in Paris, the daughter of wealthy Venezuelan parents. Her mother committed suicide when Marisol was just eleven years old. From this point on, she became reserved, speaking only when necessary throughout childhood, and maintaining long periods of silence into adulthood.

In the early 1960s, Marisol gained international recognition for her handmade wooden constructions inspired by American folk art and Pre-Columbian art. Living and working in New York City, she also drew inspiration from contemporary American life. Some of Marisol's totemic tableaux satirize the vacuous extravagances of society living. Other works explore the everyday experiences of migrant workers or mothers tending to their children. Although Marisol was considered a leading, if elusive, figure of Pop Art, her focus on social commentary and her gentle critique of class, gender and racial stereotypes set her work apart from her contemporaries.

Marisol often incorporated her own features into her sculptural installations, perhaps as a way of empathizing with a given situation, but also as part of a wider programme of self-interrogation. She said, 'There comes a point where you start asking, "Who am I?" I was trying to find out through my sculpture. That's why I made all those masks and each one of them is different. Every time I would take a cast of my face it would come out different. You have a million faces.'

Marisol's *Self-Portrait* (1961–2) appears more intent on concealment than revelation. The work features no fewer than seven different wooden faces, none of which appears to capture a strong physical likeness of the artist. Her disparate identities rest cautiously upon a simple wooden screen like coconut shies at a fairground. Six legs protrude from this brightly coloured collective body. One hitches up at the knee while the others lunge forward, flexing at the heel to create a natural barrier. The message is clear: keep out.

Marisol
Self-Portrait, 1961–2
Wood, plaster, marker, paint, graphite, human teeth, gold and plastic, 110.5 x 114.9 x 192.1 cm (43½ x 45¼ x 75⅝ in.)
Museum of Contemporary Art Chicago, Chicago

Marisol often incorporated found or readymade objects, such as hats, bags and fashion accessories, into her installations. In this work she even fixed human teeth into the mouths of her hand-carved heads. Despite these personal touches, Marisol's work gives little away. Multiple identities are suggested yet personal revelations are ultimately withheld.

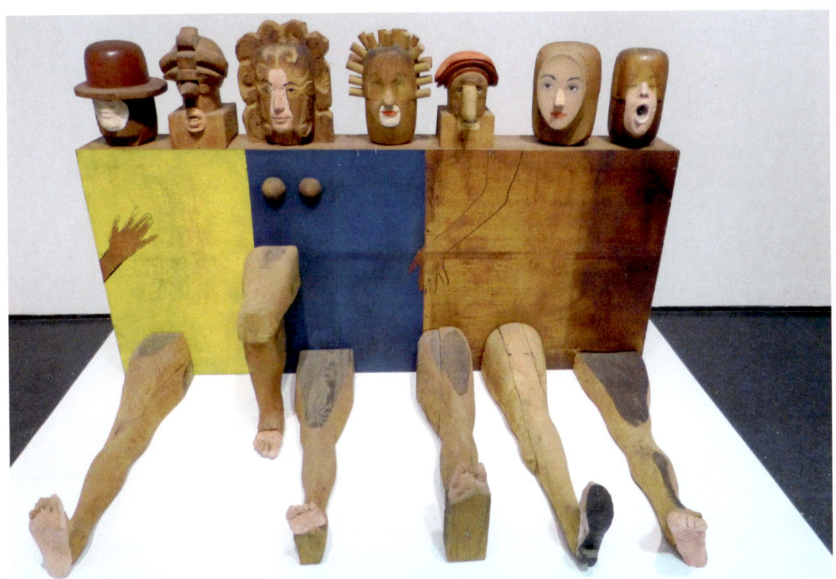

OTHER KEY WORKS

The Party, 1965–6, Toledo Museum of Art, Toledo, USA
Original wax prototype for Self-portrait ring, 1967, Museum
  of Modern Art, New York, USA

KEY FEATURES

Sculptural construction of multiple identities
Critique of class, gender and racial stereotyping
Lack of interest in autobiographical revelation
Incorporation of readymade objects and accessories
Aloof and elusive figuration

ANDY WARHOL
1928–87

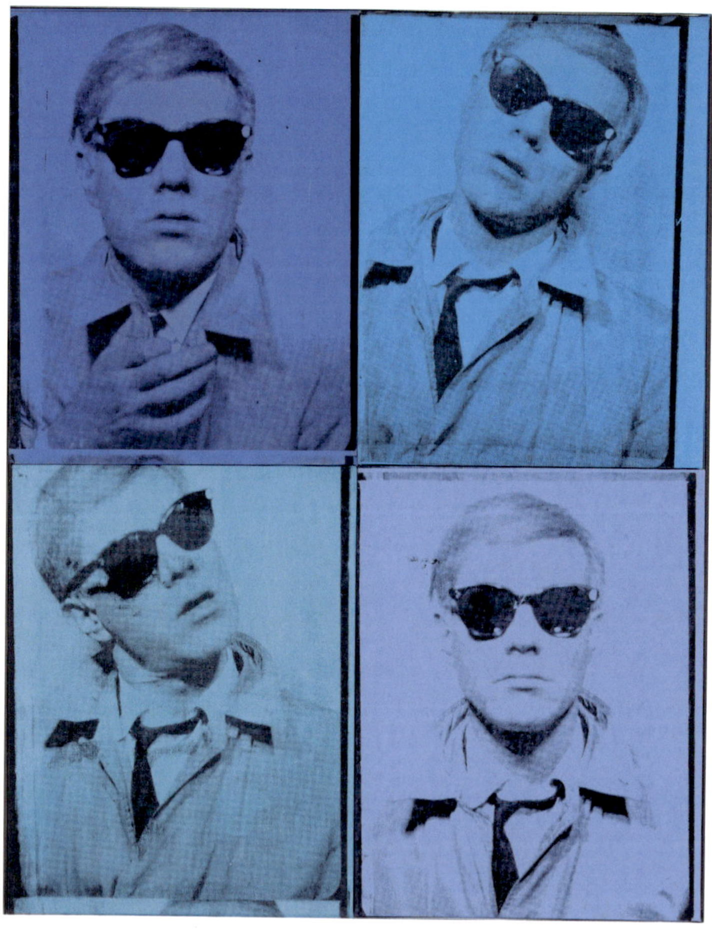

Andy Warhol's repeated silkscreen images of the rich and famous received international attention during the early 1960s. His own carefully cultivated identity also became instantly recognizable. Warhol was an icon: not just an artist, but also a filmmaker, a curator, a manager and a party-goer. He spent considerable time refining his image using make-up, collagen treatments and his signature silver-blond wig.

Self-portraiture emerged as a key strand within Warhol's practice only after his successful transition from anonymous

Andy Warhol
Self-Portrait, 1963–4
Silkscreen ink on
synthetic polymer paint
on canvas, 4 panels,
each 50.8 x 40.6 cm
(20 x 16 in.)
The Collection of Mr
and Mrs S. Brooks Barron

Warhol loved the impersonal and instant potential of photo-booth self-portraiture. Not only did he offer himself up readily to this low-quality image machine, but he also invited many celebrity sitters to portray themselves using the same process. In 1971 he invested in a Big Shot Polaroid camera, which enabled him to produce images with even greater spontaneity and speed.

commercial artist to bona fide Pop Art sensation. In 1963, Warhol donned dark glasses and a raincoat, transforming himself into a secret agent, a master of disguise. He ducked into a photo booth in Times Square, New York City, and sat for some instant self-portraiture. The four images capture the artist in a variety of poses: head askew as if hanged, full-frontal face like a mugshot, hand raised to the throat with mock theatricality. He enlarged these lowly photographs into silkscreens before transferring them onto canvas and applying brilliant shades of blue. Although *Self-Portrait* (1963–4) reveals little of Warhol's personality and character, it confirms his status as a cool cultural icon and highlights his developing skills as a mythmaker. As Warhol himself once acknowledged, 'If you want to know about Andy Warhol, just look at the surface of my paintings and films and me, and there I am. There's nothing behind it.'

Warhol's intentionally superficial and guarded self-portraiture resulted in multiple poses, guises and identities across several decades. There are, however, some moments of exposure. On the surface, his 1981–2 series of self-portraits in drag reveal a Duchampian testing of gender boundaries, but on closer inspection these images also convey an overriding sense of unguarded vulnerability. Warhol's final self-portraits of 1986 are similarly reflective. This death-fearing artist's head emerges from the darkness with skull-like foreboding and his hair sticks up on end as if in shock at that which awaits.

OTHER KEY WORKS

Self-Portrait in Drag (blond wig), 1981–2, The Museum of Fine
 Arts, Houston, USA
Self-Portrait, 1986, Solomon R. Guggenheim Museum, New York,
 USA

KEY FEATURES

Deliberate creation of an iconic artistic persona
Interest in readymade celebrity portraiture sourced from
 magazines and advertising
Deployment of instant camera processes including photo booths
 and polaroids
Use of repetition to depersonalize and distance
Acute interest in role-playing, disguise and masquerade
Experimentation with make-up and drag to explore multiple
 identities

TEHCHING HSIEH

b.1950

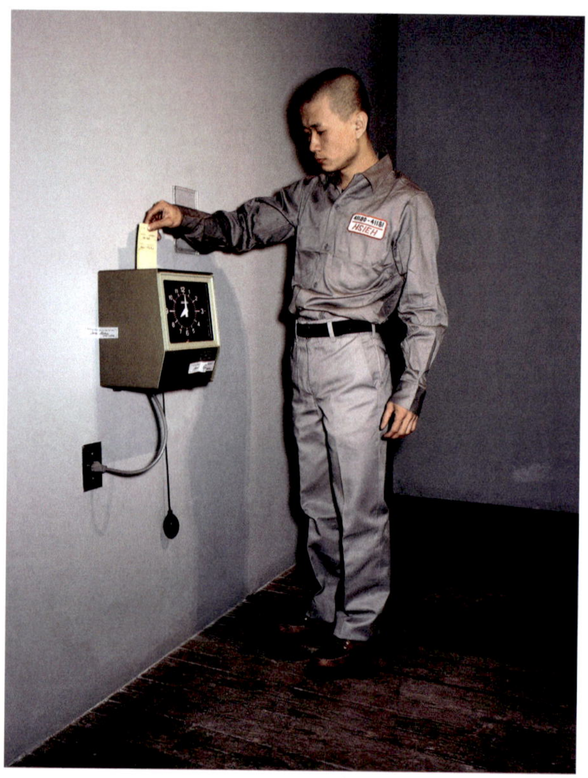

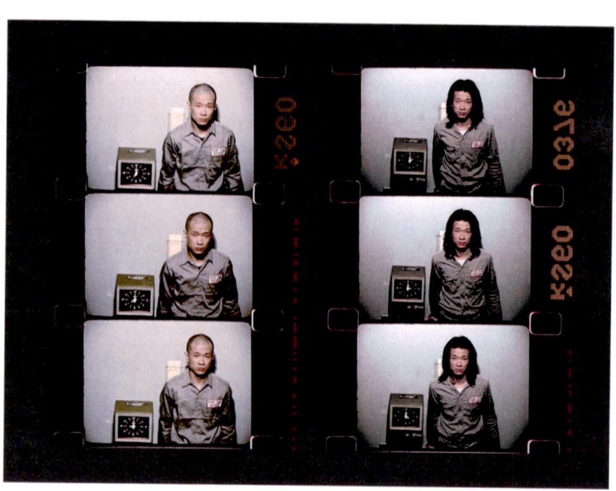

Tehching Hsieh
One Year Performance,
1980–81
Poster, letters,
photographs, time cards,
time clock, 16mm film
camera, 16mm film
(colour, silent) and
uniform, overall display
dimensions variable
Tate collection, UK

**Hsieh's early work
involved total physical
and mental commitment.
He even broke both his
ankles in the process of
making an early piece
titled *Jump* (1973).
Hsieh began this *One
Year Performance* with
a shaved head and
businesslike uniform.
By the end of the year
he looks dishevelled
and exhausted, his long,
unkempt hair evidencing
the passing of time.**

Clocking in for work is a familiar chore faced by many people every day, but it is hard to imagine the stress of clocking in every hour, on the hour, for a whole year. Tehching Hsieh undertook exactly this challenge to make *One Year Performance* (1980–81). This masterclass in presenteeism began with a simple typed statement of intent. Hsieh then installed a clock machine in his Manhattan studio and suspended a 16mm camera from the ceiling to capture his hourly mugshot. Hsieh missed just 113 out of a possible 7,800 clock-in opportunities across the year. The finished work comprises a relentless display of the punched cards alongside his trusty clock machine. A 16mm film, compressing over 7,000 images into six minutes, provides an intense whirring portrait of total physical exhaustion.

One Year Performance (1980–81) was the second of five year-long engagements undertaken by Hsieh. In his third *One Year Performance* (1981–2), Hsieh again issued a brief statement, vowing to live with just a sleeping bag and no shelter for a whole year. Taking to the streets surrounding his studio and refusing even the modest protection of a subway or a bus shelter, Hsieh embarked upon another remarkable feat of endurance. Once again, the work covers a lengthy expanse of time, with the artist becoming a dehumanized cog in an uncaring wheel. This undercurrent of living on the edge mirrors an autobiographical source. Born in Taiwan, Hsieh moved to New York City in 1974, living as an illegal immigrant for fourteen years before eventually receiving amnesty in 1988. The overall aim of Hsieh's work is to fuse art and life and to reflect on the process of passing time. He said, 'Life is a life sentence; life is passing time; life is free thinking.'

OTHER KEY WORKS
One Year Performance (Outdoor Piece), 1981–2

KEY FEATURES
Endurance and time-based performative practice, often working in isolation
Meticulous documentation of simple actions and scenarios
Reflection on universal themes concerning passing time, work, freedom and survival
Total fusion of art and life
Occupation of non-gallery spaces

CINDY SHERMAN
b.1954

'I just use myself as a model because I know I can push myself to extremes, make each shot as ugly or as goofy or silly as possible.'

As a child, Cindy Sherman loved to dress up. Later on, while studying painting at the Buffalo State College, New York, in the early 1970s, she would transform her appearance for parties, sourcing clothing from thrift stores and trying new identities for size. Sherman quickly ditched the painting career, deciding instead to pursue photography. She said, 'I was meticulously copying other art, and then I realized I could just use a camera and put my time into an idea instead.' By the time Sherman had graduated, she was beginning to explore the possibility of combining her photographic practice with her ongoing exploration of different identities and personae. She started to turn the camera on herself.

Sherman often produces work in series, pursuing a particular idea or theme across a period of time. An early body of work, the *Untitled Film Stills* (1977–80), resulted in sixty-nine small black-and-white photographs. For each work, Sherman assumed a different female stereotype as featured in many American 'B' movies of the 1950s and 1960s. She used clothing, hair and make-up to inhabit familiar roles with remarkable conviction, from the blonde bombshell and the sexy student to the jilted lover and the desperate housewife. Some of the scenes were shot in her apartment or in various locations around New York. Others were taken further afield, on the roadside in Arizona or at a friend's beach house in Long Island. The central female protagonist is always unaccompanied, yet she often appears watched, or threatened by her circumstances. Ultimately, wider narratives are suggested yet denied. In using her own body to inhabit a range of gender stereotypes across art and culture, Sherman highlights their alarming prevalence and persistence. She parodies and critiques the fixation on notions of female vulnerability, sexiness, duty or dumbness.

The majority of Sherman's subsequent work has incorporated colour, with an increase in scale and compositional complexity

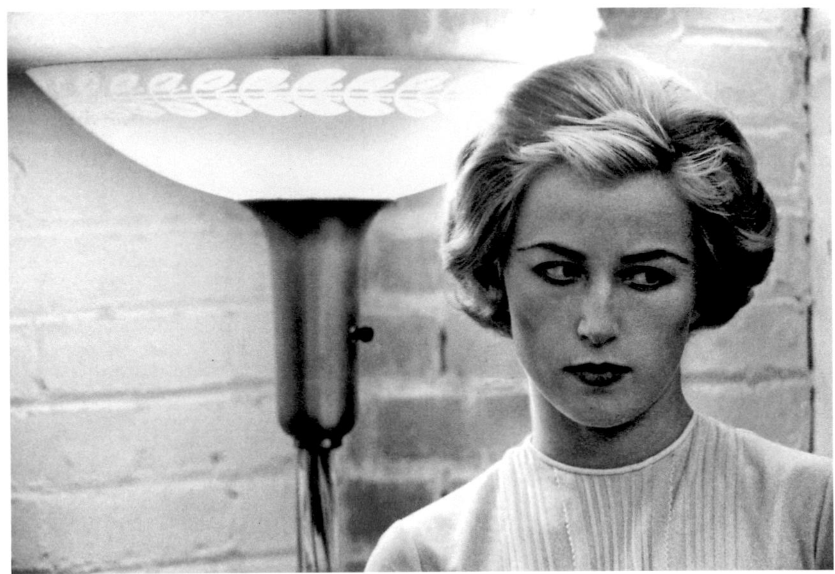

Cindy Sherman
Untitled Film Still #53,
1980
Gelatin silver print,
20.3 x 25.4 cm (8 x 10 in.)
Courtesy the artist and
Metro Pictures, New York

**In the *Untitled Film Stills*
the artist puts herself
in the shoes of actors
undertaking preconceived
roles. In this image, the
primly dressed protagonist
appears uncomfortable, as
if aware of the unwelcome
presence of another. The
image presents a familiar
filmic moment; however,
the wider narrative is not
disclosed.**

emerging as her resources grew. Oher series soon followed *Untitled Film Stills*, including *Centerfolds* (1981), *Fairy Tales* (1985) and a group of *Sex Pictures* (1992) in which the artist's body almost disappears altogether, replaced with dismembered plastic medical models. The *History Portraits* (1988–9) highlight Sherman's quest to travel back in time in search of new types. Sometimes she makes direct reference to a particular painting. *Untitled #224* (1990), for example, sees Sherman masquerading as Caravaggio's *Young Sick Bacchus* (1594), in which he himself plays the role of the god of wine. Her occupancy of a previously staged self-portrait provides an added layer of performativity. In other works, Sherman parodies generic types: the coquettish seductress, a vengeful Judith or a breastfeeding Virgin complete with preposterously spherical prosthetic breasts.

Recent work has investigated the representation of older women. Sherman has found a particularly rich source of inspiration in the close observation of affluent American ladies, all powdered and coiffured, gently lifted with a little bit of help from a specialist. Look carefully and you start to see the cracks, the imperfections, and the overzealous use of concealer. There is a tenderness here, tinged with a pervading sense of mortality.

Sherman is careful not to circumscribe her practice with conventional definitions of self-portraiture. She said, 'I really don't think that [the works] are about me. It's maybe about me not wanting to be me and wanting to be all those other characters. Or at least try them on.' A sense of privacy also underpins Sherman's processes. She prefers to work alone, acting as set and costume director, make-up artist, author and model. Characterization emerges through intense solitary reflection. She said, 'I think of *becoming* a different person. I look into a mirror next to the camera... by staring into it I try to become that character through the lens. It seems to work out. It sounds like meditation.... Something *else* takes over.'

OTHER KEY WORKS
Untitled #224, 1990, Museum of Modern Art, New York, USA

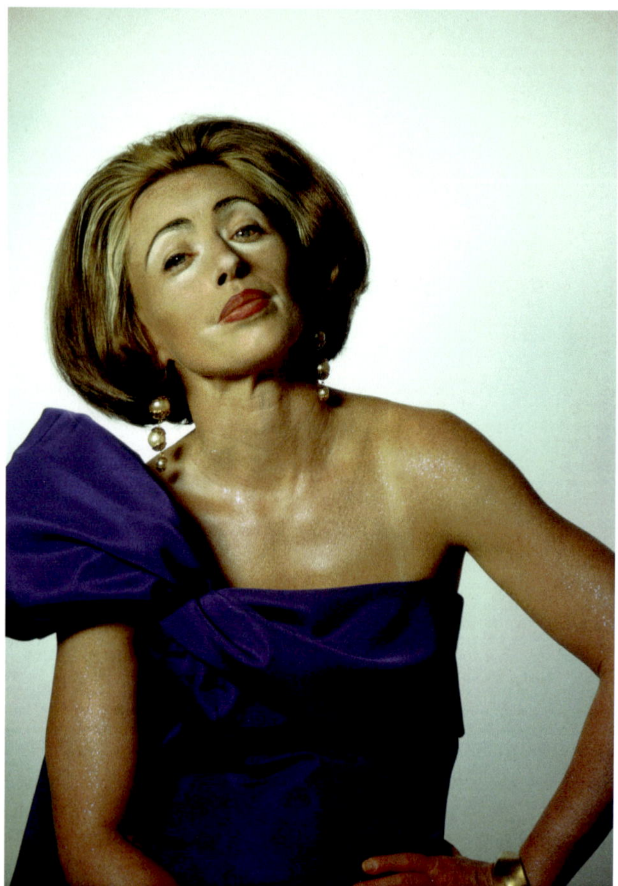

Cindy Sherman
Untitled (#400), 2000
Chromogenic colour print,
93.3 x 66 cm
(36¾ x 26 in.)
Courtesy the artist and
Metro Pictures, New York

This photograph is one of a series of *Head Shots* (2000–1) in which Sherman explored the conventions of studio portrait photography, from standard poses to soft-glow backdrops. She assumed the appearance of older women from various different backgrounds, holding it together despite the onset of ageing. Sherman invests her characters with a sense of dignity and pathos despite their slipping masks.

Cindy Sherman
Untitled #216, 1989
Chromogenic
colour print, image
221.3 x 142.6 cm
(87⅛ x 56⅛ in.),
frame 238.8 x 160 cm
(94 x 63 in.)
Courtesy the artist and
Metro Pictures, New York

**This work shares
similarities with Jean
Fouquet's *Melun Diptych*
(c.1452) in the elaborate
swathes of drapery and
the Virgin's downcast
eyes and rounded breasts.
In using photography
to capture this restaged
scene, Sherman dislodges
art history's obsession
with uniqueness and
originality. Her use
of prosthetics also
highlights the artificial
and constructed nature
of historical paintings.**

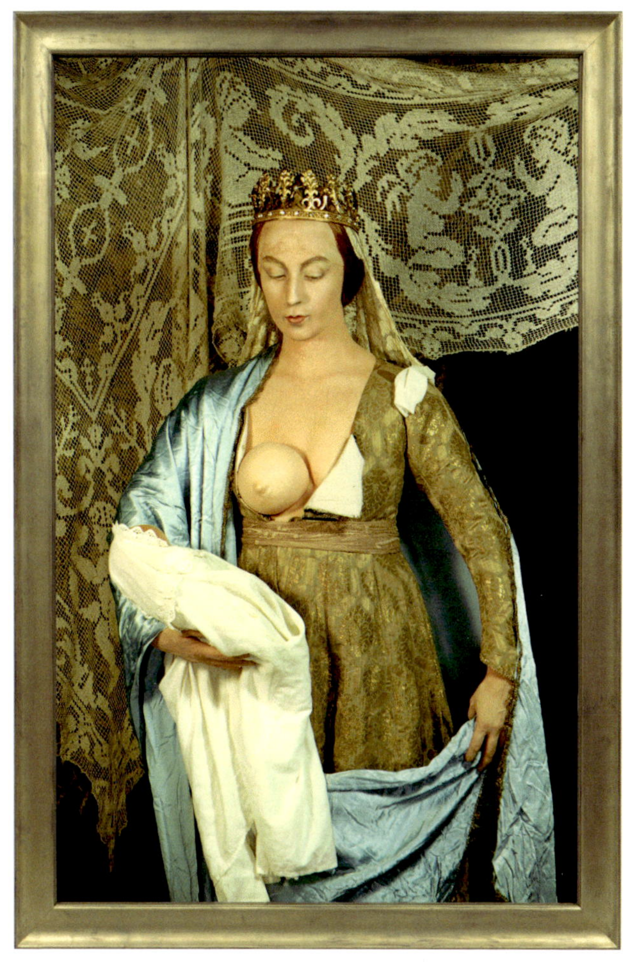

KEY FEATURES

Sustained performance-based photographic practice
Use of the self to assume a multitude of roles and identities
Feminist critique of gender stereotypes across art and culture
Extensive use of costumes, styling, prosthetics and props
Interest in the artifice of contemporary culture
Deliberate lack of self-revelation

MARC QUINN
b.1964

After completing his studies in art history at the University of Cambridge, Marc Quinn became associated with an emerging generation of so-called Young British Artists ('YBAs') during the early 1990s. Tracey Emin, Damien Hirst and Sarah Lucas, among others, pursued a playful approach to materiality, and their works reveal a shared interest in self-referential and life-or-death subjects. Quinn's predominantly sculptural practice centres on what it is to be human. His work incorporates a wide range of materials including blood, flowers and even DNA.

Quinn's early self-portrait, *Self* (1991), helped catapult his career into the spotlight. This iconic work stemmed from the artist's interest in the process of freezing and its ability to effectively stop time. Quinn had a lightbulb moment and decided he would cast his head using his own frozen blood. He enjoyed the neatness of this pure self-portraiture: the artist's likeness sculpted from the vital fluids of his own body. Ten pints of Quinn's blood were needed to fill the mould. Coincidentally, this is the quantity of blood contained within the average adult. Sliced abruptly at the neck and with eyes tight shut, this gruesome fragment has none of the elegance of traditional bust portraiture. There is no desire to capture the animated consciousness of the sitter. Instead the head appears trapped, suspended in its freezer in perpetuity, or until the unit fails.

Quinn's body has reappeared in many other works throughout his career. He has made full-body casts of himself using rubber and nylon, stringing them up from the ceiling and splaying them open like empty seed pods. These flaccid vessels recall Michelangelo's flayed skin in *The Last Judgement* (see page 22). To make *Self-Conscious 19/10/2000*, Quinn suspended a strand of his own DNA in a vial of pure alcohol. At first glance the work appears minimal, yet it actually contains Quinn's entire genetic blueprint. On one level it is an inaccurate portrayal: having recovered from alcohol dependency, Quinn no longer touches the stuff.

Marc Quinn
Self, 1991
Blood (artist's), stainless steel, Perspex and refrigeration equipment, 208 x 63 x 63cm (82 x 25 x 25 in.)
Private collection

Without a consistent source of electricity, this frozen self-portrait would quickly disintegrate. Quinn was struggling with alcoholism at the time of making this work and he acknowledges the themes of dependency and control underpinning this vulnerable object. Quinn makes a new iteration of *Self* every five years, and the series as a whole tracks his physical transformation across time.

OTHER KEY WORKS

No Visible Means of Escape IV, 1996, Tate collection, UK
Self-Conscious 19/10/2000, 2000, artist's own collection

KEY FEATURES

Sustained sculptural practice exploring our relationship to beauty,
 often through figurative works
Repeated use of casting to establish a likeness
Interest in blood as a symbol of life and renewal
Preoccupation with freezing techniques
Exploration of the relationship between interior and exterior
Interest in the drama and physicality of Baroque sculpture
Interest in the extraction and suspension of genetic material

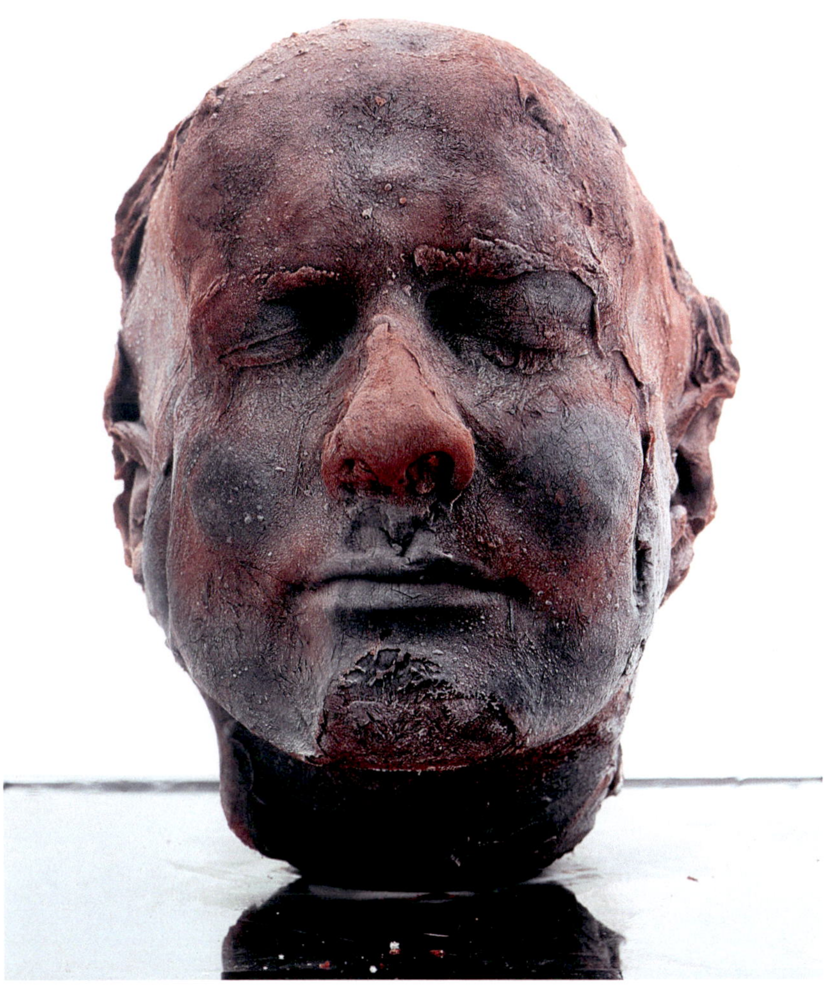

CATHERINE OPIE
b.1961

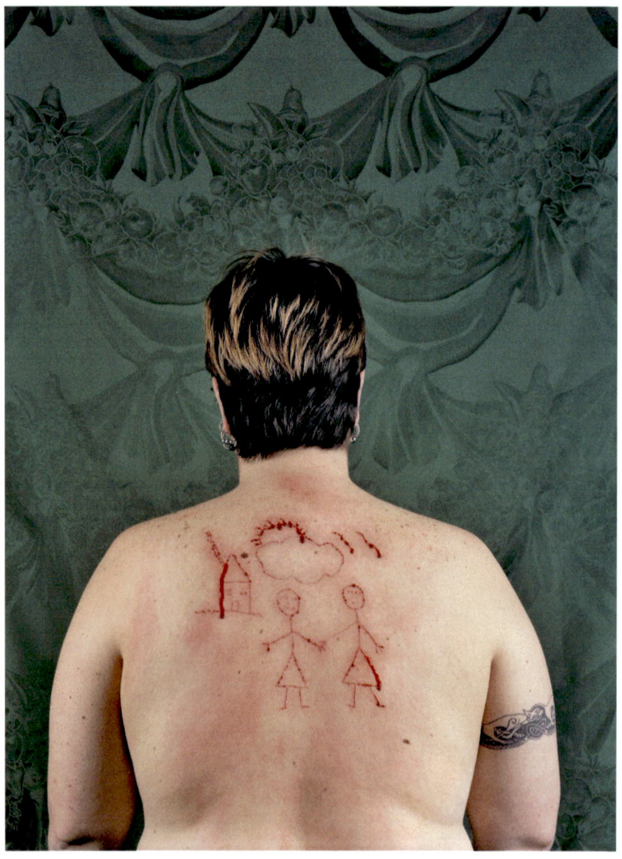

The Los Angeles-based photographer Catherine Opie once described herself as a 'kind of twisted social documentary photographer'. Her work embraces landscape and urban photography, however she is perhaps best known for her tender and empathetic portraits of her friends and associates from LGBTQIA+ communities. Drawing on the conventions of historical portraiture, she ennobles her sitters using strong lighting and lush, draped backgrounds in rich colours. Opie's formal and often full-frontal compositions also recall the dignified photographic portraiture of Lewis Hine and August Sander.

Catherine Opie
Self-Portrait/Cutting,
1993
Chromogenic print,
101.6 x 74.8 cm
(40 x 29½ in.)
Solomon R. Guggenheim
Museum, New York

Catherine Opie's photographs often incorporate art-historical references. This work, with its clear delineation of a dignified human presence set against a rich tonal background, recalls the portraits of the Northern Renaissance painter Hans Holbein. Opie's strong use of light also references Renaissance and Baroque chiaroscuro techniques.

Opie has turned to self-portraiture numerous times throughout her career, both to highlight her solidarity with her represented communities and to reflect on personal experiences. In 1993, Opie was an active member of the Los Angeles leather community. Although she felt deeply connected to this lifestyle, she also longed to secure a stable relationship, to have a child and to find domestic contentment. In *Self-Portrait/Cutting* (1993), Opie is naked to the waist. She faces away from the viewer, revealing a childlike portrayal of happy families etched into her back, raw wounds still weeping. Two figures wearing skirts hold hands, there is a pretty house, the sun is emerging from the clouds and birds fly up ahead. Opie uses her body as a blank canvas to illustrate a sense of longing and to visualize a potential future.

In 2001, Opie gave birth to a baby boy, Oliver, following intrauterine insemination. Opie's *Self-Portrait/Nursing* (2004) features the artist breastfeeding her cherished infant. This is a stately vision of contentment: the regal draped brocade, the throne-like chair, the classic union of mother and child. In referencing art-historical representations of motherhood, Opie challenges heteronormative narratives. She proposes a new iconography, one informed by inclusive interpretations of family and community.

OTHER KEY WORKS

Self-Portrait/Pervert, 1994, Solomon R. Guggenheim Museum, New York, USA

Self-Portrait/Nursing, 2004, Solomon R. Guggenheim Museum, New York, USA

KEY FEATURES

Interest in collective, sexual and cultural identities

Empathetic representation of LGBTQIA+ and outsider communities

Use of documentary photography to challenge heteronormativity

Application of art-historical conventions to ennoble the sitter

Deliberate concealment of the face

Inscription of the body through tattooing and scarification

ZHANG HUAN
b.1965

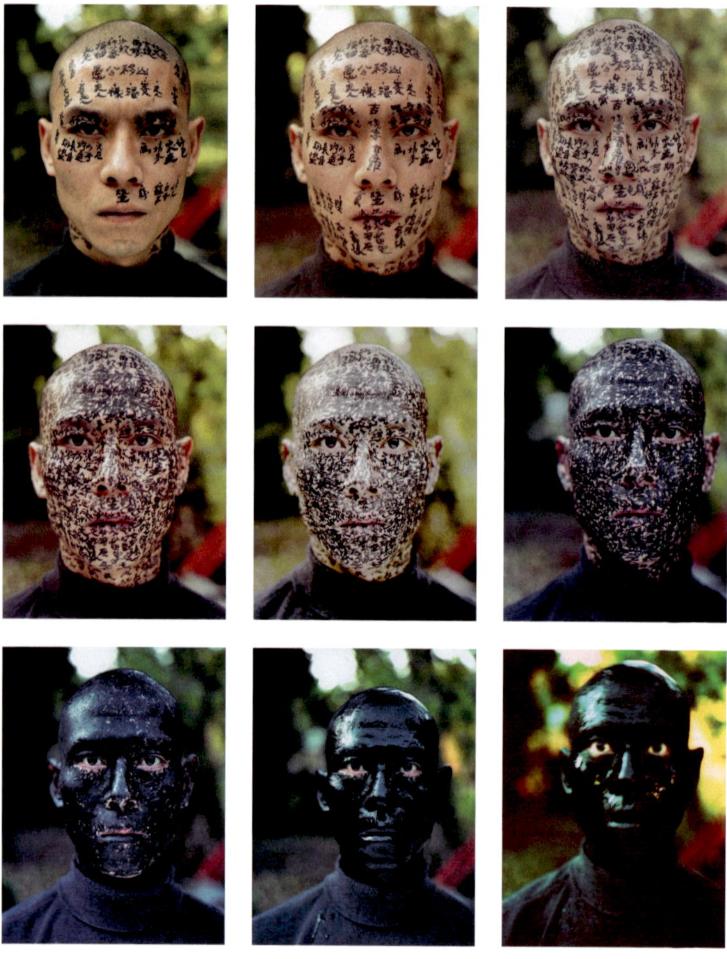

Zhang Huan grew up in poverty in a rural village in Henan province, China. His drawing ability earned him a place at art school, and he started his career as a painter before turning to performance. Zhang's early experiments with the medium involved feats of physical and mental endurance. To make *12m²* (1994), for example, he stripped naked and basted his body in fish sauce and honey before locking himself into a filthy fly-infested toilet in Beijing. The flies quickly swarmed to devour the sticky mixture. At the end of the performance, the artist jumped

Zhang Huan
Family Tree, 2000
Nine chromogenic colour
prints in polyptych,
each 127 x 101.6 cm
(50 x 40 in.)
Centre Georges
Pompidou, Paris

**Zhang's choice of a
solemn, full-frontal pose
and dignified stillness for
this work anticipates his
later experiments with
figurative sculpture. The
ink acts as a physical
manifestation of the
many invisible stories
and personal histories
that shape our identities,
wherever life takes us.**

into a nearby pond, washed himself clean and walked away. Zhang alludes to specific social and political issues in much of his work – in this case, the limited access to adequate sanitation. He also addresses poetic and spiritual concerns, often achieving a meditative state of tranquility in the face of adversity.

In 1998, Zhang moved to New York City, where he established himself as a major figure on the international art scene. *Family Tree* (2000) comprises a sequence of nine full-colour images of the artist's head and shoulders. The images document a performance for which Zhang invited three traditional calligraphers to write kanji characters on his face over a period of one day. Working from early morning until nightfall, the calligraphers were asked to maintain their composure throughout and to continue writing even when their words became illegible. They were instructed to scribe a range of Chinese proverbs and stories concerning the struggle to overcome obstacles. By the end of the day, Zhang's face was completely saturated in the glossy black ink to the point where he could barely recognize himself.

In 2006, Zhang returned to China, establishing a studio and converting to Buddhism. He began to construct large-scale meditative heads made from incense ash taken from Shanghai temples. Some of these works incorporate the artist's own features.

OTHER KEY WORKS

12m², 1994, Pace Gallery, New York
Foam, 1998, Pace Gallery, New York

KEY FEATURES

Early performance-based practice involving physical and mental
   endurance
Exploration of political and spiritual issues
Intense yet simple, reversible scenarios
Reference to proverbs and narratives to explore personal
   identities and histories
Interest in migrant experiences
Subsequent engagement with sculpture and painting to explore
   spiritual realms

YAYOI KUSAMA
b.1929

A paradox resides at the heart of Yayoi Kusama's long and successful career. On the one hand, Kusama has consciously developed and transformed her artistic identity into a global phenomenon, fuelled by her relentless work ethic and drive. Her inimitable style influenced her decision to establish her own fashion brand, Kusama Fashion Company Ltd, resulting in a brightly coloured range of clothing inspired by her trademark dots and spots. Despite this recognizable identity, much of Kusama's work is underpinned by the threat of self-obliteration. Her paintings, drawings, installations, films and performances invoke a universe of unrelenting patterns and dots, which cling to every surface like an infection.

Kusama has experienced hallucinations and bouts of depersonalization since childhood. Adapting to the trauma of living with her abusive mother, Kusama initially turned to drawing as a way of dealing with these frightening visions, capturing them on paper. Since then, her dots have appeared everywhere and on everything: on herself, on naked performers, on bulbous phallic forms and on mesmerizing installations made infinite through the use of light and mirrors. This is a wildly original and immersive practice and an ongoing process of self-therapy.

Kusama continues to produce work at a prolific pace. In recent years, she has developed a range of self-portraits using bright acrylic paints on large canvases. In these radiant and energetic works, the artist appears as a caricature or a cartoon character. In *Self-Portrait* (2008) she stares straight ahead, her full-frontal pose recalling the static intensity of a Byzantine icon. The entire picture surface is enlivened through the obsessive and precise articulation of thousands of coloured dots. Hypnotic and mesmerizing, the power of this work resides in its surface rather than in any desire to penetrate depth.

Yayoi Kusama
Self-Portrait, 2008
Acrylic on canvas,
227.3 x 181.8 cm
(89½ x 71½ in.)
Courtesy the artist
and Gagosian

Yayoi Kusama enjoys the playful and transformative potential of self-portraiture. This painting also exists as a jigsaw puzzle edition, enabling an even greater fracturing of the picture surface. In other works, the artist has assumed different features and characteristics, even appearing as a sunflower and a cat.

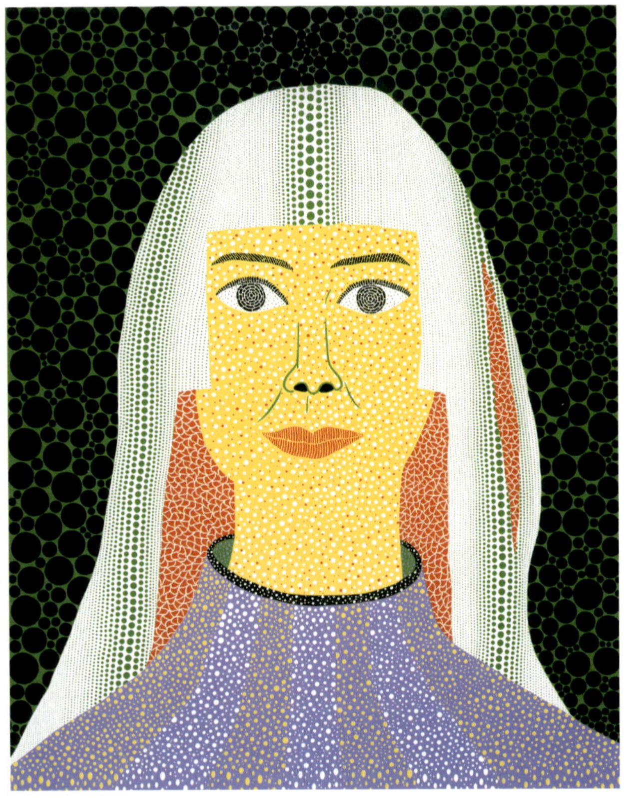

OTHER KEY WORKS

*Photograph of Collage (c.1966) with the artist reclining on
Accumulation No.2 1962*, c.1966, Museum Boijmans Van
Beuningen, Rotterdam, Netherlands

KEY FEATURES

Highly individual practice emerging from self-therapy
Incorporation of the self into radical performances and
'happenings' throughout the 1960s and 1970s
Self-conscious promotion of a strong artistic identity
Vibrant flurry of late self-portraiture
Hallucinatory use of colour and form
Playful adoption of animal and floral characteristics

ZANELE MUHOLI
b.1972

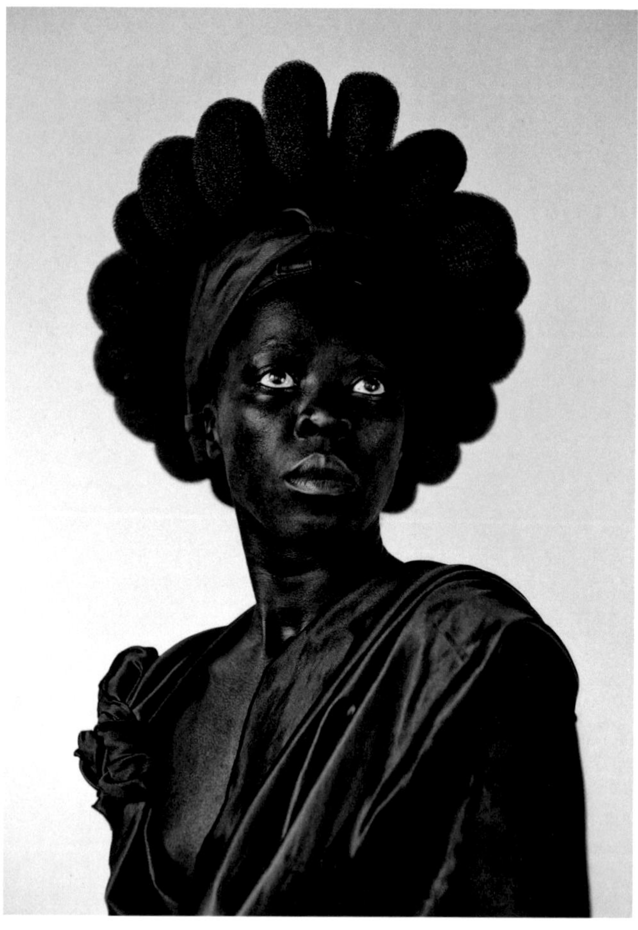

In 2014, the South African photographer Zanele Muholi decided to turn the camera on themself. This decision followed many years of documenting members of LGBTQIA+ communities in South Africa as part of a series of photographs called *Faces and Phases* (2006–). This empowering visual archive makes visible the communities and individuals who have endured a wave of hate crimes across South Africa, with black lesbians often taking the brunt of serious abuse. Muholi, who considers themself to be a visual activist rather than

Zanele Muholi
Ntozakhe II, Parktown,
2016
Gelatin silver print,
100 x 72 cm
(39⅜ x 28⅜ in.)
Courtesy the artist and
Stevenson Gallery,
Cape Town/Johannesburg

**In this image, Muholi
wears a headdress made
from hair donuts. It
radiates like a halo,
recalling Christian
iconography found in
Renaissance painting.
The gentle folds of
the drapery add to the
classical, statuesque
vibe. Muholi glances
upwards, looking beyond
the viewer and into the
distance. Their facial
expression appears both
defiant and guarded.**

an artist, turned to self-portraiture following the realization that they must express solidarity with their community. They said, 'I'm working on content that's produced by us, about us – not dependent on other so-called experts.'

Muholi's epic series of self-portrait photography bears the name *Somnyama Ngonyama*, or 'Hail the Dark Lioness'. Initiated in 2012, this series comprises 365 black-and-white photographs to reflect the year-round issues experienced as a black person. As Muholi explains, 'the black body itself is the material, the black body that is ever scrutinized and violated and undermined'. Muholi assumes an extraordinary range of alter egos across this series, using a host of everyday, domestic objects to create makeshift yet mesmerizing transformations. The titles refer to names of people known to Muholi or to characters from a deeper past. Some of the costumes recall colonial and ethnographic representations of otherness, with the clothes-peg crowns and the rubber-glove halos also referencing servitude of a domestic kind. With a confrontational gaze, Muholi wears these painful layers of meaning with determined dignity. A process of reclamation takes place, with Muholi driving the narrative. They use post-production techniques to intensify the blackness of their skin, celebrating its beauty and texture and responding to widespread media attempts to lighten black bodies. These images stretch beyond individual concerns towards collective experience and a shared desire for change.

OTHER KEY WORKS

Faces and Phases, 2006–, various collections
Bester I, Mayotte, 2015, Stevenson Gallery, Cape Town/
  Johannesburg and Yancey Richardson, New York

KEY FEATURES

Activist and political use of photography
Empowering depiction of LGBTQIA+ communities
Use of self-portraiture to challenge representations of race,
  gender and sexuality
Inventive deployment of props and costumes to explore different
  identities and tropes
Use of alter egos and names to reveal personal and political
  histories
Post-production accentuation of blackness

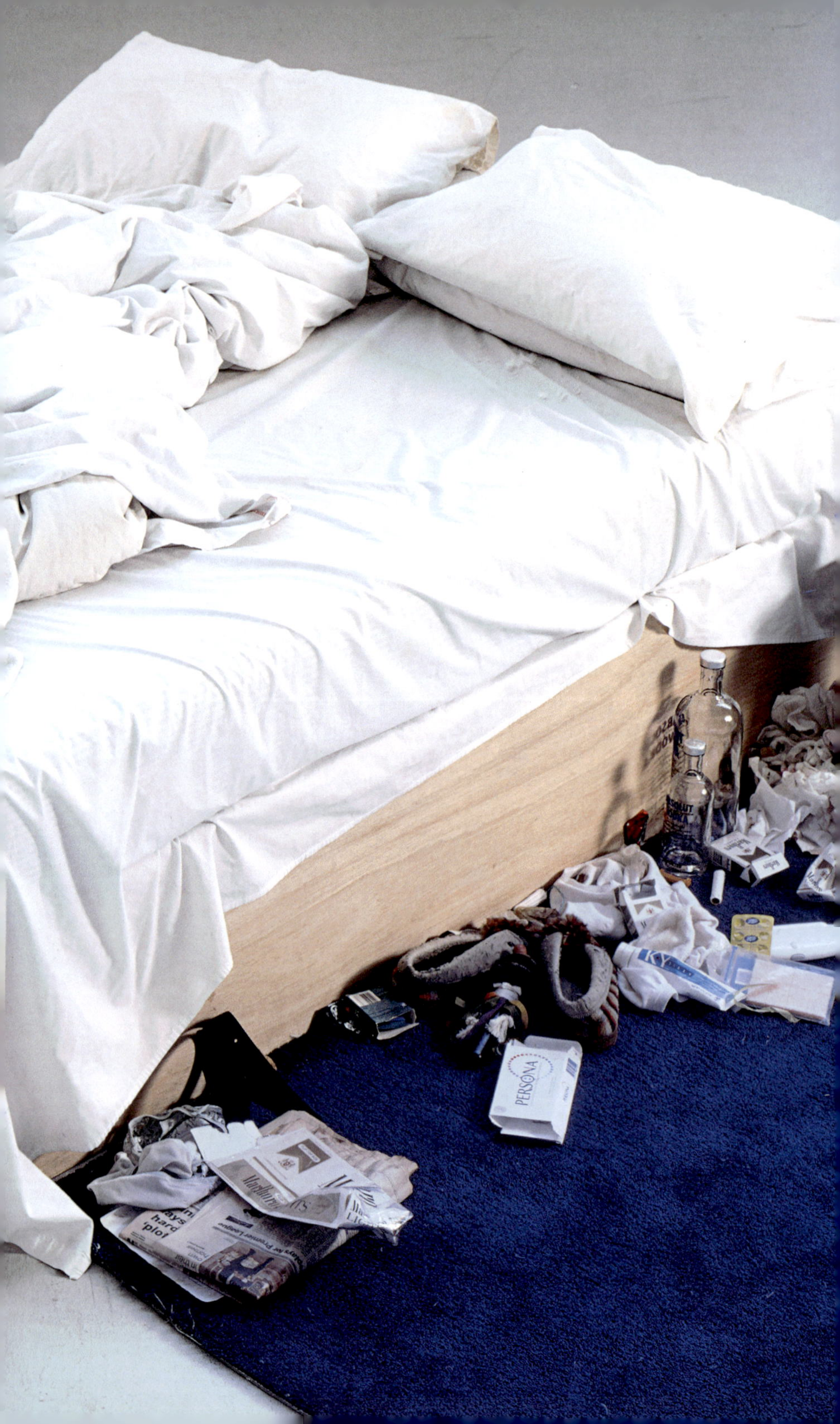

DEPARTURES

-

I work with what I know. But it goes beyond that. I start with myself and end up with the universe.

-

Tracey Emin, 1995

PIERO MANZONI
1933–63

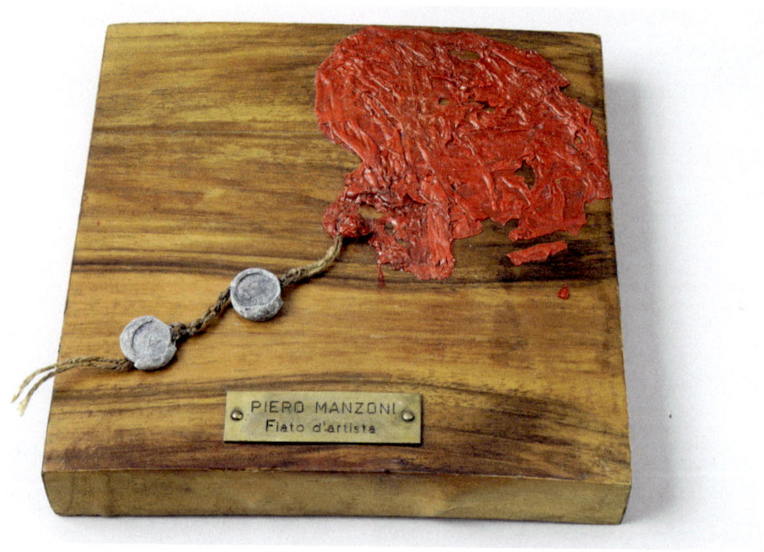

Must a self-portrait always feature an artist's face? How can the presence of the artist be conveyed in other ways? What makes an artist special and why do art objects hold so much value? The Italian artist Piero Manzoni explored many of these questions during his brief yet radical career. Picking up where Marcel Duchamp (see pages 114–15) left off, Manzoni believed in the power of ideas and the intellectual repurposing of everyday objects. In the last few years of his life, Manzoni embarked upon a series of notorious provocations, fusing sardonic wit with a material lightness of touch.

In 1960, Manzoni blew up a balloon and attached it to a wooden plinth with a small plaque engraved with the words 'PIERO MANZONI: Artist's breath'. Manzoni explained, 'When I blow up a balloon, I am breathing my soul into an object that becomes eternal.' Despite these high hopes, the balloon has disintegrated over time, leaving a sticky mess on the wooden base, and resulting in the total loss of the artist's precious exhalation. The balloon has become a symbol of failure. The museological presentation of this sad and flaccid residue recalls the painstaking preservation of holy relics. Aside from the witty concept of selling thin air, this work

Piero Manzoni
Artist's Breath, 1960
Rubber balloon inflated with artist's breath, wood, lead seal,
18 x 18 x 3.5 cm
(7 x 7 x 1⅜ in.)
Tate collection, UK

Manzoni made this work in a small edition using red, white and blue balloons. In combining perishable materials with memorializing plinths and plaques, Manzoni created miniature monuments to concepts of failure and resignation. His decision to capture his breath may have been informed by Marcel Duchamp's bottling of Parisian air in his 1919 piece, *50cc of Paris Air*.

conveys an underlying sadness and a reflection on the fragility of life, a modern-day *memento mori*.

Manzoni's father, the owner of a canning factory, once told his son that he thought his art was shit. This cutting jibe is thought to have prompted Manzoni to make his most notorious work, *Artist's Shit*, in 1961. Using the resources at his father's premises, Manzoni produced and labelled an edition of tin cans, each unit apparently containing thirty grams of his excrement. In a further comment on the commodification of art, Manzoni set the price of each can to match the price of its equivalent weight in gold. Once again, the abstract notion of artistic presence is objectified and fetishized: signed, sealed, delivered.

OTHER KEY WORKS

Artist's Shit, 1961, Tate collection, UK

KEY FEATURES

Artistic presence evidenced through traces, impressions and
  waste products
Interest in giving form and shape to ethereal concepts
Reflections on the commodification and value of artists and
  their works
Interest in minimal repetitive processes, often producing work
  in editions
Anticipates later conceptual art practices through the
  exploration of ideas and interactions

LOUISE BOURGEOIS
1911–2010

The French-American artist Louise Bourgeois produced a prolific body of drawings, sculpture, writings and prints across her long career. Although only a small proportion of her work bears the title 'self-portrait', much of her practice involves the intertwining of memories, personal narratives and family relationships to create evocative scenarios. In an early series of paintings called *Femme Maison* ('Woman House', 1946–7), female legs and torsos are topped with domestic dwellings. Part body, part architecture, these surreal characters reflect Bourgeois' position as a housewife and a mother. Her adulterous father is implicated in later installations made from oppressive tentacle forms, whereas the epic late work *Maman* (1999) reveals deep maternal respect. Made from steel and marble, this massive spider appears strong and protective, crafty and resourceful, just like Bourgeois' own mother.

During the 1960s, Bourgeois' sculptures became increasingly bulbous and anthropomorphic. Although these forms appear sexual in nature, fixed gender definitions are avoided in favour of universal expressions of attraction, repulsion and pain. *Torso, Self-Portrait* (1963–4) reflects many of these concerns. Bourgeois' decision to focus on her torso rather than her face stemmed from a desire to reflect upon personal misgivings. She explained, 'This is the way I experience my torso … somehow with a certain dissatisfaction and regret that one's own body is not as beautiful as one would like it to be. It doesn't seem to measure up to any standard of beauty.' Despite her reservations, the overall impression of this work is strength. The pear-shaped form is covered with a symmetrical arrangement of phallic and vulvic protrusions, breast-like bumps and buttock humps. Bourgeois has created a resilient and powerful kind of shield. It appears tough and protective, soft and tender all at the same time. In the hands of Louise Bourgeois, self-portraiture becomes pliant, open to transformation and metamorphosis – a source of limitless possibility.

Louise Bourgeois
Torso, Self-Portrait,
1963–4
Plaster,
62.3 x 40.5 x 18.8 cm
(24½ x 16 x 7⅜ in.)
Museum of Modern Art,
New York

This is one of only a few works by Louise Bourgeois to carry the title 'self-portrait'. Rather than focus on her face, Bourgeois chose to feature her torso, fixing various 'male' and 'female' appendages to the undulating surface to create a surreal kind of armour.

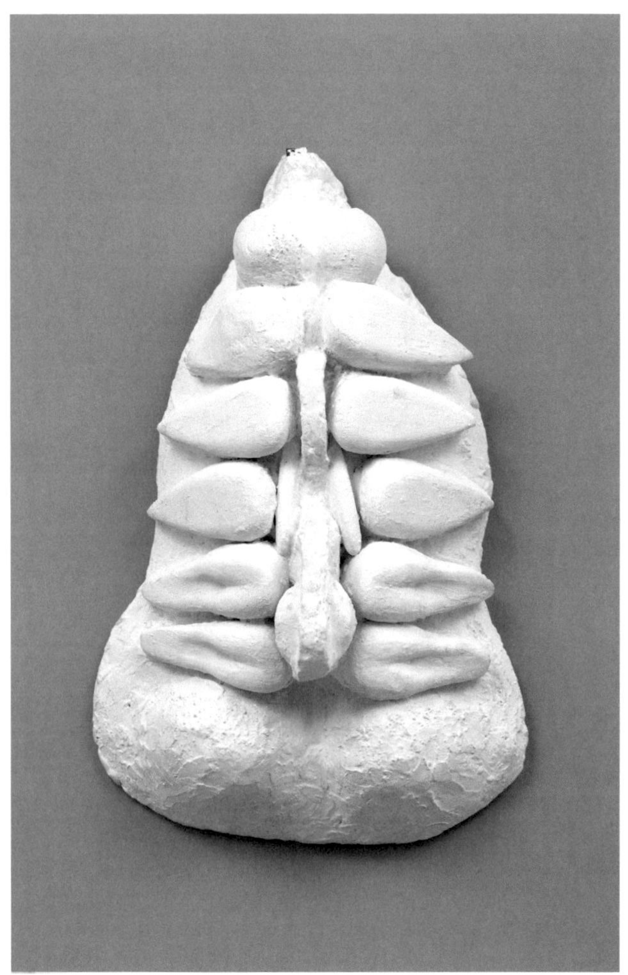

OTHER KEY WORKS

Self-Portrait, 2007, Easton Foundation, New York, USA

KEY FEATURES

Non-representational approach to self-portraiture
Extensive biographical references
Exploration of emotional and psychological states
Combination of 'male' and 'female' characteristics
Fusion of human, animal and architectural features
Interest in metamorphosis and transformation

REBECCA HORN
b.1944

In 1963, Rebecca Horn commenced her art education at Hamburg Academy of the Arts. She began making sculptures using fibreglass and polyester, unaware of the need to wear a mask when handling such toxic materials. Horn suffered serious lung poisoning and spent most of 1964 in a sanatorium. This painful and isolating period of convalescence filled her with a strong desire to communicate. She wanted to break the chains of her confinement by making physical contact with her external environment. Employing soft materials, including cotton, bandages and feathers, Horn began to extend the parameters of her body by wearing strange masks, protrusions and extensions. She undertook ritualistic performances, adopting animalistic or machine-like behaviours and capturing her actions on film. Her sensuous multidisciplinary early practice centred on a desire to trace the connections between people and their environments. Horn explored the blurred zone where 'the self' stops and 'the other' begins.

Many of Horn's performance props of the early 1970s promote touch and physical contact, albeit at one remove. The wildly extended digits of Horn's *Finger Gloves* (1972), for example, may enable her to reach to the floor with limited bending, yet ultimately these protrusions appear more restrictive than empowering. *Pencil Mask* (1972) comprises a cage-like facial lattice. A short, sharp pencil attaches to each intersection to create a novel kind of drawing machine. Horn moved her head from side to side while wearing the mask. Her sweeping, repetitive movements etched a network of graphite marks across a white wall. Horn had, in effect, created a self-portrait in reverse. Rather than using the actions of her body to portray her face, she used her face to capture the actions of her body.

Rebecca Horn
Pencil Mask, 1972
Fabric, pencils and metal,
65 x 52 x 40cm
(25⅝ x 20½ x 15¾ in.)
Tate collection, UK

Horn made a number of performative masks during the early 1970s, many of which were activated through touch. This mask is designed to capture the wearer's bodily movements as they rub up against a wall. Horn went on to make a number of masks using bird feathers in 1973. These exotic plumages threatened to tickle anyone who strayed too close.

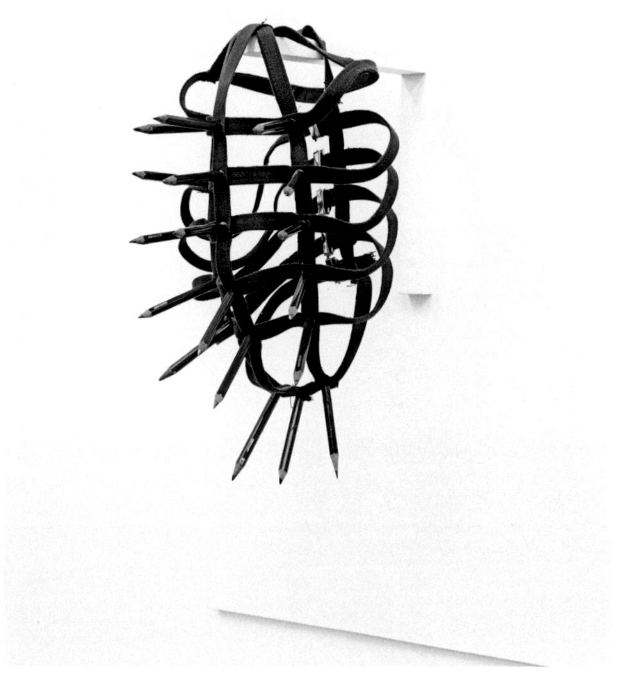

OTHER KEY WORKS

Arm Extensions, 1968, Tate collection, UK
Finger Gloves, 1972, Tate collection, UK
Cockfeather Mask, 1973, Tate collection, UK

KEY FEATURES

Focus on the sensuous, intimate space between self and other
Sculptural extension of the body using soft materials and
   prosthetic forms
Interest in masking, concealment and distancing
Exploration of the relationship between human, animal and
   mechanical actions
Ritualistic performances involving simple, repeated actions

MARTIN PURYEAR
b.1941

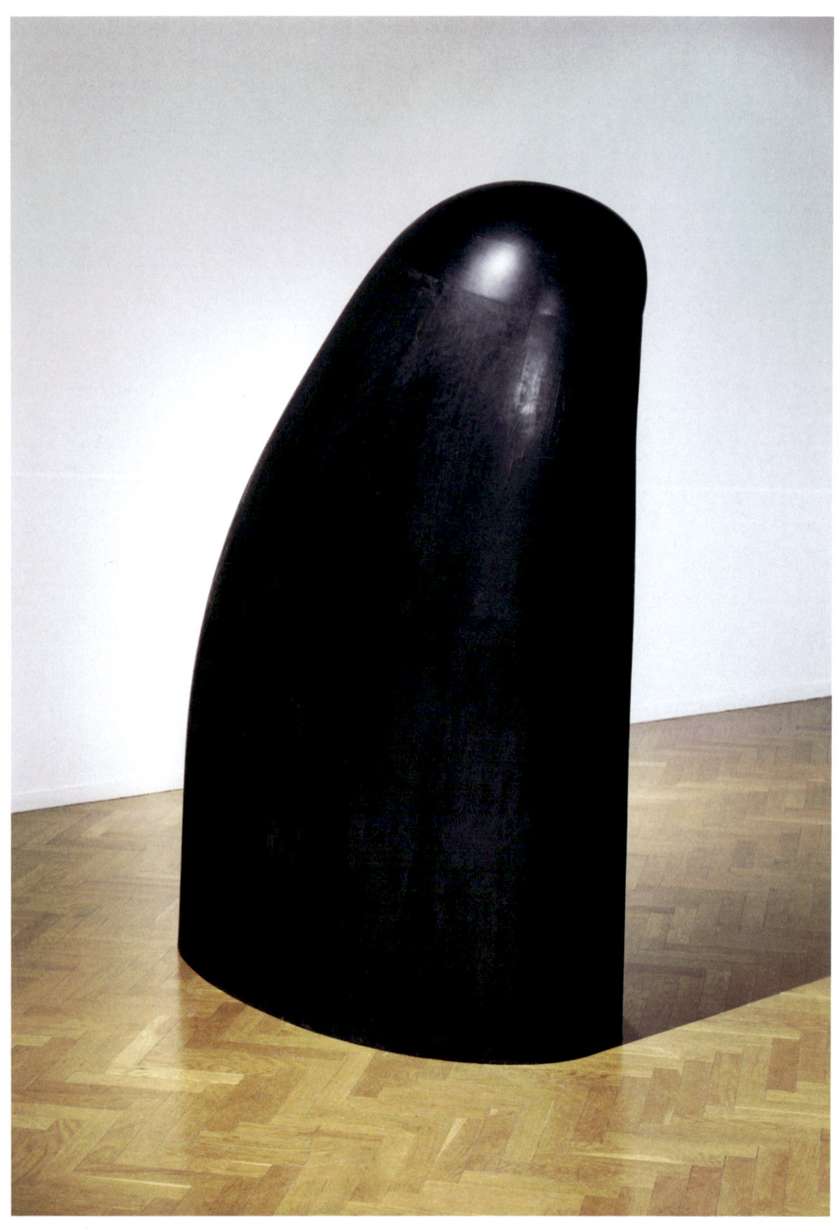

Martin Puryear
Self, 1978
Polychromed red cedar
and mahogany,
175.2 x 121.9 x 63.5 cm
(69 x 48 x 25 in.)
Joslyn Art Museum,
Omaha

Although at first glance this ambiguous form appears to have been carved, it was in fact built from a succession of horizontal and vertical wooden sheets. Furthermore, despite the suggestion of weight, the sculpture is hollow and relatively light, its shell-like structure conveying ideas of home, occupancy and belonging.

What remains when you peel away the outer shell, the face we choose to present to the world? Can an unwavering sense of self be found if we delve beneath our fleeting moods, preoccupations and circumstances? Questions such as these underpin *Self* (1978), a steadfast sculptural form made by the American artist Martin Puryear. On one level this enigmatic sculpture appears timeless, as if honed by ancient skills and natural processes. Yet the work also conveys a quiet presence, like a new thing breathing, arriving on the scene out of nowhere. As Puryear has explained, 'It looks as though it might have been created by erosion, like a rock worn by sand and weather until the angles are all gone. *Self* is all curve except where it meets the floor at an abrupt angle. It's meant to be a visual notion of the self rather than any particular self – the self as a secret entity, as a secret, hidden place.'

Born in Washington, DC, in 1941, Puryear studied sculpture at Yale University. Although he paid close attention to developments in Minimalist sculpture, he rejected its cool impersonality and avoidance of narrative. Puryear preferred to hone natural materials by hand, applying craft techniques gleaned from a global range of sources. His streamlined organic forms suggest personal narratives and prompt wider reflections on identity and race. *Self* was made at a significant moment in Puryear's development as an artist. In 1977, his Brooklyn studio was destroyed by fire, leading to a significant loss of his sculptures. Made during the following year, *Self* appears to rise up from the ground with renewed vigour. There is no face, no likeness, no desire to communicate a recognizable image, yet there is deep poetic resonance and a strong quest to reassert artistic identity and individuality.

KEY FEATURES
Post-minimal sculptural practice
Creation of ambiguous, poetic forms
Reference to personal and political narratives
Non-representational suggestion of self
Determinedly handmade, revealing the artist's touch
Mastery of craft and joinery techniques

HELEN CHADWICK
1953–96

Helen Chadwick represented herself in her work as a way of shedding fresh light on universal issues concerning memory, mortality and transformation. Her early sculptural installations and photographs often documented her performing body. However, from 1988, she increasingly investigated the inside of the body in an attempt to move beyond gender and towards greater universality. She incorporated a wide range of substances into her work, including flesh, cells, chocolate, decaying vegetable matter and even her own urine. By delving beneath the surface, Chadwick sought to shatter restrictive binary definitions and gender stereotypes. Her experimental and visceral approach influenced a younger generation of British artists to employ a wider range of materials during the 1990s.

The *Viral Landscapes* series of photographs marks Chadwick's transition from performance to the deft exploration of biological territory. To make this series, Chadwick had cell samples taken from her blood, kidney, cervix, mouth and ear. She also visited Pembrokeshire in Wales, taking photographs of the rugged coastline and making prints by swirling pigment into the frothing tides. Chadwick used computer technology to overlay her cellular and

Helen Chadwick
Viral Landscape No.3,
1988–9
C-print, powder coated steel, aluminium-faced plywood, Perspex, 120 x 300 x 5 cm (47¼ x 118⅛ x 2 in.)
Walker Art Gallery, National Museums Liverpool

Made during the AIDS crisis, this is one of a series of five panoramic photographs expressing anxiety about the risk of infection at a cellular level. Environmental concerns are also evident. To Chadwick, humanity is a direct threat to nature, a pestilent virus in need of careful control.

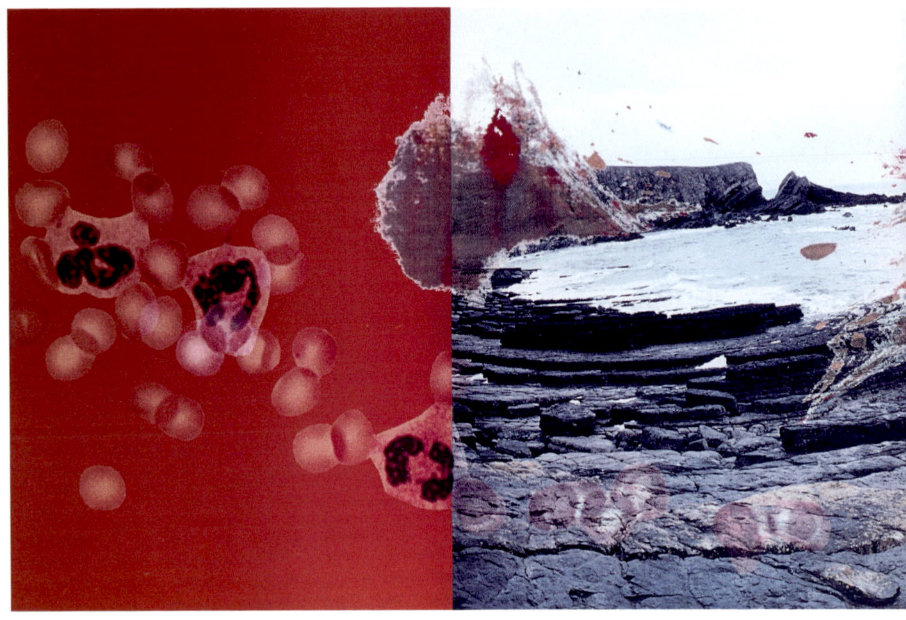

shoreline imagery onto panoramic landscape photographs. In doing so, she fused the microscopic with the macroscopic, the body with nature, and the self with the other, eroding preconceived boundaries. The works mark a departure from nineteenth-century Romantic notions of the singular artist at one remove from nature – Caspar David Friedrich's solitary figure, for example, standing on a cliff edge, commanding the scene with his powerful gaze. There is no such separation in Chadwick's work: the artist's body is immersed in her environment and indeed her cells threaten to infect the pristine landscapes. Chadwick's self is fully connected with the outside world. She is part of the natural order of things. Her actions have implications and she has responsibilities.

KEY FEATURES

Use of the self to explore universal concerns and social issues
Interest in the visceral properties of a wide range of unusual
  materials
Fusion of sculpture, photography and performance
Exploration of the inside of the human body
Challenges of binary readings and gender stereotypes
Exploration of the intersection between art, science and
  digital technology

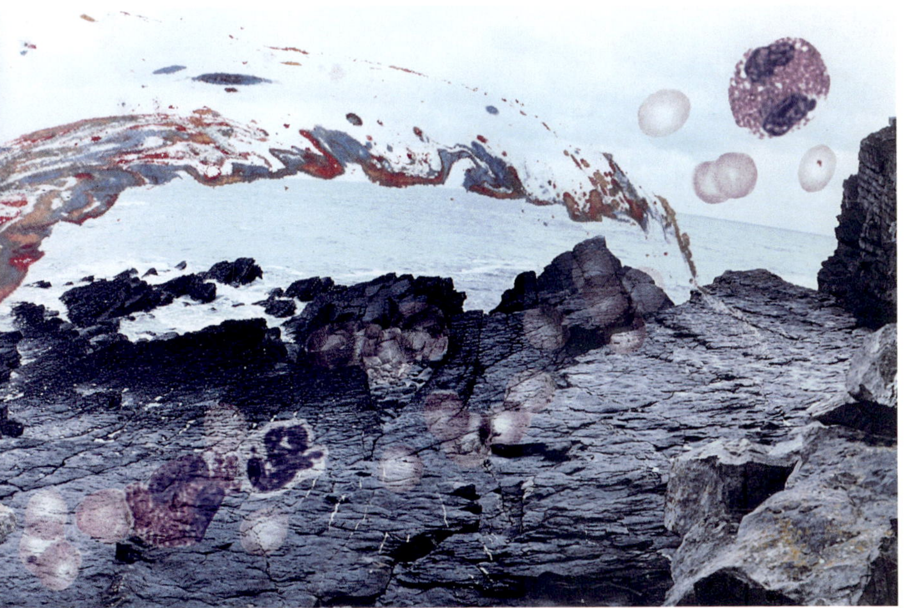

MONA HATOUM
b.1952

Mona Hatoum's Palestinian parents were uprooted from the Haifa region of Palestine during the Arab–Israeli War of 1948. Exiled from their homeland, they settled in Beirut, where Hatoum was born. She visited London in 1975, however her brief trip was ruptured by the outbreak of the Lebanese Civil War. Unable to return to Beirut, she decided to stay in London, where she continues to live and work. Hatoum's early work involved performances in which she subjected herself to constrictive conditions. Her later sculptural installations embrace a range of materials and directly implicate the viewer. Regardless of her chosen materials, much of Hatoum's work interrogates notions of displacement, alienation and the abuse of power.

Corps étranger (Foreign Body, 1994) fuses performance, installation and video. Visitors are invited to enter an enclosed cylindrical structure. An ultrasound audio recording of the artist's breathing and heartbeat adds further intrigue and intensity. A video projects onto the floor of the space: made using a camera normally reserved for endoscopy and colonoscopy examinations, the footage documents the inside and outside of the artist's body. The throbbing, slimy imagery prompts a sense of unease and repulsion. Orifices gape like ravenous mouths, ready to swallow up unsuspecting bystanders. Such horrors recall the mythical representations of women as devourers and castrators that have filtered down through art history. Perceptions of the female body as recumbent and available are also implied and critiqued.

Given its extensive analysis of the artist's body, *Corps étranger* could be described as the ultimate self-portrait, however Hatoum gives little away. She provides no information about her character and the footage could represent any woman. Furthermore, unlike many artists before her, Hatoum refuses to present a unified, contained image of herself. Instead she presents a messy, incoherent mass of pathways and exchanges. Her body is prone to invasion by various intruders: the unyielding probes of medical intervention and the repeated footfall of visitors as they traverse her territory.

Many of Mona Hatoum's installations involve the active participation of the viewer. In this work, the confined space prompts touch and intimacy. Visitors brush against one another and step onto images of the artist's body. It becomes unclear whether the foreign body in the title refers to the artist or to the encroaching presence of the viewer.

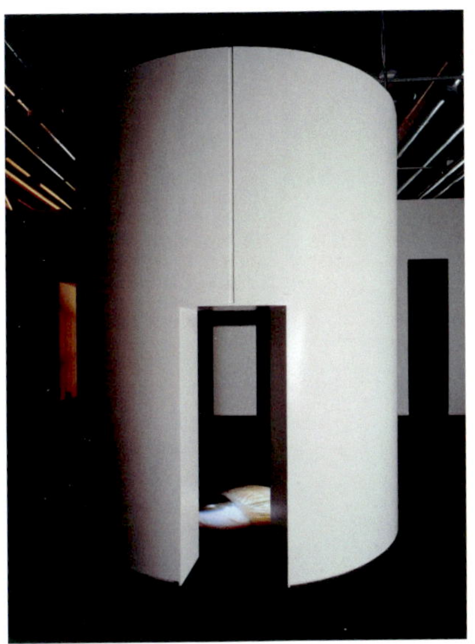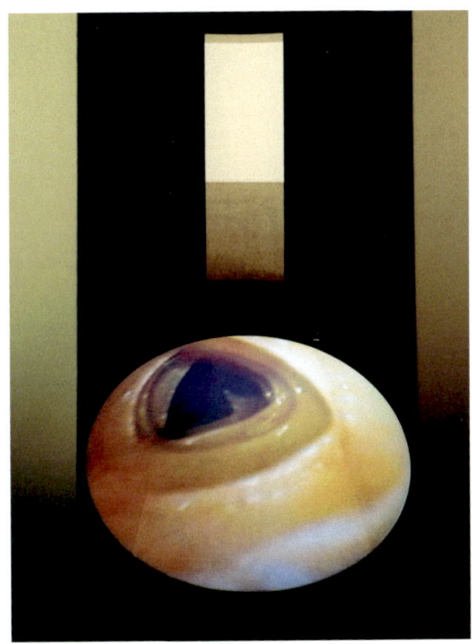

OTHER KEY WORKS

Over my dead body, 1988–2002, British Council Collection,
  London, UK
Measures of Distance, 1988, Arts Council Collection, London, UK

KEY FEATURES

Fusion of performance, video and installation
Use of the artist's body to explore race and gender politics
Investigation of the inside of the body using medical technologies
Installation approach, implicating the viewer within the action
Interest in horror, repulsion and alienation

FAITH RINGGOLD
b.1930

Faith Ringgold studied Art Education at City College, New York, unable to access the fine art course because of her gender. She went on to teach art in schools for eighteen years, never giving up on her own practice. Ringgold was determined to find an authentic means of expression for herself and her community, connecting individual and collective experiences: 'After I decided to be an artist, the first thing that I had to believe was that I, a black woman, could penetrate the art scene and that I could do so without sacrificing one iota of my blackness, or my femaleness, or my humanity.' She began searching for what she termed 'acceptable' ways to represent black skin through her paintings. Avoiding gloomy chiaroscuro shading, she applied a broader range of colours in flat, delineated zones, as evidenced in her early self-portrait of 1965.

Ringgold is perhaps best known for her story quilts. She made her first quilt with her mother in 1980, drawing inspiration from African-American quilt-making traditions and from Tibetan thangkas – exquisite paintings made on silk or cotton. The quilt provides a perfect platform for Ringgold to interweave figurative painting, intricate appliqué designs and handwritten narratives. A talented storyteller, Ringgold shares tales about herself and her community. Her characters and narrators are predominantly strong, black and female. Despite the warmth and humour of Ringgold's delivery, political reflections on a racially divided society are never far from the surface.

Self-Portrait (1998) displays Ringgold's characteristic fusion of text and pattern, abstraction and figuration. This autobiographical quilt references Ringgold's 1995 book *Seven Passages to a Flight*, which documents the artist's life in images and words. The central panel of the quilt features nine hand-painted etchings documenting personal events, moments of historical significance and flights of imagination.

OTHER KEY WORKS

Early Works #25: Self-Portrait, 1965, Brooklyn Museum, Brooklyn, USA

Change: Faith Ringgold's Over 100-Pound Weight Loss Performance Story Quilt, 1986, private collection

Faith Ringgold
Self-Portrait, 1998
Hand-painted etching and pochoir borders on linen with quilted cotton border and nylon backing, 128.4 x 109.3 cm (50½ x 43 in.)
National Portrait Gallery, Smithsonian Institution, Washington, DC

A number of the scenes represented in this quilt feature the artist and her associates in the act of flying. To Ringgold, flight represents freedom and the determination to rise above obstacles. The quilt also includes various bridge motifs, again symbolizing hope and the need to overcome moments of difficulty.

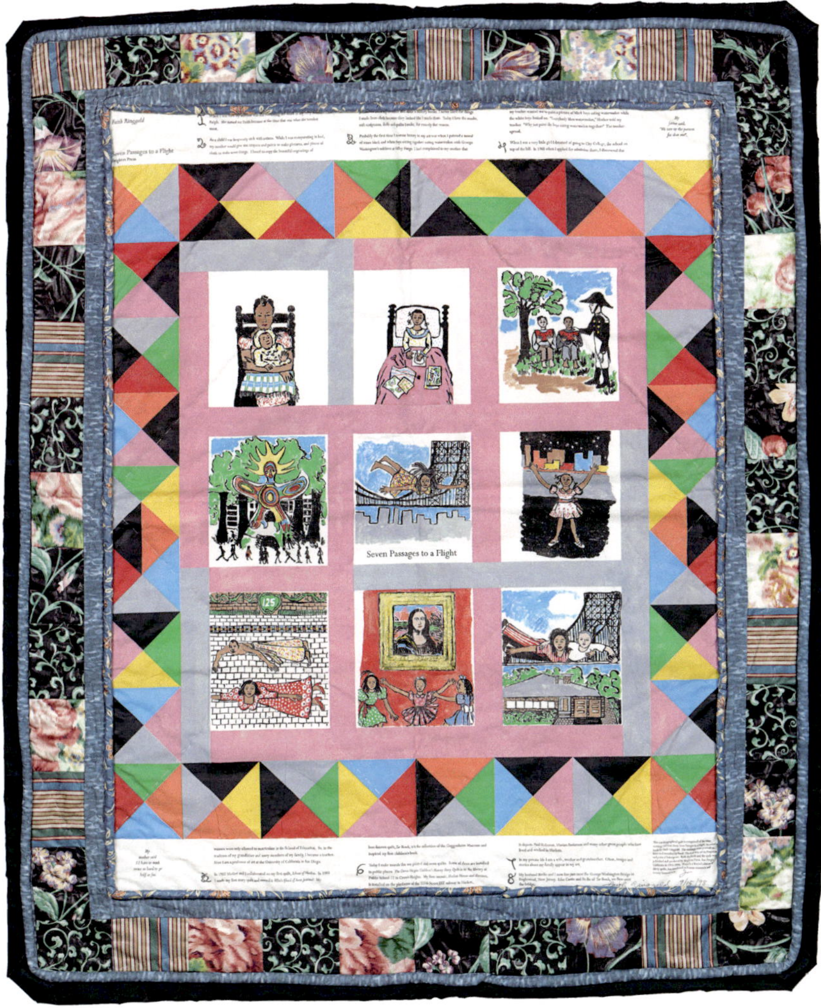

KEY FEATURES

Innovative use of the quilt as a support for writing, stitching and painting

Extensive inclusion of autobiographical and textual content

Desire to represent individual and collective identities

Focus on intersectional experiences, giving voice to strong female African-American characters

Interest in oral traditions of storytelling passed down through generations

Influence of global art histories and approaches

TRACEY EMIN
b.1963

Tracey Emin's art practice centres on herself: her experiences, traumas, break-ups and breakdowns. Using a variety of materials and processes, including painting, sculpture, text, neon, stitching, installation and film, Emin shares the intimate details of her life with a confessional intensity. At heart, Emin considers herself to be an Expressionist. Edvard Munch (see pages 72–3) is one of her favourite artists, and it is possible to discern a thread connecting the anguished figure in *The Scream* (1893), Egon Schiele's exposed, sexualized bodies (pages 94–5) and Emin's emphatic outpourings of self-disclosure.

Some of Emin's most successful installations start with the unremarkable objects associated with sleep, protection and comfort. *Everyone I Have Ever Slept With 1963–1995* (1995) comprises a blue two-berth dome tent adorned with appliquéd letters spelling out Emin's roll call of bedtime companions, sexual and platonic. Her heartfelt hand-stitching elevates this humble structure, transforming it into a shrine, a memorial to past and present relationships. Equally humble in origin is the unmade bed in Emin's iconic installation *My Bed* (1998). This work documents a difficult period of the artist's life. Emin presents a range of associated clues, inviting the viewer to join the dots like a criminal investigator. There are empty vodka bottles and cigarette packets, condoms, contraceptive pills and pregnancy tests. Soiled tissues, stained sheets, dirty knickers and used tampons. Dishevelment and disarray. Symbols of a life unravelling: quick pleasures and lengthy come downs. Emin's personal relics are presented with museological precision, frozen in time. It is a self-portrait and a still life.

Tracey Emin
My Bed, 1998
Box frame, mattress, linens, pillows and various objects, overall display dimensions variable
Tate collection. Lent by The Duerckheim Collection, 2015.
On long-term loan.

Perhaps Emin's most notorious work, *My Bed* featured in the Turner Prize exhibition of 1999. Although she did not win the prize, her unmade bed stole the headlines. The work documents a depressive moment in Emin's life during which she spent successive days in bed, enduring bad relationships and drinking alcohol.

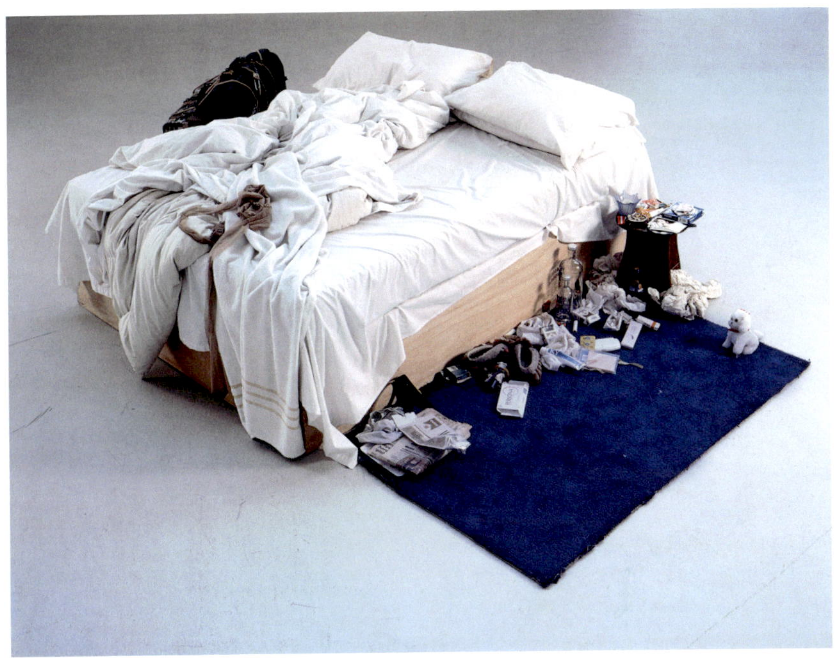

OTHER KEY WORKS

Everyone I Have Ever Slept With 1963–1995, 1995 (destroyed
  2004), Saatchi Collection, London, UK
Why I Never Became A Dancer, 1995, Arts Council Collection,
  London, UK

KEY FEATURES

Self-revelatory practice embracing a range of media
Strong narrative impulse and frequent incorporation of text
Analysis of traumatic experiences and difficult relationships
Expressionist interest in heightened emotion and feeling
Adaptation of everyday objects to convey autobiographical
  content and heightened realism

PAWEŁ ALTHAMER
b.1967

An innovative approach to self-portraiture occupies the heart of Paweł Althamer's sculptural and performance-based practice. For his final show at the Academy of Fine Arts in Warsaw, Althamer presented a life-size sculpture of himself made from wax and hair. Rather than make a personal appearance for the crit, Althamer left a copy of a short film documenting his exodus from the school and his departure from the city. At the end of the film he is seen wandering into the woods and disappearing altogether. Althamer has continued to explore this intriguing terrain between sculpture and performance, presence and absence, using a variety of playful and maverick methods.

Many of Althamer's works occupy public space and involve processes of abandonment and desertion. For example, to make *Self-Portrait as a Businessman* (2002), Althamer arrived in a Berlin city square one evening dressed smartly in corporate attire. He stripped naked, leaving his clothing, mobile phone and briefcase near a public fountain before vacating the scene altogether. The heaped belongings provide an enduring trace of the artist, albeit a very faint one, for the suit already marked a departure from Althamer's usual fashion choices. With the later installation *Balloon* (2007), it was impossible to avoid the artist. This 21-metre (69-foot) long balloon self-portrait hovered above a Milanese park like a sore thumb. Naked and exposed, this ungainly Gulliver was tethered to the ground, unable to escape the amused gaze of his Lilliputian public.

Althamer's participatory and collaborative practice has pushed the limits of self-portraiture even further. Often working with marginalized groups, he invites participants to engage in playful and deviant acts, some so slight they are hard to spot. By working with others, Althamer gains a deeper insight into his own identity. Indeed, he considers these interventions to be a radical form of self-portraiture, one arising from collective creativity and orchestrated chaos.

Paweł Althamer
Balloon, 1999–2011
Nylon, polyester, acrylic, ropes, helium,
3.66 x 21 x 6.71 m
(12 x 69 x 22 ft)
2007 installation at Fondazione Nicola Trussardi, Milan

Althamer collaborated with aeronautical specialists and manufacturers of helium balloons to make this enormous inflatable self-portrait. Measuring over 20 metres long, this gargantuan representation of the artist's naked body hovered above Parco Sempione in Milan for one month, tethered by ropes to prevent its departure into space.

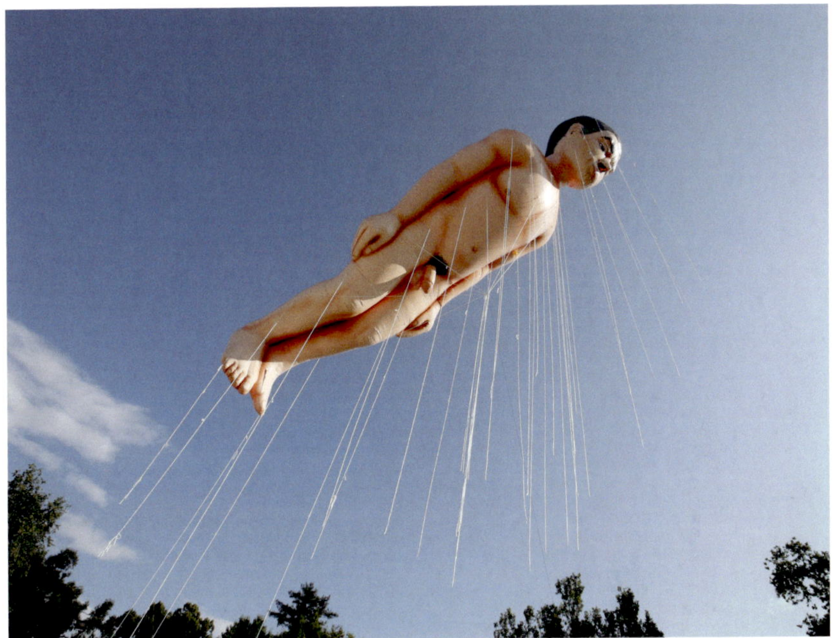

OTHER KEY WORKS

Self-Portrait as a Businessman, 2002, with additions 2004, Tate collection, UK

KEY FEATURES

Innovative combination of figurative sculpture and performance
Interest in the intersection between presence and absence, self and other
Engagement with communities to reveal collective actions and identities
Playful interventions in public spaces
Exploration of the artist as shaman, author and orchestrator

ABRAHAM CRUZVILLEGAS
b.1968

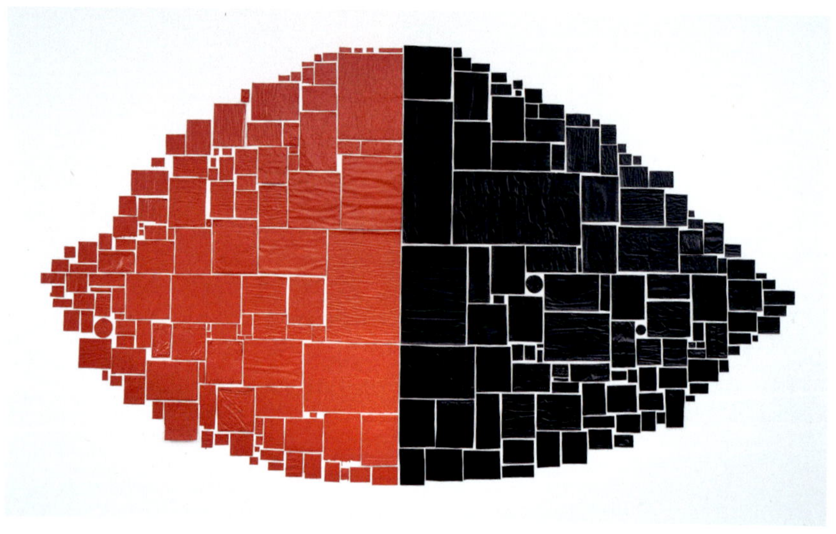

Abraham Cruzvillegas grew up in Ajusco, a southern suburb of Mexico City. Against the odds, its settlers built an informal architecture on inhospitable volcanic rock using ad-hoc building methods and sheer determination. A similar resourcefulness informs Cruzvillegas' approach as an artist. He lives by the dictum of making something out of nothing. Sourcing his materials locally, he draws inspiration from different places and communities as he travels.

Since 2007, Cruzvillegas has explored his concept of *autoconstrucciòn* or 'self-building'. This approach involves his resourceful adaptation of found materials to reveal the 'inner lives' of things. With a nod to Marcel Duchamp (see pages 114–15), Cruzvillegas' playful adaptation of the stuff of everyday life results in surprisingly self-revelatory work. The fragmentary, unfinished nature of his homespun sculptures and installations reflects the contradictory and evolving aspects of his own identity:

Abraham Cruzvillegas
Itchy blind self portrait drinking a Colimita beer by the patio, under the shade of the Pomarrosa tree, remembering the late Valentín Campa after reading Terry Eagleton's 'Hope without optimism' while I listen to the beautiful version of 'La Martiniana' with Tinito y Porfirio's duet, but really wanting to have some cashews before going for dinner, whatever the Paleolithic menu at Lardo could include..., 2016
Black and red acrylic paint on newspaper clippings, cardboard, photographs, drawings, postcards, envelopes, tickets, vouchers, letters, drawings, posters, flyers, cards, recipes, napkins and steel pins on wall, variable dimensions (installation of 456 pieces)
Courtesy of the artist and kurimanzutto, Mexico City/New York

This 'blind' self-portrait features a hoard of collected paper ephemera. The back of each item is painted before being pinned neatly to a wall. In an active process of interpretation, members of the public are invited to turn individual elements over to reveal a range of clues. The poetic title highlights Cruzvillegas' interest in language and his ongoing practice as a writer.

'Something definitely unfinished, something that is building itself forever – fragmentary, contradictory, weak, unstable, dark, transparent, warm, stupid, delicious, chaotic, crippled. It's movement and life, it's love,
it's sex, it's me.'

In recent work, Cruzvillegas has explored the notion of blind self-portraiture. Turning his back on restrictive notions of likeness, he has discovered other ways to express his identity. To make each blind self-portrait Cruzvillegas amasses a stack of paper mementos. These tickets, napkins, notelets and photographs build a picture of a life of travel and places visited. He paints the back of each item using a limited colour palette before pinning his source material to the wall in intricate, amorphous arrangements. Visitors are invited to peek behind each token, piecing together the clues. The long, poetic titles allude to personal chains of thought, inviting us on another kind of journey, a further step away from limiting definitions of self-portraiture.

OTHER KEY WORKS

AC: Blind Self-Portrait: Glasgow Cove Park, 2008, Tate collection, UK

KEY FEATURES

Playful incorporation of found objects to explore individual and collective identities
Strong collecting impulse, salvaging discarded materials
Development of the concept of *autoconstrucciòn* (self-building) as an ongoing self-referential process
Interest in concealment, overturning the revelatory conventions of self-portraiture
Embodiment of social and political narratives
Fusion of local and global references

RYAN GANDER
b.1976

What is the relevance of self-portraiture today? After centuries of expression, has the genre finally run out of steam? Ryan Gander has subjected self-portraiture to a process of re-imagination and reinvention. Rejecting all preconceptions, Gander has opened up new ways of thinking about the self, particularly in relation to others and to the outside world.

Born in Chester in 1976, Ryan Gander studied interactive art at Manchester Metropolitan University before completing his studies at the Jan van Eyck Academie in Maastricht. His internationally recognized conceptual practice centres on a playful process that he terms 'imagineering'. A prolific conjurer and channeler of ideas, Gander refuses to limit himself to art-world materials and processes. The idea dictates the outcome. The idea might lead to a sculpture, an installation or a painting, but it could equally emerge as writing, fashion, trainer design, cocktail-making, an animatronic talking mouse or an art school. Gander considers art to be a field of unlimited creative possibility, not just for himself, but also for anyone willing to join him on the journey.

Gander's refusal to accept limitations is reflected in his desire to eliminate any trace of a signature style. He has produced work under the guise of several alter egos in an attempt to avoid getting stuck in a subjective rut. Working collaboratively has also enabled Gander to maintain a spirit of openness. Autobiographical references do, however, emerge across the practice, but these are interwoven with fictional stories and other perspectives. For example, Gander made *Both before and after, I had to write your obituary* (2008) with fellow artist Bedwyr Williams. Using

Ryan Gander
Self-Portrait VIII, 2012
Toughened glass, paint,
overall installation
1.92 x 2.73 m
(62¼ x 9 ft),
each palette depth 30 cm
(11⅞ in.)
RISD Museum, Rhode
Island

In September 2011, Gander decided to make one self-portrait every day for a year. This work documents the eighth month of his endeavour. The thirty days of April are presented as a minimal grid of toughened glass palettes, each bearing the traces of Gander's activity. The actual self-portraits are permanently removed from view, either destroyed or locked in the artist's archive.

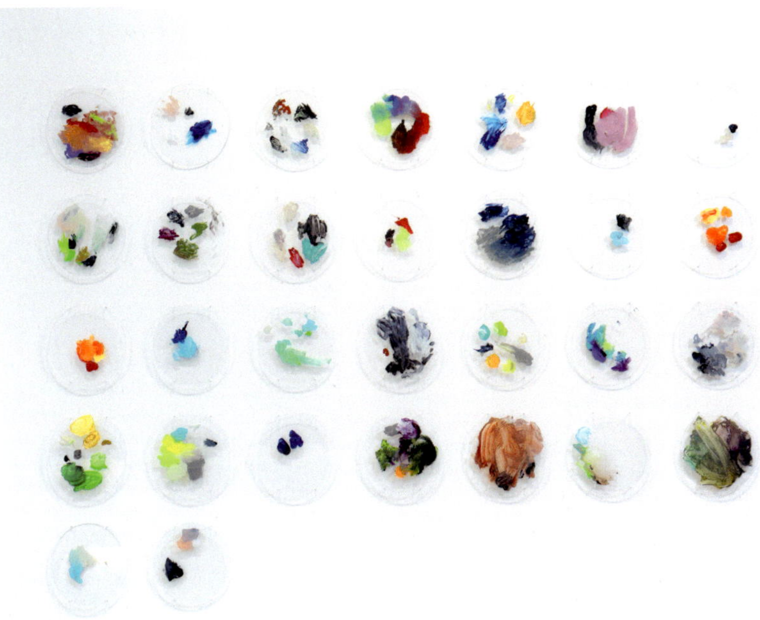

a newspaper column format, the two artists wrote each other's eulogy. They reflected back on their lives from the vantage point of the year 2050, applying a retrospective form of writing to imagine an as yet undisclosed future. In other works, Gander has taken direct inspiration from his children. *I is... (I)* (2012) features a marble resin cast of his daughter's home-made den. This memorial to a piece of makeshift architecture draws on precious moments to celebrate the unbounded creativity of childhood.

In addition to his playful adaptation of autobiographical content, Gander has also developed new ways to explore portraiture and self-portraiture. He has painted portraits of himself and others, often working from memory to capture past experiences and interactions. He uses a new disc of toughened glass as his palette for each work. Intriguingly, the finished paintings will never be seen: they are discarded or permanently stowed in the artist's archive. Instead, the palettes steal the limelight, presented in minimal grids or chaotic salon hangs – an explosion of bright colour and abstract gesture. Gander has explained the significance of the palette, saying 'The palette represents all the paintings that could have been, not the painting that I decided on. The self-portrait palettes are like a tongue-in-cheek dig at how ridiculous it is to build clumsy egocentric monuments to yourself, which is what so many artists do.' Instead of providing all the answers, Gander prompts the viewer to fill in the gaps, to imagine the painting and the events leading up to the scenario. These works also invite us to reflect upon the fleeting nature of our experiences and memories, and the relationships we have with others and with ourselves.

A recent series of works appears to endorse letting go of the past in order to move forward. *I be … (X)* (2016) is one of a number of pieces featuring stately antique mirrors draped in marble-resin cloths. The viewer's expectation of self-scrutiny is thwarted by the presence of solid, impermeable folds. The mirror, the primary tool of self-portraiture for many centuries, appears redundant, unable to function. Liberated from representational responsibility, self-portraiture is now free to pursue fresh directions. Gander invites his audience to consider an important question: what can *I* be? *I* can be anything imaginable.

OTHER KEY WORKS

Ryan Gander and Bedwyr Williams, *Both before and after, I had to write your obituary*, 2008, Collection of Bedwyr Williams
I is … (I), 2012, Lisson Gallery, London, UK

KEY FEATURES

Conceptual art practice based on ideas and 'imagineering'
Invitation for active audience engagement and interpretation
Combination of autobiographical references and fictional stories
Layering of past and present, art-historical and everyday experiences
Rejection of the traditional conventions of self-portraiture
Interest in hiding and concealment

Ryan Gander
I be … (X), 2016
Antique mirror,
marble resin,
171 x 120 x 25 cm
(67⅜ x 47¼ x 9⅞ in.)
Lisson Gallery, London

This work stems from a series of pieces featuring stately antique mirrors draped in marble-resin cloths. As with many of Gander's works, art-historical allusions collide with contemporary references to prompt new ways of thinking. In this case, self-recognition is thwarted by classical drapery, a reminder of the enduring and essentially human propensity for narcissism.

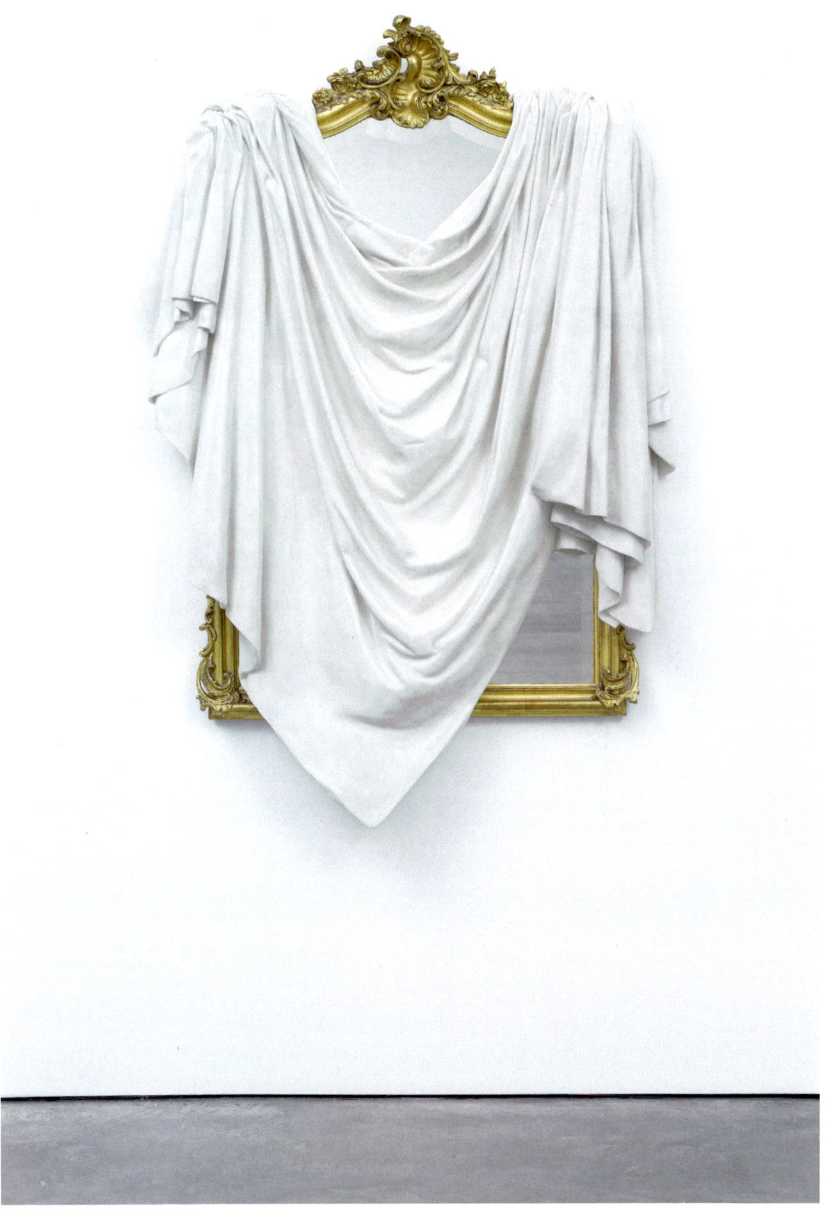

GLOSSARY

Allegory: a narrative or scene containing hidden meanings. For example, a character could symbolize a particular virtue or a political position.

Altarpiece: a painting, relief or sculpted work presented behind the altar in a Christian church.

***Assistenza* self-portraiture**: the discreet, anonymous insertion of a self-portrait into a larger scheme. For example, the representation of the artist as an anonymous bystander in a crowd scene.

Baroque: a style of art prevalent in Europe between the early 1600s and the 1740s. Much baroque art features theatrical gestures, a strong sense of movement and dramatic chiaroscuro lighting.

Bust portrait: a portrait format featuring the head and shoulders of the sitter.

Bust sculpture: the three-dimensional representation of the head and shoulders of a person. Bust sculptures can be sculpted or cast and can be made from a range of materials including marble, wax, plaster, bronze, wood and terracotta.

Caricature: an exaggerated or distorted portrayal of a person or thing, often to mock or satirize.

Chiaroscuro: Strong tonal contrasts of light and dark within a painted composition.

Conceptual art: an art movement that first emerged during the late 1960s. Conceptual artists use ideas and theoretical concepts as the source material for their work. Moving beyond traditional skills and the production of finished objects, conceptual art can assume many forms and outcomes.

Endurance art: a form of performance art involving the extreme physical or mental endurance of the artist. These performances can involve pain or social isolation and can take place over a long period of time. See also *performance art*.

Etching: a process of printmaking whereby acid is used to cut into an exposed metal surface, leaving furrowed lines that can be filled with ink to produce a print.

Expressionism: a generic approach to art involving the use of heightened, non-naturalistic colour and gestural paint handling to convey strong emotions. An extension of Romantic and Post-Impressionist principles, Expressionist art predominated in the early twentieth century. German Expressionism refers to the Expressionist art produced by *Die Brücke* (The Bridge) and *Der Blaue Reiter* (The Blue Rider) artist groups, among others.

Feminist art: a category of art that emerged in the late 1960s and early 1970s. Drawing on feminist theory and ideas, feminist artists use a variety of materials and perspectives to challenge stereotypes and to fight inequality in the art world and across wider society.

Fresco: a type of mural painting made by working into freshly laid lime plaster. The painting effectively becomes part of the wall.

Full-frontal portrait: a portrait in which the sitter looks straight ahead without turning to one side or the other.

Full-length portrait: a portrait representing the entire figure, from head to toe. Historically, this format was reserved for wealthy, aristocratic patrons.

Genre painting: a type of painting depicting ordinary people undertaking everyday tasks. Genre painting was often considered lowly when compared with other forms of painting, such as *history painting*. Genre was a popular form within seventeenth-century Netherlandish art.

Half-length portrait: a portrait capturing the top half of a person, from the head to the waist.

History painting: a genre of painting involving the depiction of historical, mythological or religious scenes. Often large in scale, history paintings were considered the highest form of art for many centuries.

Installation art: a work of art occupying or responding to a particular space. Installation art rose to prominence in the late 1950s and remains a popular art form within contemporary practice.

Installations can take many forms and often feature a wide range of materials. The active engagement of the audience is a recurrent feature.

Likeness: the quality of bearing a strong physical resemblance to someone or something.

Mannerism: an approach to art emerging in sixteenth-century Italy before spreading across Europe. Picking up where Michelangelo and Raphael left off, Mannerist artists sought even greater idealization in their work, resulting in stylized bodies, elongated limbs and self-conscious elegance.

Maulstick: a stick with a padded leather ball at one end. The ball rests gently against the bare canvas to steady the artist's hand while painting.

Memento mori: Latin for 'remember you must die'. *Memento mori* paintings feature a range of objects that symbolize the fragility of life and the inevitability of death, including skulls and snuffed candles. See also *vanitas*.

Narcissism: an excessive interest in the self often involving particular admiration of one's own physical appearance. The term stems from Ancient Greek mythology: Narcissus fell in love with his own reflection in a pool of water. Narcissism features strongly in psychoanalytic theory, as evidenced in Sigmund Freud's 1914 essay *On Narcissism*. See also *psychoanalysis*.

Performance art: a time-based form of art involving actions undertaken by the artist or by other people. Performance art often involves live presentations in front of an audience, with photography and film often used to document the action. Although the specific term only came into common use during the 1970s, a performative spirit can be discerned in much twentieth-century art practice.

Photorealism: a style of painting involving the faithful representation of photographic material. Often featuring banal or anonymous scenes, photorealism rejects notions of painterly expression and emotional investment. Photorealism first rose to prominence in the late 1960s and enjoyed a resurgence during the 1990s.

Post-Impressionism: a loose term to describe work made by a range of artists working in the late nineteenth century who sought to move beyond the optical effects of Impressionism and towards heightened emotions, painterly expression and the symbolic use of colour and form.

Profile portrait: a portrait format focusing on the side view of a person.

Psychoanalysis: a group of theories and techniques developed by the Austrian neurologist Sigmund Freud. These theories centre on the impact of unconscious states and childhood influences on subsequent wellbeing.

Renaissance: French for 'rebirth'. The Renaissance was a revolutionary period of artistic and scientific development that transformed Europe during the fifteenth and sixteenth centuries. Spearheaded by renewed interest in classical ideas and inventions, the Renaissance took hold first in Italy and later in northern Europe. Renaissance art is divided into two key phases: Early Renaissance and High Renaissance.

Romanticism: a term used to describe a wide range of art, music and literature produced during the nineteenth century. Romantic art often reflected the spirited creativity of individual artists, heightened emotions and deep personal connections with nature.

Selfie: a photograph taken of oneself usually on a smartphone or similar portable device and shared using social media.

Silverpoint: a type of drawing made by dragging a silver rod across the picture surface to leave a deposit trail.

Still life: a work of art depicting a range of inanimate objects, often including flowers, food and household goods. Still-life paintings often convey symbolic meanings and explore themes of mortality and the futility of human life. See also *memento mori* and *vanitas*.

Surrealism: an art movement spearheaded by the French writer André Breton in the 1920s. Surrealist artists and writers explored subconscious and irrational states with the intention of liberating their art from pictorial conventions.

Tabernacle: a special cabinet designed to store consecrated offerings for religious ceremonies.

Three-quarter-length portrait: a portrait depicting a person from the head to around the knee.

Three-quarter profile portrait: a portrait that captures a turn of the head, halfway between a *profile portrait* and a *full-frontal portrait*. Many artists have used a three-quarter profile for self-portraiture as this pose reflects the natural turn of the head needed to observe oneself in a mirror.

Trompe-l'oeil: French for 'trick of the eye'. A representation so convincing it appears real.

Vanitas: a vanitas still-life painting features a range of familiar objects, each item symbolizing the worthless vanity of human exploits and pleasures. Goblets of wine, books, musical instruments, coins and globes are recurrent motifs in vanitas paintings. See also *memento mori*.

FURTHER READING

Bell, Julian and Liz Rideal, *500 Self-Portraits* (Phaidon Press, London, 2018)

Billeter, Erika and Roger Marcel Meyou, *Self-Portrait in the Age of Photography* (Benteli Verlag, Bern, 1985)

Bond, Antony and Joanna Woodall, *Self-Portrait: Renaissance to Contemporary* (National Portrait Gallery, London, 2005)

Borzello, Frances, *Seeing Ourselves: Women's Self-Portraits* (Thames & Hudson, London/New York, 2014)

Brilliant, Richard, *Portraiture* (Reaktion, London, 1991)

Cumming, Laura, *A Face to the World: On Self-Portraits* (HarperPress, London, 2010)

Doy, Gen, *Picturing the Self: Changing Views of the Subject in Visual Culture* (I.B. Tauris, London, 2004)

Feather, Jessica, *Face to Face: Three Centuries of Artists' Self-Portraiture* (National Museums & Galleries, Merseyside, 1999)

Hall, James, Wolfgang Ullrich and Pierre Vaisse, *Facing the World: Self-Portraits (and Selfies) from Rembrandt to Ai-Weiwei* (Snoeck Publishers, Cologne, 2016)

Hall, James, *The Self-Portrait: A Cultural History* (Thames & Hudson, London/New York, 2014)

Jones, Amelia and Tracey Warr, *The Artist's Body* (Phaidon, London, 2000)

Koerner, Joseph, *The Moment of Self-Portraiture in German Renaissance Art* (University of Chicago Press, Chicago, 1993)

Melchior-Bonnet, Sabine, *The Mirror: A History* (Routledge, New York/London, 2001)

Meskimmon, Marsha, *The Art of Reflection* (Columbia University Press, New York, 1996)

Natter, Tobias G., *The Self-Portrait from Schiele to Beckmann* (Prestel, New York/London, 2019)

Porter, Roy (ed.), *Rewriting the Self: Histories from the Renaissance to the Present* (Routledge, New York/London, 1996)

Schneider, Norbert, *The Art of the Portrait* (Taschen, Cologne, 2002)

Storr, Will, *Selfie: How we became so self-obsessed and what it's doing to us* (Picador, London, 2017)

Sturgis, Alexander (ed.), *Rebels and Martyrs: The Image of the Artist in the Nineteenth Century* (National Gallery, London, 2006)

Vasari, Giorgio, *Lives of the Artists* (2nd edition 1568) (Penguin Classics, London, 2003)

West, Shearer, *Portraiture* (Oxford University Press, Oxford, 2004)

Woodall, Joanna (ed.), *Portraiture: Facing the Subject* (Manchester University Press, Manchester, 1997)

Woods-Marsden, Joanna, *Renaissance Self-Portraiture* (Yale University Press, New Haven, 1998)

INDEX

Main entries are in **bold**.

PICTURE ACKNOWLEDGEMENTS

2 Courtesy the artist and Gagosian **8** Royal Collection, UK **11**, **12**, **13** National Gallery, London **14**, **15** Uffizi Gallery, Florence. Photo Alinari/Shutterstock **16** Lorenzkirche, Nuremberg **17** Lorenzkirche, Nuremberg. Photo B. O'Kane/Alamy Stock Photo **19** Albertina, Vienna **20** Museo Nacional del Prado, Madrid **21** Sammlung Alte Pinakothek, Munich **22** Sistine Chapel, Vatican **25** Kunsthistorisches Museum, Vienna **26** Museum of Fine Arts, Boston. Emma F. Munroe Fund (60.155) **28** Museum-Zamek, Lancut, Poland **29** Pinacoteca Nazionale, Siena **30** Galleria Borghese, Rome **32** Royal Collection, UK **33** Rijksmuseum, Amsterdam **34** Kenwood House, London, English Heritage **36**, **37** Staatliche Kunsthalle, Karlsruhe **39** Private Collection **41** Private Collection, Eaton Hall, Cheshire **42** National Gallery of Art, Washington, DC. Gift of Mr. and Mrs. Robert Woods Bliss (1949.6.1) **45** Rijksmuseum, Amsterdam **46** National Gallery, London. Photo Mariano Garcia/Alamy Stock Photo **47** Kenwood House, London, English Heritage **48** Museo Nacional del Prado, Madrid **50** Museum of the Home, London **51** National Portrait Gallery, London **53** Uffizi Gallery, Florence **54** National Gallery, London **57** Musée du Louvre, Paris **58** Minneapolis Institute of Art, Minneapolis. The Ethel Morrison Van Derlip Fund (52.14) **59** Metropolitan Museum of Art, New York. Gift of Mrs. Francis Ormond, 1950 (50.558.33) **60** Courtauld Gallery, London **63** Private Collection **64** Musée d'Orsay, Paris **65** Musée Fabre, Montpellier **66** Courtauld Gallery, London **68** National Gallery, London **69** Kunstindustrimuseet, Copenhagen **70** Menard Art Museum, Komaki, Japan **73** Munch Museum, Oslo **75** Museum of Modern Art, New York. The Modern Women's Fund (730.2012). Digital image, The Museum of Modern Art, New York/Scala, Florence **76** Philadelphia Museum of Art, Philadelphia. 125th Anniversary Acquisition. Purchased with funds contributed by C. K. Williams, II, 1999 (1999-50-1). Dorothea Tanning © ADAGP, Paris and DACS, London 2021 **79** Harry Ransom Center, Austin, Texas. Photo Album/Scala, Florence. © Banco de México Diego Rivera Frida Kahlo Museums Trust, Mexico, D.F./DACS 2021 **80**, **82**, **83** Collection Jewish Historical Museum, Amsterdam **84** Ateneum Art Museum, Helsinki **86** Private Collection. © The Lucian Freud Archive/Bridgeman Images **88** Paula Modersohn-Becker Museum, Bremen **91** Hamburger Kunsthalle (2940). Photo Elke Walford/Scala, Florence/bpk, Bildagentur für Kunst, Kultur und Geschichte, Berlin **92** Tretyakov Gallery, Moscow. Zinaida Serebriakova © ADAGP, Paris and DACS, London 2021 **95** Leopold Museum, Vienna. Photo Art Collection 2/Alamy Stock Photo **97** Collection of Navina and Vivan Sundaram **99** Private Collection. © The Lucian Freud Archive/Bridgeman Images **101** Walker Art Center, Minneapolis. © Chuck Close, courtesy Pace Gallery **103** © Ulay/Marina Abramović. Courtesy of the Marina Abramović Archives/DACS 2021 **104** Institute of Contemporary Art, Miami. Courtesy Galerie Lelong & Co. © The Estate of Ana Mendieta Collection, LLC. and ARS, NY and DACS, London 2021 **107** San Francisco Museum of Modern Art, San Francisco. Courtesy Galerie Lelong & Co. © The Estate of Ana Mendieta Collection, LLC and ARS, NY and DACS, London 2021 **109** Museu d'Art Contemporani de Barcelona (MACBA), Barcelona. Government of Catalonia long-term loan. Formerly Salvador Riera Collection. Photo Adagp Images, Paris/Scala, Florence. © The Estate of Jean-Michel Basquiat/ADAGP, Paris and DACS, London 2021 **110** Saatchi Collection, London. © Jenny Saville. All rights reserved, DACS 2021 **112** Jersey Heritage Trust, UK. Bridgeman Images **115** J. Paul Getty Museum, Los Angeles. © Succession Marcel Duchamp/ADAGP, Paris and DACS, London 2021/© Man Ray Trust/ADAGP, Paris and DACS, London 2021 **117** Jersey Heritage Trust, UK. Bridgeman Images **118** Metropolitan Museum of Art, New York. Photo Peter Horree/Alamy Stock Photo **119** Jersey Heritage Trust, UK **121** Collection Museum of Contemporary Art Chicago. © Estate of Marisol/ARS, NY and DACS, London 2021 **122** Collection of Mr. and Mrs. S. Brooks Barron. Photo Christie's Images, London/Scala, Florence. © 2021 The Andy Warhol Foundation for the Visual Arts, Inc./Licensed by DACS, London **124** © Tehching Hsieh. Courtesy the artist, Sean Kelly Gallery, New York, and Tate Modern, London **127**, **128**, **129** Courtesy the artist and Metro Pictures, New York **131** Private Collection. Image © Marc Quinn **132** © Catherine Opie, courtesy Regen Projects, Los Angeles **134** Edition of 8 © Zhang Huan, courtesy Pace Gallery **137** Courtesy the artist and Gagosian **138** © Zanele Muholi. Courtesy Stevenson, Cape Town/Johannesburg and Yancey Richardson, New York **140** Image courtesy Saatchi Gallery, London. Photo Prudence Cuming Associates Ltd. © Tracey Emin. All rights reserved, DACS/Artimage 2021 **142** Tate, London. Piero Manzoni © DACS 2021 **145** Museum of Modern Art, New York. Mr. and Mrs. Joseph Slifka Fund (249.1983). Digital image, The Museum of Modern Art, New York/Scala, Florence. Louise Bourgeois © The Easton Foundation/VAGA at ARS, NY and DACS, London 2021 **147** Tate, London. Rebecca Horn © DACS 2021 **148** © Martin Puryear. Courtesy Matthew Marks Gallery **150–51** Walker Art Gallery, National Museums Liverpool. Helen Chadwick © The Estate of the Artist. Courtesy Richard Saltoun Gallery, London **153** Photo Centre Pompidou, MNAM-CCI, Dist. RMN-Grand Palais/Philippe Migeat. © Mona Hatoum 2021 **155** National Portrait Gallery, Smithsonian Institution, Washington, DC. (NPG.2004.25). © Faith Ringgold/ARS, NY and DACS, London, Courtesy ACA Galleries, New York 2021 **157** Image courtesy Saatchi Gallery, London. Photo Prudence Cuming Associates Ltd. © Tracey Emin. All rights reserved, DACS/Artimage 2021 **159** Courtesy the artist and Foksal Gallery Foundation, Warsaw **160** Courtesy of the artist and kurimanzutto, Mexico City/New York. Photo John Wilson White, 2016. © Abraham Cruzvillegas & kurimanzutto, Mexico City/New York **163** © Ryan Gander. Courtesy Ryan Gander and Lisson Gallery. Photo Jack Hems **165** © Ryan Gander. Courtesy Ryan Gander and Lisson Gallery. Photo Ken Adlard

-

To Simon, Mary and
Jem Skirrow
Special thanks to my parents,
Ann and Anthony Rudd

-

First published in the
United Kingdom in 2021 by
Thames & Hudson Ltd, 181A High
Holborn, London WC1V 7QX

First published in the United States
of America in 2021 by Thames &
Hudson Inc., 500 Fifth Avenue,
New York, New York 10110

The Self-Portrait © 2021
Thames & Hudson Ltd, London
Text © 2021 Natalie Rudd

Design by April

All Rights Reserved. No part of this
publication may be reproduced or
transmitted in any form or by any
means, electronic or mechanical,
including photocopying, recording
or any other information storage
and retrieval system, without prior
permission in writing from the
publisher.

British Library Cataloguing-in-
Publication Data
A catalogue record for this book is
available from the British Library.

Library of Congress Control
Number 2020940846
ISBN 978-0-500-29581-6
Printed and bound in China by
Toppan Leefung Printing Ltd

Be the first to know about our
new releases, exclusive content
and author events by visiting
thamesandhudson.com
thamesandhudsonusa.com
thamesandhudson.com.au

Front cover: Zanele Muholi, *Ntozakhe II, Parktown*, 2016 (detail of page 138). © Zanele Muholi. Courtesy of Stevenson, Cape Town/Johannesburg and Yancey Richardson, New York

Title page: Yayoi Kusama, *Self-Portrait*, 2008 (detail of page 137). Courtesy the artist and Gagosian

Chapter openers: page 8 Artemisia Gentileschi, *Self-Portrait as the Allegory of Painting*, c.1638–9 (detail of page 32). Royal Collection, UK; **page 34** Rembrandt van Rijn, *Self-Portrait*, c.1665 (detail of page 47). Kenwood House, London, English Heritage; **page 60** Vincent van Gogh, *Self-Portrait with Bandaged Ear*, 1889 (detail of page 66). Courtauld Gallery, London; **page 86** Lucian Freud, *Interior with Hand Mirror (Self-Portrait)*, 1967 (detail of page 99). Private Collection. © The Lucian Freud Archive/Bridgeman Images; **page 112** Claude Cahun, photograph from the series *I am in training don't kiss me*, c.1927 (detail of page 117). Jersey Heritage Trust, UK. Bridgeman Images; **page 140** Tracey Emin, *My Bed*, 1998 (detail of page 157). Image courtesy Saatchi Gallery, London. Photo Prudence Cuming Associates Ltd. © Tracey Emin. All rights reserved, DACS/Artimage 2021

Quotations: page 9 Reproduced in Julian Bell and Liz Rideal, *500 Self-Portraits* (London: Phaidon, 2018), p.74; **page 35** Michel de Montaigne, 'On Solitude', 1580, *Essays I: 39*, p.270, reproduced in James Hall, *The Self-Portrait: A Cultural History* (London: Thames & Hudson, 2014), p.157 **page 61** Reproduced in Julian Bell and Liz Rideal, *500 Self-Portraits* (London: Phaidon, 2018), p.274; **page 87** Reproduced in Sir Lawrence Gowing, *Lucian Freud* (London: Thames & Hudson, 1984), pp.190–91; **page 113** Claude Cahun, *Aveux non avenus* (Paris: Éditions du Carrefour, 1930); **page 141** Reproduced in Frances Borzello, *Seeing Ourselves: Women's Self-Portraits* (London: Thames & Hudson, 2016), p.221